ADVENTURES IN PARANORMAL INVESTIGATION

ADVENTURES IN PARANORMAL INVESTIGATION

Joe Nickell

THE UNIVERSITY PRESS OF KENTUCKY

Publication of this volume was made possible in part by
a grant from the National Endowment for the Humanities.

Scholarly publisher for the Commonwealth,
serving Bellarmine University, Berea College, Centre
College of Kentucky, Eastern Kentucky University,
The Filson Historical Society, Georgetown College,
Kentucky Historical Society, Kentucky State University,
Morehead State University, Murray State University,
Northern Kentucky University, Transylvania University,
University of Kentucky, University of Louisville,
and Western Kentucky University.

Editorial and Sales Offices: The University Press of Kentucky
663 South Limestone Street, Lexington, Kentucky 40508-4008
www.kentuckypress.com

11 10 09 08 07   1 2 3 4 5

Library of Congress Cataloging-in-Publication Data

Nickell, Joe.
Adventures in paranormal investigation / Joe Nickell.
p. cm.
Includes bibliographical references and index.
ISBN 978-0-8131-2467-4 (hardcover : alk. paper)
1. Parapsychology. I. Title.
BF1001.N53 2007
130—dc22

CONTENTS

CONTENTS

ACKNOWLEDGMENTS

I AM MOST GRATEFUL TO John and Mary Frantz, whose generous establishment of an investigative fund helped make possible many of the investigations presented in this book.

I am also indebted to my colleagues at the Center for Inquiry (CFI) in Amherst, New York, home of the Committee for Skeptical Inquiry (CSI) and publisher of *Skeptical Inquirer* science magazine: Paul Kurtz, chairman; Barry Karr, executive director; Kendrick Frazier, editor; David Park Musella, editorial assistant; and Lisa Hutter, art director. Providing help with financial and other matters were Paul Paulin and Pat Beauchamp, along with the many other staffers whose day-to-day assistance is invaluable.

Timothy Binga, director of libraries for CFI, provided ongoing research assistance—often beyond the call of duty—and Paul E. Loynes provided crucial production help, including manuscript preparation. Tom Flynn also provided valuable assistance.

Working with me on specific investigations were my dear friend, the late Robert A. Baker; John F. Fischer; Martin Mahner; Benjamin Radford; and Vaughn Rees. And as always, I am indebted to the professional staff at the University Press of Kentucky, including Stephen M. Wrinn, Ann Malcolm, Ila McEntire, Leila Salisbury, Mack McCormick, Wyn Morris, copyeditor Linda Lotz, and others.

In addition to those mentioned in the text, I am grateful to many others who assisted in various ways: the Lily Dale Museum—especially the late Joyce LaJudice, Ron Nagy, and Beverly Anderson—for access to historical spiritualist materials; in Australia, Barry Williams and Ian Bryce; in Germany, Amardeo Sarma, Christoph Bordlein, and Detlev Luck; in Italy,

Paula de Gobbi, Francesco Chiminello, and Matteo Fillipini (in Venice), Stefano Bagnasco, Andrea Ferrero, Claudio Pastore, Beatrice Mautino, and Mariano Tomatis (in Turin), and Luigi Garlaschelli (who accompanied me to Naples); Andrew A. Skolnick, former executive director of the Commission for Scientific and Mental Health; Dr. Wallace Sampson, editor of *The Scientific Review of Alternative Medicine*; the Boston Public Library and the Middleboro, Massachusetts, Public Library (Betty Brown, reference librarian); and others, including Philip Befumo Jr. (product manager of United Mineral & Chemical Corporation, Lyndhurst, N.J.), Martin Braun, Ed and Diane Buckner, Jenny Everett (*Popular Science*), John Gaeddert, Ranjit Sandhu, and John Zachritz.

To my many other friends and associates, and to those who call themselves fans, I express my sincerest gratitude.

Finally, I am grateful for the support and indulgence of my family: my wife Diana, our daughter Cherette, and grandsons Chase and Tyner. They are the loves of my life.

INTRODUCTION

I AM NOW IN MY FOURTH DECADE as a paranormal investigator—apparently, the only full-time professional one in the world. Ironically, I recall one of my childhood heroes, Sherlock Holmes, explaining to his new friend Dr. Watson (in *A Study in Scarlet*): "Well, I have a trade of my own. I suppose I am the only one in the world. I'm a consulting detective." I followed Holmes in shaping my career around my interests and abilities. I began as a stage magician and "mentalist" (1969–1973), became a private investigator for a world-famous detective agency (1973–1975), and (many roles and adventures later) obtained a Ph.D. in English (1987), focusing on literary investigation and folklore.

Meanwhile, I began investigating paranormal mysteries—those beyond the range of science and normal human experience. At first, it was only an avocation. In 1969 I sat in on a séance that attempted to contact the spirit of Houdini, while coproducing a radio special on the life of the great magician and pioneering paranormal investigator; in 1972 I solved my first important case, that of Toronto's Mackenzie House haunting. After many additional investigations and personas (see my Web site, www.joenickell.com), I began my association with the Committee for the Scientific Investigation of Claims of the Paranormal (CSICOP), which has since been renamed the Committee for Skeptical Inquiry (CSI). I moved from consultant (1984) to fellow (1988) to member of the Executive Council (1993) to a salaried position as senior research fellow (1995). My office is in the Center for Inquiry in Amherst, New York, flanked by a small lab and a "situation room."

I travel around the world, lured by its strangest enigmas, but I engage in neither the hype of so many mystery-mongering writers nor the dismissals of self-styled "debunkers." Instead, I investigate claims with the intent of solving them. I take a rational, scientific approach, following the evidence objectively and remembering certain basic principles: that the burden of proof is on the claimant; that extraordinary claims require extraordinary proof—that is, the evidence must be commensurate with the nature of the claim; and that the simplest tenable explanation—that is, the one that requires the fewest assumptions—is most likely correct (the rule of Occam's razor).

Taken largely from my "Investigative Files" column in *Skeptical Inquirer* and *Skeptical Briefs*, this collection of cases (the third in a series, following *Real-Life X-Files* [2001] and *The Mystery Chronicles* [2004]) examines claims ranging from alien abductions to zoological enigmas. We visit snake charmers in Morocco, explore legendary castles in Germany, view "miraculous" relics in Italy, go undercover to examine quack cancer cures in Mexico, and search for an elusive lake monster in Canada. We encounter "spirit" writing, mystery artifacts, supposed psychic phenomena, crop circles, phantom ships, allegedly healing springs, UFOs, and even a ghost-town curse.

It is time now to turn the page and begin the first adventure. Again, we can hear Sherlock Holmes urging (in *The Adventure of the Abbey Grange*): "Come, Watson, come! The game is afoot. Not a word! Into your clothes and come!"

HAUNTED PLANTATION

How would you like to spend the night—alone—in the most haunted house in America? That was the question posed to me by the producers of a documentary for the Discovery Channel. I readily agreed and was on location on August 14–15, 2001. Also there to investigate (although they did not spend the night) were Jeff Reynolds and a colleague, Krista Mattson, from Ghost Tracker Investigations (a branch of North Florida Paranormal Research, Inc.), who carried in lots of impressive ghost-hunting equipment.

The Myrtles

The site was the Myrtles Plantation Bed and Breakfast in St. Francisville, Louisiana, northwest of Baton Rouge (figure 1). The antebellum estate reportedly "holds the dubious record of more ghostly phenomena per square inch than anywhere else in the country," or so claims Barbara Sillery (2001) in her book *The Haunting of Louisiana*. She labels the Myrtles "America's Most Haunted Home." Reportedly, there are apparitions, unexplained noises, a mysteriously rumpled bed, photos with orbs and shadowy figures, an oil portrait whose features become animated, a bloody handprint on the adjacent wall, doors that inexplicably open or close, and fingerprints in the silvering of a mirror, among other phenomena.

The Myrtles Plantation was the home of David Bradford, a lawyer and the "most violent leader" of the 1794 Whiskey Rebellion, a protest against a tax on distilled spirits. The uprising consisted largely of western Pennsylvania and Virginia farmers, most of Scots-Irish descent, who made whiskey from their grain. The rebellion was put down by the militia under the orders of President George Washington, and Bradford "escaped down the Mississippi River" (*Collier's Encyclopedia* 1993, s.v. "Whiskey Rebellion").

Bradford established the Myrtles and built the plantation house in 1796 on

1

Figure 1. The picturesque—but supposedly haunted—house at the Myrtles Plantation is nestled among trees hung with Spanish moss. (Photo by Joe Nickell)

a Spanish land grant (Spain owned Louisiana from 1762 to 1800). According to a historical marker on the grounds, "the architecture, elaborate plaster work and lacy ironwork make this twenty room mansion one of Louisiana's most unusual plantation homes." Bradford's fourteen-year-old daughter married Judge Clarke Woodruff, who played a role in one purported ghost story at the Myrtles (discussed presently).

The plantation was acquired in 1834 by a jovial Scotsman, Ruffin Gray Stirling, whose family eventually included nine children. One girl, Sarah, married a St. Louis attorney named William Winter, and the couple settled at the Myrtles. In 1871 Winter was shot and—according to legend—staggered upstairs, reaching the seventeenth step before expiring. Allegedly, the "labored footsteps" of Winter's ghost could be heard on the stairs until they ceased in 1985 (Kermeen 2002, 9). Of course, one must wonder how a nonphysical entity such as a ghost would be able to produce these noises and other physical phenomena.

The Legend of Chloe

Many of the alleged ghostly occurrences at the Myrtles are attributed to one of the plantation's slaves, Chloe (also spelled Cloey [Rule 2001]). According to a doubtful, garbled tale, she was the aforementioned Judge Woodruff's concubine. Either because she was eventually rejected by the judge for another woman and feared being "sent to the working fields" or because she was "seeking to increase her influence and power," Chloe began eavesdropping on Woodruff's private conversations. When she was caught at this, she was punished by having one of her ears cut off (her *left* ear, according to one source). As a consequence, she wore a turban to conceal the defect (a *green* turban, divined one writer). In retaliation, Chloe poisoned the birthday cake of Woodruff's nine-year-old daughter by adulterating the batter with juice from oleander leaves. Some accounts claim that this was done for vengeance; others state that Chloe only planned to make everyone sick so that she could either nurse them back to health, and thus win the judge's gratitude, or administer a magic cure so that the family would regard her "as a powerful voodoo priestess," and thus regain her favored status. However, the poisoning resulted in the death of Mrs. Woodruff and two of her daughters. As a consequence, Chloe was hanged—supposedly by fellow slaves, either as retribution or out of fear of the judge's wrath. At least one source has somehow learned that after the hanging "Chloe's body was weighted with rocks and dropped in the nearby Mississippi River."

In reality, none of the sources I have come across offers any evidence that the Chloe tale is true, attributing it—if at all—to legend. Some sources quote the present owner of the Myrtles, Teeta Moss, or *her* apparent source, Hester Eby, who has rehearsed the story for many years. Eby has outlasted three owners, each of whom no doubt appreciated her ability to enthrall tourists with the colorful account and other spine-tingling assertions.

Court archives in St. Francisville fail to substantiate the existence of Chloe (Frank 2001; Williams 2003). Although there are variants (as folklorists say) of the Chloe tale, most do not seem to be based on any long-standing tradition. Instead, they appear to be the result of the garbling of details by careless writers. For instance, Hauck (1996), apparently following Roberts (1995), gives

Chloe's name as Cleo. (I suspect that someone spelled *Chloe* as *Cloe*, which was then "corrected" to *Cleo*.)

Frances Kermeen, who owned the Myrtles for eight and a half years and wrote her own version of the story, either did not know Chloe's name or did not think it worth mentioning, simply referring to her as "a beautiful mulatto housemaid." This version is also different in more significant respects. The slave girl is not caught eavesdropping but rather is discovered keeping a sexual rendezvous with Judge Woodruff—although the motif of the door being flung open, this time by the wronged wife, remains. There is no mention of a severed ear, a green turban, or revenge, although the poisoning episode is retained, along with the denouement: "the pathetic slave was hung in the morning" (Kermeen 2002, 7–8). Kermeen cites "a book published in 1882" that says of the Myrtles: "The lights are never extinguished at the plantation. When the lights are all out, something always happens." Kermeen does not further identify this book (according to another source, it was published in 1900), but the salient point is that it apparently does not mention the Chloe tale. This suggests that the story is of more recent origin.

Most significantly, historians insist that Sarah Woodruff and her daughters actually died in a yellow fever epidemic (Hamilton 1990). In brief, the Chloe story seems to be the product not of folklore but of *fakelore*.

Ghostly Phenomena?

In any event, various ghostly goings-on have been reported—even hyped—at the Myrtles. For example, guests have heard banging noises. At one point on the *Haunted Plantation* documentary, such noises were quite audible. But then the television audience learned that the pounding was actually being caused by me, slamming a loose shutter against a drainpipe to demonstrate one possibility. In fact, mysterious noises can be caused by sundry factors. As the noted paranormal investigator and magician Milbourne Christopher (1970) observed, they are often attributable to low-hanging tree branches, drafts, children's pranks, and similar mundane causes. He added, "Woodwork affected by a change of temperature has frightened superstitious occupants of both old and new houses."

Some guests and employees at the Myrtles have seen ghostly apparitions, commonly while in bed. Some occurred in a room where a little girl reportedly died in 1868, despite the ministrations of a local "voodoo queen." According to Kermeen (2002, 12), "She may appear as a shadow dancing across walls, or you may awake to find her working her voodoo on you." Actually, such nocturnal sightings are merely waking dreams, a common type of hallucination that occurs in the twilight between wakefulness and sleep and typically includes bizarre imagery (Nickell 1995, 2001). For example, one guest, a writer, "swore that he awoke to find two blond-haired little girls standing at the foot of his bed" (Norman and Scott 1995, 139).

Some apparitional experiences at the Myrtles have been reported during waking activities, including one by tour guide Hester Eby (Sillery 2001). However, evidence shows that apparitions are linked to periods of reverie. They typically occur while the observer is in a relaxed state or performing routine work. Such a mental state may be conducive to images welling up from the subconscious and being superimposed on the visual scene—a sort of mental double exposure (Nickell 1995, 2001).

Numerous other phenomena have been reported by superstitious staff and guests. Well-publicized experiences prompt additional reports, creating a sort of bandwagon effect. Here are my explanations for some of the most well known of them.

The rumpled bed. One of the bedrooms in the plantation house is known as the "Room of the Rumpled Bed." According to Teeta Moss, housekeeping staff are forever straightening the bedcovers because "someone"—presumably the ghost of Chloe—repeatedly rumples them (Sillery 2001). Armed with the hypothesis that the phenomenon was due to children playing, a napping staffer, a frisky pet, or a household prankster, I decided to monitor the bed during my stay at the Myrtles. I constantly looked in on the room and took several photographs—even during the wee hours of the morning, when I climbed out of bed and padded about the premises. Except for me, the place was deserted; even the ghosts had apparently left. The supposedly haunted bed remained undisturbed.

Ghost photos. Mrs. Moss showed me some photographic enlargements of the house's exterior that depict what she and others believe is a female figure, presumably the legendary Chloe. Unfortunately, the original negatives are unavailable, and the enlargements have been copied from prints. Some were actually color photocopies, and when I examined one black-and-white enlargement with a magnifier, I found that it had a halftone-screen pattern; on inquiry, I learned that it had been copied from a printed postcard. Such photographic "evidence" is therefore virtually meaningless. Nevertheless, taking the pictures at face value, the shadowy figures that some perceive are, in my opinion, what are known as *simulacra*. That is, they are the result of the percipient's ability to discern images in random patterns (e.g., foliage), like seeing shapes in clouds or inkblots.

Nonfigural "ghost" images at the Myrtles are typically "orbs," those round balls of light that are often associated with haunted places. However, skeptics have shown that these effects typically result from particles of dust, water droplets, and the like reflecting the camera's flash (Nickell 2002). Some of these images in the photos taken by guests and ghost hunters at the Myrtles may have been caused by tiny flying insects, reflections from glossy paint or varnish, and other mundane causes (*Haunted* 2002). In addition to orbs, other glitches in photos that ghost trackers believe are caused by spirit "ectoplasm" can be caused by flash rebounding from the camera strap, hair, jewelry, a finger, and so on.

Ghost-detection phenomena. In addition to still and video cameras, amateur ghostologists use various other glitch-prone equipment—such as electromagnetic field (EMF) meters—to supposedly detect the energy from ghosts. They breathlessly report "high readings" and "significant spikes" on EMF devices and other equipment. Alas, these ghost buffs are invariably nonscientists who know little about their devices and what they are really recording, and they do not use scientific protocols and controls. They seem to think that if they use high-tech equipment they are performing science, but they are actually engaging in pseudoscience. None of the varied instruments they use are designed for ghost detection. There is no scientific evidence that ghosts exist, let alone that they emit electromagnetic radiation or have other detectable properties.

The animated portrait. Hanging in the foyer on the second floor of the Myrtles is an oil painting of an unidentified man whose features reportedly become animated (figure 2). Teeta Moss (2001) told me that she has seen its expression change from happy to sad, although she has never documented the

Figure 2. This oil portrait reportedly changes expression, and its eyes follow passersby. (Photo by Joe Nickell)

alleged transformation. She and others have also reported that the man's eyes follow them when they pass by. I monitored this painting throughout my stay at the Myrtles and took many photos. The countenance never changed, but I can explain why some believe that it does. The subject's expression is analogous to that of Leonardo's celebrated *Mona Lisa,* with its enigmatic smile and ambiguous facial expression. In the Myrtles painting, the gentleman's slight smile and "sad" eyes combine to give him an expression that may subjectively appear to shift. As for the claim that the man's gaze follows viewers, one can easily see for oneself that any two-dimensional portrait in which the subject's eyes gaze directly at the viewer produces the same effect. It is the result of a three-dimensional view being "fixed" in the two-dimensional representation.

The bloody handprint. According to one source (Taylor 2000), an infrared photograph taken of the portrait "revealed what seemed to be a bloody handprint on the wall next to the painting." This alleged photo is no longer extant, and Hester Eby recalled that the bloody handprint was on the painting itself

7

rather than on the wall. In any case, my inspection of the area with an infrared video camera (as part of my documentation of the interior of the plantation house during my nighttime sojourn) failed to substantiate the presence of any handprint—bloody or not. The purported rationale for the bloody handprint is also missing. Although Taylor (2000) claims that "four people have been murdered in that room over the years," and legend says that ten people have been murdered on the property, historians state that only one murder can be documented at the Myrtles: that of William Winter, mentioned earlier (Hamilton 1990; *Haunted* 2002).

Handprints on a mirror. There are, however, clearly discernible handprints in the front hallway—on a mirror with an ornate, gilded frame. Guide Hester Eby stands beside the mirror as she tells of the local superstition current at the time of Chloe's alleged poisoning of Mrs. Woodruff and the two girls. If mirrors were not covered with black cloth, Eby says, it was believed that the spirits of the dead could be trapped inside. "During the time of the poisoning of Sarah and her daughters, there was so much confusion that this mirror was left uncovered. It's believed those people's souls still live inside this section of the mirror" (Sillery 2001, 22).

Indeed, utilizing a lighted magnifier to examine the mirror's discolored silvering, I discovered the presence of dermal ridges and specifically identified one fingerprint as a "plain whorl" pattern (as illustrated in Nickell and Fischer 1999, 119). However, the handprints are along the outer edges of the mirror, consistent with where the glass would have been handled by workmen. This points to the likelihood that grimy hands affected the silvering, either before or after it was applied. Eby maintains that although the glass looks old, it is not, and that "each time a new glass has been placed back into that frame, the handprints reappear" (Sillery 2001, 22). However, *MSNBC Investigates* (2001) stated that the handprints returned when the mirror was "resilvered," not replaced.

Swinging doors. Among numerous other claims of ghostly shenanigans at the Myrtles (which seem to be reported faster than ghost-book authors can repeat them) are doors that mysteriously open and shut. During my explorations of the house, I discovered that one bathroom door—which had supposedly shut on one person—had been hung off balance, causing it to close by itself; another door swings open by itself, for the same reason. Drafts are another possible explanation for some moving doors.

Hoaxes and Hype

Not all spooky phenomena at the Myrtles have an innocent explanation, however. Consider the events that took place at the Murder Mystery Weekend on January 24, 1985—the 114th anniversary of William Winter's murder. As the actor playing Winter feigned death, the lights went out! When they came back on, guests found that some paintings in the house had become askew, and others were upside down. One (which was supposedly out of reach of a prankster) was even "crying." These occurrences have the earmarks of hoaxing and are an especially doubtful admixture of phenomena: part "poltergeist," part mystery-drama staging, and part weeping-icon effect—the last perhaps accomplished by someone armed with a water pistol.

Hoaxing aside, mere suggestion can prompt many people to experience ghosts, such as when Hester Eby suggests to visitors that they might feel a spooky tap on the shoulder. She acknowledges, "We always get skeptics, but I really think people are interested in the ghosts and the mystery" (*Haunted* 2002). Her employer, Mrs. Moss (2001), admitted to me that the "haunted thing" (the idea that the place has resident ghosts) was the "hook" to bring in business. The weathered signboard at the entrance bills the plantation house as "The Home of Mystery and Intrigue." And an advertising flyer emphasizes the haunted-house aspect and, in addition to daily tours, offers "Mystery Tours" each Friday and Saturday evening.

Individual differences also help explain why some guests seem to be targeted by ghosts. Not only are some people more inclined to believe in ghosts, but some are more imaginative than others. In a continuing study that I am conducting on reported ghost encounters, I find a good correlation between the level of encounters and the number of traits associated with fantasy proneness (Nickell 2001). This also held true at the Myrtles (*Haunted* 2002), supporting psychologist Robert A. Baker's adage, "There are no haunted places, only haunted people."

References

Christopher, Milbourne. 1970. *ESP, Seers and Psychics,* 164–73. New York: Thomas Y. Crowell.

Collier's Encyclopedia. 1993. New York: P. F. Collier.

Frank, Diana (ABC News Productions). 2001. Telephone communication with Joe Nickell, August 22.

Hamilton, Anne Butler. 1990. The exorcism of the Myrtles. *Louisiana Life,* January–February, 36–40.

Hauck, Dennis William. 1996. *Haunted Places: The National Directory,* 194–95. New York: Penguin Books.

The Haunted Plantation. 2002. Discovery Channel, April 4.

Kermeen, Frances. 2002. *Ghostly Encounters: True Stories of America's Haunted Inns and Hotels,* 5–29. New York: Warner Books.

Moss, Teeta. 2001. Interview by Joe Nickell, August 14.

MSNBC Investigates. 2001. August 12.

The Myrtles Plantation. www.geocities.com/TimesSquare/Bridge/9622/RiverRoad .html (accessed 2001).

Myrtles Plantation Bed and Breakfast. www.hauntedhouses.com/states/1a/house.htm (accessed 2001).

The Myrtles Plantation in Louisiana. http://njnj.essortment.com/myrtlesplantatio_ rioa.htm (accessed 2001).

Nickell, Joe. 1995. *Entities: Angels, Spirits, Demons and Other Alien Beings.* Amherst, N.Y.: Prometheus Books.

———. 2001. Haunted inns. In *Real-Life X-Files,* 289–300. Lexington: University Press of Kentucky.

———. 2002. Circular reasoning: The "mystery" of crop circles and their "orbs" of light. *Skeptical Inquirer* 26, no. 5 (September–October): 17–19.

Nickell, Joe, and John F. Fischer. 1999. *Crime Science: Methods of Forensic Detection.* Lexington: University Press of Kentucky.

Norman, Michael, and Beth Scott. 1995. *Historic Haunted America,* 137–40. New York: Tom Doherty Associates.

Roberts, Nancy. 1995. *Haunted Houses: Chilling Tales from Nineteen American Houses,* 3rd ed., 134–39. Old Saybrook, Conn.: Globe Pequot Press.

Rule, Leslie. 2001. *Coast to Coast Ghosts: True Stories of Hauntings across America.* Kansas City, Mo.: Andrews McMeel Publishing.

Sillery, Barbara. 2001. *The Haunting of Louisiana,* 17–26. Gretna, La.: Pelican Publishing.

Taylor, Troy. 2000. The Myrtles Plantation. www.prairieghosts.com/myrtles.html.

Williams, Helen (director, West Feliciana Historical Society). 2003. Interview by Joe Nickell, July 3.

CROP CIRCLE CAPERS

Controversy over the phenomenon of crop circles—typified by swirled, circular depressions in wheat and other cereal crops—has flourished since it first captured media attention in England in the late 1970s. The controversy soon spread to North America, where it continues. Two cases—one in southwestern Ontario, Canada, and the other in Solano County, California—directly involved my office. The cases are instructive in illustrating how misinformation about the paranormal is created, packaged, and sold.

Background

In its early years, "circlemania" attracted a number of self-styled researchers called "cereologists" (after Ceres, the Roman goddess of grains or agriculture). Also dubbed "croppies," they have advanced a number of theories to account for the proliferating, evolving designs of crop circles, ranging from the mystical (earth spirits and occult energies) to the science-fictional (alien hieroglyphics) and the pseudoscientific (ionized wind vortices) (Nickell and Fischer 1992; Nickell 2002; Guiley 1991).

Actually, as forensic analyst John F. Fischer and I demonstrated in 1991, several factors pointed to hoaxing as the most likely explanation: crop circles were more prevalent in southern England, had proliferated in the wake of media reports, were increasing in complexity each season, and exhibited a "shyness" effect (i.e., the mechanism was never seen in operation). Just before we went to press, two retired artists, Doug Bower and Dave Chorley, admitted that they had pioneered the making of crop circles, using planks and cord. To prove their claim, they fooled cereologist Pat Delgado, who declared a pattern they had produced for a British tabloid to be genuine. Soon, others admitted that they had been infected with the circle-making bug.

The croppies, however, could not be dissuaded by such simple evidence—

11

especially since that would require admitting how gullible they had been. They defended their untenable position with clouds of smoke and arrays of mirrors. Indeed, as often happens with paranormal issues, the croppies attracted a tiny number of low-level, maverick scientists who lent an air of credibility to the nonsense. At least their pronouncements have been afforded much ink and airtime by the infotainment media—all at the expense of authentic scientific inquiry.

Unlike scientists who seek to solve mysteries (science is from the Latin *scientia*, "knowledge"), the self-anointed cereologists—like other paranormalists—are trafficking in the "unexplained." They engage in a logical fallacy called arguing from ignorance: "We don't know what causes certain crop circle anomalies," they say, "so this crop circle must be a genuine one, possibly formed by aliens or wind vortices." They explain a minor mystery (real or perceived) by manufacturing a greater one—what the ancients called straining at a gnat and swallowing a camel.

Ontario Dumbbell

Among several crop circles that appeared in southwestern Ontario in August 2003 was a 170.5-foot dumbbell-shaped formation in a wheat field in Elgin County (figure 3). It appeared on the farm of eighty-one-year-old Lawrence Holland, located between Iona and Wallacetown. Croppies were soon on site, getting all the media attention they could.

Kevin Christopher, then public-relations director of CSI, had been in touch with a reporter for the *London (Ontario) Free Press*, Marissa Nelson, who expressed an interest in accompanying me to investigate the formation. On August 21, with *Skeptical Inquirer* managing editor Benjamin Radford, I drove to London to rendezvous with Nelson at the newspaper offices. On the way, Ben and I outlined our investigative strategy. As he took notes, I added some predictions: (1) that the lay pattern of the wheat would show which of the two circles had been made first, (2) that the wheat of the dumbbell's connector bar would be flattened in the direction of the second circle, and (3) that the second circle's depressed wheat would overlap the lay of the connector. Ben agreed that this sequence was the most likely scenario for a hoaxed dumbbell formation.

We picked up Nelson and press photographer Ken Wightman and contin-

Figure 3. View (from atop a combine) of the dumbbell-shaped crop circle formation in south-western Ontario. (Photo by Lawrence Holland)

ued to the Holland farm. When we arrived, we first examined the formation's lay pattern and found it to be exactly as predicted. We had brought a "stalk stomper"—a rope and plank device (figure 4)—and shared with Mr. Holland some of what we had learned from making crop circle formations ourselves (see Christopher 2002). An onlooking neighbor became incensed at our skepticism, and she asked rather shrilly, "How do you explain it [the formation] facing north?" Actually—as I emphasized by pulling from my pocket a lensatic (sighting) compass—the formation was not aligned with true north but rather with magnetic north (Nelson 2003b). And in fact, the alignment was only approximate, being off by about four degrees. Moreover, the first circle's axis was out of alignment with the main axis by some eleven degrees. These misalignments are clearly shown in a diagram of the formation, yet the cereologist who drew it claims that the "circles align to magnetic north" (Rock 2003). (Apparently, there is more than one type of crop circle dumbbell.) The neighbor also wondered how the circle had been made in the dark, supposedly during a foggy night, but Mr. Holland believes that "the formation appeared on a clear night around the full moon" (Nelson 2003b).

The cereologists and other visitors to the site discovered other "mysteries" as well. For example, the flattening had supposedly occurred without breaking the plants (young wheat stalks are quite resilient), but there was indeed some breakage, probably due to the maturity of the crop. Some "twisting below the seed head" was found "in the occassional [sic] stalk" inside the formation, but this "anomaly" was also found outside, at least "near the formation" (Emery 2003a, 2003b). The mystery mongers had their day, but Mr. Holland was quick to understand our evidence that the formation had been made in three stages, quite apparently by hoaxers. Reported Marissa Nelson (2003b):

> While Holland at first thought the circles were the result of a freak whirlwind, he's changed his mind.
>
> "Thanks for coming," he says, shaking Nickell's hand after watching the brief crop circle demonstration.
>
> "Thanks for explaining it."

Solano Circles

Another crop circle case that received considerable media attention began on June 28, 2003, when a Solano County, California, farmer named Larry Balestra discovered a large array of crop circles in his wheat field. Soon afterward, four teenagers from Fairfield confessed to creating the formation. In the wake of the hoax, the *San Francisco Chronicle* quoted me as saying that the media helped fuel the crop circle craze. The *Chronicle*'s excellent coverage also featured a quote from Balestra, who stated that crop circles were the product of people "with too much time on their hands" (Davidson 2003). The teenagers confirmed both assessments, admitting that they had learned how to make crop circles from a television documentary and had been motivated in part by summer boredom (Moy 2003b).

The brouhaha started to die down but was given new life when self-styled researchers from a pro-paranormal organization called Psi Applications

Figure 4. The author demonstrates the use of a "stalk stomper" device for the making of crop circles. (Photo by Benjamin
Radford)

claimed that the Solano crop circles were too sophisticated to have been done
by the teen hoaxers. A CSI press release written by Kevin Christopher challenged those claims and quoted me as saying that they amounted to "blatant
mystery mongering." I cited considerable corroborative evidence, including
the fact that the boys had a history of mischief making and had been on pro-
bation at the time. One boy's mother confirmed that when the teens arrived
home in the early-morning hours on the day the circles appeared, they had

with them the proper circle-making equipment, including stalk stompers and ropes. Only after the *Vallejo Times-Herald* reported that the youths were in possession of blue tape was it confirmed that the farmer's wife, Lisa Balestra, had discovered pieces of blue tape in the circles. The teens also knew that there had been little moonlight on the night the circles were made, and they revealed other firsthand knowledge, such as the fact that wheat lies down more easily than grass. They showed a reporter "practice" circles they had made elsewhere, as well as a "wrinkled paper" bearing a diagram of the Solano formation (Moy 2003a, 2003b; Christopher 2003).

Psi Applications, according to one reporter, concentrated "on trying to debunk the hoax [the teenagers' confession] rather than explain who or what" had produced the circles (Garofoli 2003). However, even if croppies could disprove the teenagers' claim, they would still be faced with the likelihood that someone else was responsible, since we know that hoaxers do make crop circles, and no other mechanism has been scientifically confirmed. As I told Fox television's *Fox Report* (December 30, 2003), we know that teenagers make crop circles, and in fact, a 1992 crop circle competition in England was won by—teenagers!

References

Christopher, Kevin. 2002. CSI field investigations: 2002 crop circle experiments. *Skeptical Briefs* 12, no. 3 (September): 3–5.

———. 2003. Skeptics dispute Psi Applications' Solano crop circle report. CSI press release, December 5.

Davidson, Keay. 2003. Real culprit behind crop circles? Skeptics point to the media. *San Francisco Chronicle,* July 12.

Emery, Joanna. 2003a. Field report—Wallacetown, Ontario, August 15. www.cccrn .ca/wallacetown03reports.html (accessed August 19, 2003).

———. 2003b. Site photos. www.cccrn.ca/wallacetown03photos.html (accessed August 19, 2003).

Garofoli, Joe. 2003. Crop circles called out of teens' league. www.sfgate.com (accessed December 4, 2003).

Guiley, Rosemary Ellen. 1991. *Harper's Encyclopedia of Mystical and Paranormal Experience,* 126–28. New York: HarperCollins.

Moy, Catherine. 2003a. Bay Area media converges on alleged makers of crop circles. *Vallejo (Calif.) Times-Herald,* July 11. www.timesheraldonline.com (accessed July 14, 2003).

———. 2003b. Circles the work of Fairfield teens. *Vallejo (Calif.) Times-Herald,* July 11. www.timesheraldonline.com (accessed July 14, 2003).

Nelson, Marissa. 2003a. Circles crop up for third time in area. *London (Ontario) Free Press,* August 14.

———. 2003b. Mystery or myth? *London (Ontario) Free Press,* August 23.

Nickell, Joe. 2002. Circular reasoning: The "mystery" of crop circles and their "orbs" of light. *Skeptical Inquirer* 26, no. 5 (September–October): 17–19.

Nickell, Joe, and John F. Fischer. 1992. The crop-circle phenomenon: An investigative report. *Skeptical Inquirer* 16, no. 2 (Winter): 136–49.

Rock, Matt. 2003. Diagram, Iona/Wallacetown, Ontario, Canada. www.ccrn.ca/wallacetown03diagrams.html (accessed August 19, 2003).

RORSCHACH ICONS

PEOPLE ARRIVE IN DROVES TO VIEW THEM: holy images that appear—many believe miraculously—in the most unlikely places. They include the figure of the Virgin Mary formed by a stain on the bathroom floor of a store, the face of Jesus in a giant forkful of spaghetti illustrated on a billboard, and the likeness of Mother Teresa on a cinnamon bun served in a coffee shop (Nickell 1997, 1998). Such images are commonly reported, and if the depictions are of religious figures, they may be popularly termed "apparitions" or "religious visions" (e.g., Virgin Mary 2003). However, they are quite different from the internalized conceptions of "visionaries," which are typically unseen by ordinary folks. Rather, these are more or less visible to everyone, representing simply the inkblot or the picture-in-the-clouds effect: the mind's tendency to "recognize" common shapes in random patterns.

Simulacra

These images are known as *simulacra,* and the tendency to see them is called *pareidolia,* a neurological-psychological phenomenon by which the brain interprets vague images as specific ones (DeAngelis 1999; Novella 2001). Often the discerned image is a face because, as Carl Sagan (1995, 47) explains, "As soon as the infant can see, it recognizes faces, and we now know that this skill is hardwired to our brains." Sagan (1995, 46) notes:

> The most common image is the Man in the Moon. Of course, it doesn't really look like a man. Its features are lopsided, warped, drooping. There's a beefsteak or something over the left eye. And what expression does the mouth convey? An "O" of surprise? A hint of sadness, even lamentation? Doleful recognition of the traits of life on Earth?

18

Certainly the face is too round. The ears are missing. I guess he's bald on top. Nevertheless, every time I look at it, I see a human face.

Other secular simulacra include the "face on Mars" (Morrison 1988), as well as various shapes—a camel, a butterfly, and a portrait of comedian Bob Hope—in a woman's potato chip collection (Nickell 1998, 137). One famous granite formation, New Hampshire's Old Man of the Mountains profile, was a 700-ton, 1,200-foot-high simulacrum until it collapsed into rubble (Laughlin 2003).

Of course, simulacra can be faked. For example, crudely artistic images appeared repeatedly on the floor of a peasant woman's home in Belmez de la Moraleda, Spain, in 1972 (Nickell 1998, 39). A large portrait of Christ—looking amateurishly airbrushed, complete with a neat, oval-ringed halo—supposedly formed "miraculously" in 2000 on the wall of Palma Sola Presbyterian Church in Bradenton, Florida, after workers used pressurized water to clean the bricks (Christ image 2000). Deliberate hoaxes, however, seem to be rare.

Pious Imagination

Not surprisingly, many reported simulacra are religious. For example, a Muslim girl in England reportedly found an Arabic message, "There is only one God," in the seed pattern of a sliced tomato (Message 1997). Religious simulacra are perhaps more often associated with Catholic or Orthodox tradition, which emphasizes icons and other holy images. Historically, excessive veneration of images was thought to represent idolatry, a violation of the commandment against graven images. Objections to this practice led to the iconoclastic crisis in the Byzantine Empire (AD 724–843) and were among the issues involved in the Protestant Reformation (Eliade 1995; Nickell 1997). Today, theologians and clerics are usually quick to dismiss such images, one priest wisely attributing them to "pious imagination" (Nickell 1998, 34). However, they remain intensely popular among the superstitious faithful, and another priest, though warning against image worship, is hopeful that simulacra created by nature "can provide us with a mirror into the transcendence of something larger than ourselves" (Cox 2001).

Images of Mary are especially prevalent, as shown by the number of clippings in my bulging "simulacra" file (e.g., Virgin Mary 2003). She has appeared in a splotch of tree fungus in Los Angeles, a fence post in Sydney, a tree stump and a refrigerator door in New Jersey, a mottled rust stain on a water heater in Arizona, a bedroom wall in Nova Scotia, the bark of an elm tree in Texas, and so on. One of my favorites is the form of the Virgin of Guadalupe in spilled ice cream (Stack 2000).

Images of Jesus are also frequently perceived—for example, in the foliage of a vine-covered tree in West Virginia, in rust stains on a forty-foot-high soybean oil tank in Ohio, on a grimy window in an Italian village, and in the discoloration on a San Antonio living-room ceiling, among numerous others. In 1995 television viewers saw the face of Jesus in a photo taken by the Hubble space telescope showing stars being born in a gas cloud some six trillion miles long (Nickell 1997, 5). A sacred-heart figure of Jesus (as well as the Easter bunny) is even outlined in the wood-grain pattern of my office door.

St. Bartholomew's

Religious simulacra have been sighted since at least the third century A.D. (Rogo 1982, 113). In 1932 one "suddenly appeared" on a wall of St. Bartholomew's Church in Manhattan (Hauck 1996). Actually, it was suddenly discerned. The rector of the Episcopal church, the Reverend Dr. Robert Norwood, had just concluded a Lenten sermon titled "The Mystery of Incarnation." As he stated: "I happened to glance at the sanctuary wall and was amazed to see this lovely figure of Christ in the marble. I had never noticed it before. As it seemed to me to be an actual expression on the face of the marble of what I was preaching, 'His Glorious Body,' I consider it a curious and beautiful happening" (Calkins 1982). The figure was described as about one and a half feet tall, delineated in the variegations of the sepia marble directly above the door of the sanctuary.

Armed with Norwood's description, colleague Austin Dacey and I visited St. Bart's in search of the image. Few there had heard of it except for Becca Earley, who trains the church's tour guides. She did not know the exact location, but over the years, she had discovered multiple simulacra—various faces and figures—in the sanctuary's expanse of marble. She termed it "one enormous slab of Rorschachs" (Earley 2003). Using the published description,

Figure 5. In the sanctuary of St. Bartholomew's Church in Manhattan, a figure of Jesus emerging from his tomb has been divined in the patterned marble. (Photo by Joe Nickell)

we quickly found the image, which—to the imagination—might look like a white-robed figure emerging from a tomb (figure 5). Seemingly unaware of the simulacra phenomenon, Norwood had told the *New York Times* (February 24, 1932): "How this Christ-like figure came to be there, of course, I don't know. It is an illusion that grows before the vision. Has thought the power of life? People can scoff but the figure is there."

21

Holy Tortilla

A classic example of the genre was reported in 1978 at Lake Arthur, New Mexico. While Mrs. Maria Rubio was making burritos, she noticed the pattern of skillet burns on the tortilla. "It is Jesus Christ!" exclaimed the pious woman, and other family members agreed. After a priest reluctantly blessed the tortilla, she built a shrine for it, and thousands flocked from across the United States to witness the purported miracle and pray for divine assistance in curing ailments (Nickell 1998, 37).

In 1993 I appeared with Mrs. Rubio's daughter (among others) on a segment of the *Oprah Winfrey Show* about miracles. The audience did not seem to take the young woman seriously, and later she sat in the show's green room looking, I thought, somewhat dejected. She brightened when I showed interest in her photos, and she invited me to visit her mother's shrine. A decade later, with colleague Vaughn Rees, I did. The supposedly sacred object is displayed in a small outbuilding in Mrs. Rubio's backyard. Alas, it is at best a former miracle, for the image is no longer recognizable.

The Clearwater Virgin

Among the simulacra to get widespread media attention was the one that appeared in late 1996 on the glass facade of a building in Clearwater, Florida. Composed of flowing lines that suggested the veiled head and shoulders of a faceless woman, the image was believed by the faithful to depict the Virgin Mary. It was curiously iridescent, its "rainbow colors" adding to the effect (Cox 2001). Although never sanctioned by the local diocese, the image drew an estimated million visitors over the next several years. The building was purchased by the Shepherds of Christ Ministries—an Ohio-based Catholic revivalism group—and dubbed the Virgin Mary Building (Cox 2001). On March 1, 2004, the three uppermost panes of the window were broken by a vandal. A troubled teenager confessed to using slingshot-propelled ball bearings to do the damage. Because he was acting out of personal frustration, rather than any religious motivation, he was not charged with a hate crime (Tisch 2004).

Shortly thereafter (on March 20), I was in the area to give a talk and had the opportunity to visit the site with Dr. Gary Posner. He had investigated and tracked the Clearwater "miracle" claims and written a definitive article about them (Posner 1997). A local chemist, Charles Roberts, had examined the window and, based on his forty years of experience in analyzing glass, explained that the iridescent stain had been produced by water deposits combined with weathering, yielding a chemical reaction like that seen on old bottles. "The culprit seems to be the sprinkler," Roberts concluded (Norton 1996; Posner 1997). Indeed, as I walked around the glass-faced building with Dr. Posner and another local skeptic, astronomy professor Jack H. Robinson, we could see that there were iridescent flow patterns on other windows, each at a sprinkler location. One, on the west wall, had been dubbed the "Buddha" (Posner 1997).

The Milton Madonna

In June 2003 thousands of pilgrims and sightseers were drawn to a hospital in Milton, Massachusetts, where an image had appeared on a second-floor window. Most people envisioned it as Mary cradling the infant Jesus, but some thought that she was standing among clouds, and others saw her astride a globe or atop a mountain (Virgin vision 2003).

I briefly commented on the phenomenon on CNN (July 13), and I traveled to Milton to conduct an on-site investigation before appearing on Boston television and later on BBC radio (together with a church spokesman). I interviewed a hospital information officer (Schepici 2003), took photographs (figure 6), and talked with various pilgrims. I saw no need to disguise my identity and was soon recognized by one of the Catholic evangelicals with whom I discussed the phenomenon.

Various claims and rumors about the Milton Madonna were untrue. For instance, the discoloration did not suddenly appear; rather, it had begun five years earlier when the seal of the double-paned window broke, allowing moisture from the brickwork to mix with a moisture-absorbing sealant. (The window is behind a permanent partition, so it could not be reached from the inside.) Nor was this the only discolored window on the premises; one at the end of the building, bearing a cloudy shape that some saw as a "fetus," had been replaced earlier. A rumor that the replacement window had cracked (as if in divine protest) was untrue. Also untrue was the notion—spread by antiabortion zealots—that the Madonna image had appeared to warn the hospital not to perform abortions; the facility does not even have an obstetrics unit (Heuer 2003; Schepici 2003).

Figure 6. A "Madonna" appearing on the window of a hospital at Milton, Massachusetts, in June 2003 drew some 25,000 faithful in a single weekend. (Photo by Joe Nickell)

Nevertheless, after an estimated 25,000 persons visited the site the first weekend, hospital officials issued a statement noting that "a substantial safety issue has arisen that jeopardizes the ability of the Hospital to do its charitable work, to treat the sick and infirm" (Milton 2003). When devotees refused to heed the hospital's request to limit viewing to the hours of 5:30 to 8:30 P.M., officials responded by covering the window with a tarp and removing it only during that period (Redd 2003). Subsequently, a "cross" was discovered on the hospital's chimney, and other images were divined in nearby tree foliage.

Soon, however, attendance began to diminish, and a spokesman for the Boston Archdiocese, the Reverend Christopher Coyne, concluded that the phenomenon was neither a mystery nor a miracle (Heuer 2003). Indeed, the same can be said of all simulacra.

References

Calkins, Carroll, ed. 1982. *Mysteries of the Unexplained,* 304. Pleasantville, N.Y.: Reader's Digest Association.

Christ image drawing faithful. 2000. *Florida Times-Union* (Jacksonville), May 3.

Cox, Billy. 2001. Miraculous images give people hope. *Florida Today,* February 4.

DeAngelis, Perry. 1999. Mother Mary comes to me. *New England Journal of Skepticism* 2, no. 4 (Fall): 1, 13–15.

Earley, Becca. 2003. Interview by Joe Nickell and Austin Dacey, October 10.

Eliade, Mircea, ed. 1995. *The Encyclopedia of Religion.* New York: Simon & Schuster Macmillan.

Hauck, Dennis William. 1996. *Haunted Places: The National Directory.* New York: Penguin Books.

Heuer, Max. 2003. Miracle, schmiracle: Church skeptical of Milton's Mary. Bostonherald.com, June 29.

Laughlin, Larry. 2003. Old Man's loss heartfelt in New Hampshire. *Buffalo News,* May 5.

Message from God written in a tomato. 1997. *Daily Mail* (England), June 12.

Milton Hospital media statement. 2003. June 16.

Morrison, David. 1988. Seeing faces on Mars. *Skeptical Inquirer* 13, no. 1 (Fall): 76–80.

Nickell, Joe. 1997. Those tearful icons. *Free Inquiry* 17, no. 2 (Spring): 5, 7, 61.

———. 1998. *Looking for a Miracle: Weeping Icons, Relics, Stigmata, Visions and Healing Cures.* Amherst, N.Y.: Prometheus Books.

Norton, Wilma. 1996. Science tests Madonna of windows. *St. Petersburg Times,* undated clipping.

Novella, Robert. 2001. Believing is seeing. *New England Journal of Skepticism* 4, no. 1 (Winter): 1, 16–17.

Posner, Gary P. 1997. Tampa Bay's "Virgin Mary apparition." *Free Inquiry,* Spring, 4, 6.

Redd, C. Kalimah. 2003. Milton Hospital puts Virgin Mary under wraps. www.globe .com, June 20.

Rogo, D. Scott. 1982. *Miracles: A Parascientific Inquiry into Wondrous Phenomena.* New York: Dial Press.

Sagan, Carl. 1995. *The Demon-Haunted World: Science as a Candle in the Dark.* New York: Random House.

Schepici, Susan. 2003. Interview by Joe Nickell, July 7.

Stack, Megan K. 2000. Virgin seen in spilled ice cream. Associated Press, January 14.

Tisch, Chris. 2004. Teen held in Virgin Mary smashing. www.sptimes.com, May 12.

Virgin Mary hits Sydney beach again. 2003. *Age,* February 2. www.theage.com (accessed February 3, 2003).

Virgin vision in glass. 2003. *Fortean Times* 174 (October): 5.

POSTMORTEM ON
"ALIEN AUTOPSY"

Britain's *Manchester Evening News* termed it a hoax that "fooled the world" (Salford 2006), but that is not exactly true: *Skeptical Inquirer* magazine was on to the "alien autopsy" film from the outset. In fact, my article on the case (Nickell 1995) inaugurated my "Investigative Files" column. Now, however, the reputed creator of the fake extraterrestrial corpse used for the "autopsy" has publicly confessed.

The Skeptics

The film—purporting to depict the postmortem examination of an extraterrestrial who died in a UFO crash at Roswell, New Mexico, in 1947—was part of a "documentary" that aired on the Fox television network (figure 7). Skeptics and many UFOlogists quickly branded the film a hoax. Among numerous observations, they noted that the film bore a bogus, nonmilitary code mark; that the injuries sustained by the extraterrestrial were inconsistent with an air crash; and that the person performing the autopsy held the scissors like a tailor rather than a pathologist (who is trained to place the middle or ring finger in the bottom of the scissors hole and use the forefinger to steady the blades). Houston pathologist Ed Uthman (1995) faulted the film for lacking what he aptly termed "technical verisimilitude."

Other pathologists agreed. Cyril Wecht (1995), former president of the National Association of Forensic Pathologists, described the viscera in terms that could apply to supermarket meat scraps: "I cannot relate these structures to [an] abdominal context." Nationally known pathologist Dominick Di Maio (1995) was even more succinct: "I would say it's a lot of bull." And Hollywood special-effects expert Trey Stokes (whose film credits include *The Blob, Batman Returns,* and *Tales from the Crypt*) told CSICOP that the alien corpse behaved

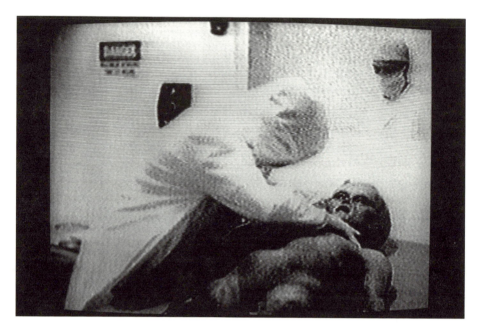

Figure 7. TV-screen image from the "alien autopsy" film. (Courtesy of *Skeptical Inquirer* magazine)

like a dummy, seemingly lightweight and "rubbery" and therefore moving unnaturally when handled (Stokes 1995).

The Perpetrator

Belatedly, a Manchester sculptor and special-effects creator, John Humphreys, now claims that the Roswell alien was his handiwork and that it was destroyed after the film was shot. He made this revelation just as a new movie, *Alien Autopsy,* was being released in April 2006. Humphreys re-created the original creature for this new film, which retells the making of the 1995 hoax autopsy film. A pair of British television celebrities play the original producers, Ray Santilli and Gary Shoefield. Santilli now claims that the 1995 film was a re-creation of genuine footage that was damaged when its container was opened after forty-eight years (Horne 2006).

As Humphreys told the BBC, "Funnily enough, I used exactly the same process as before. You start with the stills from the film, blow them up as large as you can. Then you make an aluminum armature, which you cover in clay, and then add all the detail." The clay model was used to produce a mold that yielded a latex cast. The body cavities were filled, Humphreys admitted, with chicken entrails, sheep brains, and the like, purchased from a meat market near the north London flat where the film was shot (Horne 2006).

Are Humphreys's claims credible? Indeed, he is a graduate of the Royal Academy and a special-effects model maker; his credits include *Max Headroom* and *Doctor Who.* His re-creations are so good that there is no doubt that he could have made the originals. And examples of his work displayed on his Web site are stylistically consistent with the hoaxed aliens. Humphreys also admitted that he played the role of the pathologist in the original autopsy film; his identity was concealed by a contamination suit.

The Roswell Saga

The alien autopsy hoax represented the culmination of several years' worth of rumors, urban legends, and outright deceptions purporting to prove that flying saucer wreckage and the remains of its humanoid occupants were stored at a secret facility—that is, (nonexistent) Hangar 18 at Wright Patterson Air Force Base—and that the small corpses were autopsied there or at another site. Among the hoaxes were the following:

- A 1949 science fiction movie, *The Flying Saucer,* purported to contain scenes of a captured spacecraft; an actor posing as an FBI agent swore that the claim was true.
- In 1950 writer Frank Scully reported in *Behind the Flying Saucers* that the U.S. government possessed no fewer than three Venusian spaceships, together with the humanoid corpses found on board. Scully had been fed the tale by two con men who had hoped to sell a petroleum-locating device allegedly based on alien technology (Clark 1993).
- In 1974 Robert Spencer Carr began to promote one of the crashes from the Scully book and claimed firsthand knowledge of where the pickled aliens were stored. But as the late claimant's son told me, and subsequently informed *Skeptical Inquirer* readers (Carr 1997), Carr was a spinner of yarns and made up the entire story.

- In 1987 the author of a book on Roswell released the notorious "MJ-12 documents," which seemed to prove the crash-retrieval story and expose a high-level government cover-up. Unfortunately, document experts readily identified the papers as inept forgeries (Nickell 1995; Nickell and Fischer 1990).
- In 1990 Gerald Anderson claimed that while rock hunting in the New Mexico desert in 1947, he and family members came upon a crashed saucer with injured aliens among the still-burning wreckage. Anderson released a diary in which his uncle had purportedly recorded the event. Alas, forensic tests showed that the ink used to write the entries had not been manufactured until 1974 (Nickell 2001, 120).

The most elaborate Roswell hoax, and the one that probably reached the largest audience, was the "alien autopsy" film. It will be remembered as a classic of the genre. The truth about the "Roswell incident"—that the crashed object was a secret U.S. spy balloon, part of Project Mogul, that was attempting to monitor emissions from anticipated Soviet nuclear tests—continues to be obscured by hoaxers, conspiracy cranks, and hustlers. We should recall Paul Kurtz's statement from back in 1995: "The Roswell myth should be permitted to die a deserved death. Whether or not we are alone in the universe will have to be decided on the basis of better evidence than that provided by the latest bit of Roswell fakery" (Nickell 1995, 19).

References

BBC home page. www.bbc.co.uk/manchester/content/articles/2006/04/07070406_alien_interview_features.html (accessed April 18, 2006).

Carr, Timothy Spencer. 1997. Son of originator of "alien autopsy" story casts doubt on father's credibility. *Skeptical Inquirer* 21, no. 4 (July–August): 31–32.

Clark, Jerome. 1993. UFO hoaxes. In *Encyclopedia of Hoaxes,* ed. Gordon Stein, 267–78. Detroit: Gale Research.

Di Maio, Dominick. 1995. Appearance on *American Journal,* September 6.

Horne, Marc. 2006. *Max Headroom* creator made Roswell alien. *Sunday Times* (Britain), April 25. http://www.timesonline.co.uk/article/0,,2087–2136617,00.html (accessed April 25, 2006).

Humphreys, John. Official Web site. http://www.john-humphreys.com/index.html (accessed April 18, 2006).

Nickell, Joe. 1995. Alien autopsy hoax. *Skeptical Inquirer* 19, no. 6 (November–December): 17–19.

———. 2001. *Real-Life X-Files: Investigating the Paranormal.* Lexington: University Press of Kentucky.

Nickell, Joe, and John F. Fischer. 1990. The crashed-saucer forgeries. *International UFO Reporter,* March–April, 4–12.

Salford man admits alien autopsy fake. 2006. *Manchester Evening News,* April 6. www .manchesteronline.co.uk/men/news/showbiz/s/210/21 (accessed April 6, 2006).

Stokes, Trey. 1995. Personal communications, August 29–31.

Uthman, Ed. 1995. Fox's "alien autopsy": A pathologist's view. Usenet, sci.med .pathology, September 15.

Wecht, Cyril. 1995. Quoted on *Alien Autopsy: Fact or Fiction?* Fox, August 28 and September 4.

SNAKE CHARMING

FROM THE SNAKE-CHARMING "MIRACLE MEN" of the East to their Western counterparts who "take up serpents" in certain Christian rituals or perform in sideshows, many have demonstrated their supposed power over the feared reptiles.

Eastern Tradition

Figure 8 is a sketch I made in the Medina in Marrakech, Morocco, in 1971. I was drawn to the scene by the peculiar flute music. The performer was putting on a snake show while his assistant used his tambourine as a collection tray. As shown in the soft-pencil rendering, one of the charmer's stunts was to approach a cobra in a squatting position, one hand on the ground and the other holding a tangle of serpents with which he teased the cobra.

In India the itinerant *Jadu* (magic) performer occasionally does herpetological tricks. For example, he might transform a piece of rope into a snake (after wrapping the rope in cloth, of course, as he no doubt makes the switch) (Siegel 1991, 186). My friend Premanand, an Indian conjurer and skeptic, knows many such feats. One, described in his *Science versus Miracles* (1994, 36), is a rod-to-serpent feat like that of the Pharaoh's sorcerers related in Exodus (7:9–15). The snake's head and tail are held in either hand, and the reptile is stretched straight. Firm pressure on the head by the thumb and index finger causes the snake to stiffen, making it look like a rod. Then it is thrown to the ground, whereupon it recovers, and the rod is "transformed" into a snake.

The Indian snake charmer performs in the open air and uses his flute music to cause a deadly hooded cobra to rise and sway rhythmically. A number of additional snakes, released from baskets and jute bags by his assistants, may be similarly entranced. When the music stops and the performer extends a stick toward the cobra, it strikes quickly. The snake charmer may even have the

Figure 8. Moroccan snake charmer teases a cobra with a tangle of snakes. (On-site sketch by Joe Nickell)

deadly reptiles crawling over his arms, and he concludes his act by dramatically capturing each snake.

Actually, although snakes do have hearing organs, it is the movement of the charmer, swaying to the melody, that the cobra follows. By ceasing to pipe and sway, the charmer causes the cobra to pose motionless; then, by extending the stick, he provokes it to strike. In some cases, the cobras are drugged or have their venom sacs removed or their mouths sewn shut. But skilled performers can and do handle these lethal reptiles. From long experience, they understand how cobras behave, know their striking distance, and rely on the snakes' shortsightedness.

In concluding his act, the charmer often deliberately provokes a cobra with the movements of one hand and then, as it prepares to strike, quickly grasps it behind the head with the other. By taking advantage of the snake's natural tendency to hide, he places it in a basket or bag (Gibson 1967, 70–73; Gardner 1962, 51–52).

Western Religion

In the West, certain Christian charismatics believe that their faith gives them immunity to serpents, just as they are given the ability to speak in tongues and the power to heal by the laying on of hands. They are inspired by two New Testament passages. In Luke (10:18–19), Jesus says to some followers: "Behold, I give unto you power to tread on serpents and scorpions, and over all the power of the enemy: and nothing shall by any means hurt you." And in a passage in the Gospel of Mark (16:16–18), when Jesus appears to his disciples after his resurrection, he says: "He that believeth and is baptized shall be saved; but he that believeth not shall be damned. And these signs shall follow them that believe: In my name shall they cast out devils; they shall speak with new tongues; they shall take up serpents; and if they drink any deadly thing, it shall not hurt them; they shall lay hands on the sick, and they shall recover." However, the latter passage may be spurious—an addition of the second century (Larue 1990, 212).

The modern practice of snake handling seems to have originated in 1909 with one George Went Hensley, an illiterate Church of God preacher. Hensley was sermonizing about the passage from Mark at an outdoor service near

Cleveland, Tennessee, when a box of rattlesnakes was overturned next to his pulpit. Hensley picked up the snakes and continued preaching—thus earning a reputation as "the original prophet of snake handling" (Yardley 1992).

No major Pentecostal denomination now endorses snake handling, and it has been specifically rejected by the Church of God. Even so, some rural congregations continue the practice, including the Free Pentecostal Holiness Church (with churches in Virginia, Kentucky, Tennessee, and North Carolina) and various independent churches scattered throughout Appalachia. The churches are invariably small, rural edifices, like one in Alabama that was converted from a store and filling station (Nickell 1998, 117).

Adherents of the practice insist that taking up serpents should be done only when worshippers truly feel that the Holy Spirit is upon them. This caution may reflect more shrewdness than piety, however. Although poisonous snakes are certainly dangerous and must be handled carefully, knowledgeable snake handlers are aware that unless snakes are hot, hungry, or frightened, they move little and are relatively unaggressive (Parsons 1990, 15). Also, snakes raised from hatchlings can become accustomed to handling. Large snakes grasped firmly behind the neck are unable to bite, and "once they are off the ground they are much less likely to bite and can usually be held safely" (Mattison 1991, 56–57). In addition to these general practices, there are some that apply to particular species of snakes that handlers can use to their advantage (see Nickell 1998, 119). The extent to which trickery is employed is debatable, but there are occasional allegations of the use of defanged snakes.

When a snake handler is bitten, it is often blamed on his or her lack of faith. When a devout member of the sect dies from a snakebite, the others must resort to some other rationalization (Nickell 1998, 120–21). Although snakebites should certainly be treated, the fact is that the amount of venom injected, and thus the severity of the reaction, varies: with a mild snakebite, the strike is a glancing one, causing only minimal pain; a moderate snakebite causes some localized pain and swelling but not a general feeling of illness; a severe snakebite causes excruciating pain, discoloration and swelling, and generalized illness. The effect of a snakebite can also vary considerably depending on the health and size of the victim, the speed of venom absorption, and the location of the bite; fortunately, most bites are on the extremities, and venom is rarely injected directly into a blood vessel, which could be fatal. Multiple bites are most dangerous, since venom can be injected with each bite, and the attack of several snakes could be life-threatening. Remaining calm is essential, since panic causes the venom to spread more quickly, as snake handlers know well (Nickell 1998, 119; Smith and Brodie 1982, 9–10).

Ironically, snake handling's "original prophet," George Went Hensley, died in 1955 of a snakebite sustained during a religious service (Yardley 1992).

Sideshows

Snakes are also part of circus and carnival exotica. They have been included in menageries and featured in sideshows. The standard snakes for the latter are Indian pythons and Central American boa constrictors, which are dangerous "only if you let them get a coil around your neck or chest and then only if you are alone and can't find the head or tail" (Gresham 1953, 141–42).

A link with the East is sometimes acknowledged in sideshow presentations. A young Indian woman—Saidor A. Isoha—appeared in 1890s publicity photographs by Karl Hagenbeck, whose German circus was among the most important shows in Europe. She once staged public fights, pitting a cobra against a mongoose. As William G. FitzGerald (1897) reported in the London magazine the *Strand*, "This was a little costly, however, for the cobra was always killed." Saidor reportedly gave up her cobras after watching a man suffer a terrible death from a cobra bite. She dressed in colorful Indian costumes and wore metal bracelets on her wrists and upper arms, working with six Indian and three African pythons plus three boa constrictors, all in the eight-to twelve-foot range. Wrote FitzGerald (1897): "She has a real affection for her snakes, and they for her. One large python will form himself into a living turban about her head."

Most of the European and American sideshow snake charmers have been women. The combination of scantily clad ladies and their fang-bearing charges is a subtly erotic one—a beauty-and-the-beast theme that has proved irresistible to sideshow banner artists. In researching my book *Secrets of the Sideshows* (Nickell 2005), I occasionally met one of these performers (figure 9). Obviously (as with eating fire, lying on a bed of nails, and similar tortures I endured for my research), I lived to tell about it.

Figure 9. The author poses with sideshow snake charmer Ginger Donahue and her friend. (Author's photo by Benjamin Radford)

Note

Portions of this chapter were adapted from my *Looking for a Miracle* (1998) and *Secrets of the Sideshows* (2005).

References

FitzGerald, William G. [1897]. The fabulous creation. *Strand* (London). Reprinted in James Taylor and Kathleen Kotcher. 2002. *James Taylor's Shocked and Amazed!— On and Off the Midway,* 90–113. Guilford, Conn.: Lyons Press.

Gardner, Dick. 1962. *The Impossible.* New York: Ballantine Books.

Gibson, Walter. 1967. *Secrets of Magic: Ancient and Modern.* New York: Grosset & Dunlap.

Gresham, William Lindsay. 1953. *Monster Midway.* New York: Rinehart & Company.

Larue, Gerald A. 1990. *The Supernatural, the Occult, and the Bible.* Buffalo, N.Y.: Prometheus Books.

Mattison, Chris. 1991. *A–Z of Snake Keeping.* New York: Sterling Publishing.

Nickell, Joe. 1998. *Looking for a Miracle.* Buffalo, N.Y.: Prometheus Books.

———. 2005. *Secrets of the Sideshows.* Lexington: University Press of Kentucky.

Parsons, Alexandra. 1990. *Amazing Snakes.* New York: Alfred A. Knopf.

Premanand, B. 1994. *Science versus Miracles*. Delhi, India: Indian CSICOP.

Siegel, Lee. 1991. *Net of Magic: Wonders and Deceptions in India*. Chicago: University of Chicago Press.

Smith, Hobart M., and Edmund D. Brodie Jr. 1982. *A Guide to Field Identification: Reptiles of North America*. New York: Golden Press.

Yardley, Jim. 1992. Mark of the serpent, and poison and pulpit. *Atlanta Constitution*, February 9.

ABRAHAM LINCOLN'S
SPIRIT WRITING

ALTHOUGH PURPORTED COMMUNICATION with the dead is ancient, modern spiritualism began in 1848 at Hydesville, New York, when two schoolgirls, Maggie and Katie Fox, pretended to communicate with a ghost who identified himself as a murdered peddler. Four decades later the sisters confessed their trickery and even publicly demonstrated how they had faked the "spirit rappings." In the meantime, however, spiritualism had spread across the United States and beyond. Magicians such as Harry Houdini (1874–1926) were instrumental in exposing phony mediums who produced so-called materializations, spirit writing and photography, and other bogus phenomena (Nickell 1988; 2001, 195, 259–60).

Spirit Writing

Alleged spirit writing takes two major forms. In automatic writing—sometimes called trance writing—"scripts [are] produced without the control of the conscious mind." In this case, some entity, such as an angel or a spirit, supposedly guides the individual's hand. The other type of spirit writing, known as slate writing, is allegedly a "direct" form in which the entity itself wields the chalk or pencil. Typically, according to one authority (Shepard 1984):

> The medium and the sitter take their seats at opposite ends of a small table, each grasping a corner of an ordinary school slate, which they thus hold firmly pressed against the underside of the table. A small fragment of slate-pencil is first inclosed [*sic*] between slate and table, for the use of the supposed spirit-writer. Should the seance be successful, a scratching sound, as of someone writing on a slate, is heard at the end of a few moments; three loud raps indicate the conclusion of the message, and on the withdrawal of the slate, it is found to be

partly covered with writing—either a general message allegedly from the spirit world, or an answer to some question previously written down by the sitter.

Proponents of automatic writing admit that it has been "the source of innumerable cases of self-delusion," but slate writing has an even more notorious history. The phenomenon of slate writing was claimed to have been discovered by Henry Slade (d. 1905). Although he claimed that the script had been created under conditions that precluded trickery, thereby proving its authenticity as a spirit-created document, in fact, it was easily produced by a variety of magic tricks. Mediums—including Slade himself—were repeatedly caught faking the phenomenon (Shepard 1984; Houdini 1924).

Keeler the "Medium"

I have been able to study various types of writings, drawings, and paintings allegedly produced by spirits (Nickell 2001, 18–27, 259–75). Recently, I examined a specimen of slate writing allegedly done by the spirit of Abraham Lincoln through the mediumship of one Pierre Louie Ormand Augustus Keeler (figure 10), who was active for more than fifty years, beginning in the late 1870s (Keeler 1938).

Keeler performed a variety of feats, including producing physical phenomena while he was behind a curtain with his hands supposedly secured. For example, English naturalist Alfred Russel Wallace (1823–1913) reported that "a waistcoat was handed to me over the curtain, which proved to be the medium's, though his coat was left on and his hands had been held by his companion all the time" (Wallace 1905). Wallace was probably unaware that this stunt has many versions and is a well-known magicians' trick (Hull 1915). Others were convinced that Keeler was merely "a clever trickster," and in at least one séance he was "accidentally seen writing on a slate held in his lap under the table." This occurred at the Lily Dale spiritualist camp in western New York in 1907, and the observer was the noted psychic investigator Hereward Carrington (Shepard 1984). According to *The Encyclopedia of Occultism and Parapsychology* (Shepard 1984): "In retrospect, it is difficult to

Figure 10. Pierre Louie Ormand Augustus Keeler, under whose mediumship slate writing was produced—allegedly. (Photo by Joe Nickell from original at Lily Dale Museum)

doubt that Keeler's phenomena, as with so many other exponents of slate-writing, must have been fraudulent."

Keeler also used a pair of slates in conjunction with a feat called "pellet reading," in which messages appeared on a pellet of paper that had been secured between hinged, locked slates, the key to which Keeler placed in his pocket (Shepard 1984). Keeler had a summer cottage at Lily Dale, and his journal contains an entry for a séance he held on October 7, 1894: "Portrait in oil of Abraham Lincoln given on canvas inside of slates in six minutes" (Keeler 1894, 12). I envision this as a swatch of canvas measuring about eight by ten inches, since its whereabouts are now unknown.

Magicians have exposed and duplicated numerous slate secrets, such as the construction of trick slates, the use of confederates, the switching of paper pellets by sleight of hand, and so forth (e.g., Houdini 1924, 79–110).

Figure 11. Slate with a message purportedly from the spirit of Abraham Lincoln. (Photo by Joe Nickell)

The "Lincoln" Slate

Keeler's alleged Lincoln script is exhibited in a display case at the Lily Dale Museum and labeled "THE 'LINCOLN' SLATE / Through the mediumship of P. L. O. A. Keeler" (figure 11). Written in chalk, the message reads:

> We come to you Sir because we see you are spreading the truth in the right way. I understood this phenomenon while in earth life, and had I lived, should of proclaimed it to the world. Press fo[r]ward My Brother. Never let thy step stray from the path of progress and truth. Your Friend
>
> Abraham Lincoln

The specific conditions under which it was produced are unknown.

If this was indeed Lincoln writing, his saying that he "understood this phenomenon" would likely refer to the fact that his wife, Mary Todd Lincoln, attended séances. One was even held in the White House's Red Parlor, and Lincoln stumbled upon the session and watched with curiosity. On another occasion, he accompanied Mary to a séance at a private home. The president, however, was a skeptic, and one biographer has suggested that his limited involvement in spiritualism was due to a desire "to protect his gullible wife" (Temple 1995, 199; Nickell 2001, 113–14). She had turned to spiritualism in her grief over the death of their eleven-year-old son, Willie, in 1862. According to Lloyd Lewis's *Myths after Lincoln* (1973, 301), "In these dark hocus-pocuses Mrs. Lincoln found comfort, and Lincoln let them go on for a time, careless of whether the intellectuals of the capital thought him addle-pated or no."

Keeler's Lincoln slate text is one of the many examples of skeptics purportedly endorsing spiritualism posthumously. The most outrageous case is the series of communications supposedly from arch-antispiritualist Houdini, in which he recanted his doubts even though the great magician had personally caught one medium after another at their tricks (Polidoro 2001). I sat in on such a séance, held in a dimly lit radio studio in Toronto in 1969. The medium went into a "trance" in record time, and then gave an unconvincing speech allegedly from Houdini who implicitly realized from the great beyond the error of his former disbelief.

Textual Analysis

Even apart from the self-serving nature of the Lincoln message—which is an endorsement not only of spiritualism but also of Keeler himself—the message does not seem authentically Lincolnesque. First of all, Lincoln typically signed his missives "A. Lincoln," reserving the more formal "Abraham Lincoln" for presidential documents such as the Emancipation Proclamation, military orders, and the like (Hamilton 1996, 14; Lorant 1957).

Several elements of the text are suspicious, including the use of *thy* in the last sentence: "Never let thy step stray from the path of progress and truth." *Thy*, an archaic form of *your*, is uncharacteristic of Lincoln; he avoided such archaisms even in works in which he used especially formal language, such as the Gettysburg Address and letters of consolation to relatives of slain soldiers (Nickell 1992). However, *thy* is often used by pretentious writers trying to sound poetical or hoping to effect a pseudobiblical tone, as in this platitudinous—and supposedly otherworldly—advice. Most significant is the slate writer's use of *should of* for *should have.* That grammatical error is unimaginable for Lincoln.

Handwriting Study

If the slate were genuine, the handwriting should be Lincoln's, since the writings were supposedly done by the spirit's own hand. In fact, a 1938 article on Keeler in the *Psychic Observer* is illustrated with "a reproduction of a slate-writing" from a Keeler séance, consisting of thirty-five "signatures" supposedly from the spirit world. They appear under the statement, "We all send glad greetings / We have no special messages." The spirit signees included a number of now mostly obscure spiritualists, along with one noted skeptic, orator Robert Green Ingersoll (Keeler 1938). Lacking the original signatures, however, we must conclude that they could have been merely freehand forgeries, as that of Ingersoll appears to be.

In fact, the slate handwriting is clearly not that of Abraham Lincoln. Even at first glance (see figure 11), we can see that the writing has a backward slant, which may be symptomatic of affectation, left-handedness, or disguise (Nickell 1996, 14–15). Lincoln's own script (figure 12)—which I have had many occasions to examine—is slanted normally.

Moreover, the specific individual characteristics are not those of Lincoln. For example, he habitually made the initial *A* of his signature in two parts: first, rendering the tented body of the letter with a series of movements, and second, after lifting the pen, producing the crossbar with the beginning stroke of his *L* (see figure 12). In contrast, the alleged spirit text's *A* of the unlikely *Abraham* was written without any lifting of the chalk, resulting in a double-looping configuration that belies Lincoln's authorship. (Lincoln did sometimes make a continuous *A*, but not for his signature, and in any case, the chalked *A* fails to resemble his in other respects.)

Another marked difference between the questionable spirit text and examples of Lincoln's handwriting is the form of the capital *S* and the initial lowercase *s.* Those on the slate tend to be the printed form of both, assuming that the large *S* of *Sir* is indeed a capital; the only exception among the six

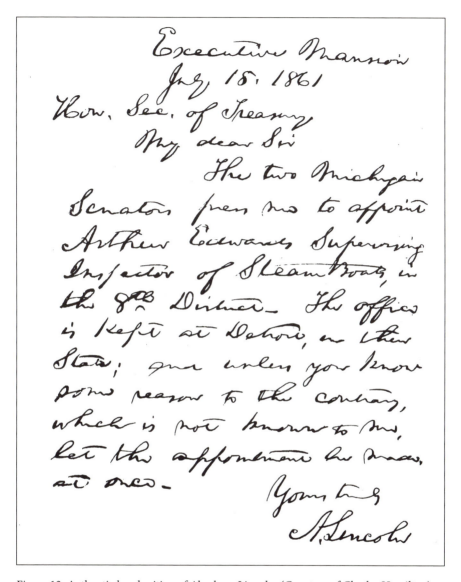

Figure 12. Authentic handwriting of Abraham Lincoln. (Courtesy of Charles Hamilton)

instances is that of *should*, which has the more usual cursive *s.* Lincoln's own handwriting consistently exhibits cursive forms, one for the capital *S,* another for the lowercase letter.

Yet another difference is the basic form of the lowercase *a*'s. Those in the

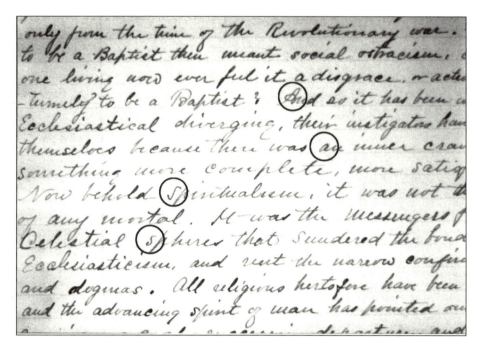

Figure 13. Handwriting from Keeler's 1894 personal journal. (Photo by Joe Nickell)

slate text are made in the common way, with the body of the letter consisting of an oval made from the top (with or without a connecting stroke). In contrast, Lincoln—rather distinctively—usually began his *a*'s from the bottom, often extending well below the baseline (see, for example, the word *and* in line 11 of figure 12).

These significant differences—and there are many more—demonstrate that the alleged spirit writing on the Keeler slate is not in the handwriting of Abraham Lincoln. But whose script is it? Although it was chalked, scrawled, written backhandedly (possibly disguised), and only a limited sample, the previously mentioned features can be seen in the script in Keeler's journal (figure 13), penned either by Keeler or by someone else taking down his trance utterances. In brief, the Lincoln message is bogus and was probably scrawled by Keeler or a confederate during the séance. Had it been prepared in advance, no doubt the writer would have at least attempted to imitate Lincoln's distinctively rugged script, rather than producing a scrawled, backhanded writing that bears no resemblance to it.

References

Hamilton, Charles. 1996. *Great Forgers and Famous Fakes,* 1–37. Lakewood, Colo.: Glenbridge Publishing.

Houdini, Harry. [1924]. *A Magician among the Spirits,* 138–39. Reprint, New York: Grosset & Dunlap, 1972.

Hull, Burling. 1915. *Rope Ties and Chain Releases,* 25–26. New York: Magnotrix Novelty.

Keeler, P. L. O. A. 1894. Journal titled "Recordings of Readings Given by P. L. O. A. Keeler, 1894." On display at Lily Dale Museum, Lily Dale, N.Y.

Keeler—slate writer/fifty years service. 1938. *Psychic Observer,* September 10.

Lewis, Lloyd. 1973. *Myths after Lincoln.* Gloucester, Mass.: Peter Smith.

Lorant, Stefan. 1957. *Lincoln: A Picture Story of His Life.* New York: Harper & Brothers.

Nickell, Joe. 1988. *Secrets of the Supernatural: Investigating the World's Occult Mysteries,* 47–60. Buffalo, N.Y.: Prometheus Books.

———. 1992. *Ambrose Bierce Is Missing and Other Historical Mysteries,* 99–109. Lexington: University Press of Kentucky.

———. 1996. *Detecting Forgery: Forensic Investigation of Documents.* Lexington: University Press of Kentucky.

———. 2001. *Real-Life X-Files: Investigating the Paranormal.* Lexington: University Press of Kentucky.

Polidoro, Massimo. 2001. *Final Séance: The Strange Friendship between Houdini and Conan Doyle.* Amherst, N.Y.: Prometheus Books.

Shepard, Leslie, ed. 1984. *The Encyclopedia of Occultism and Parapsychology,* 2nd ed. Detroit: Gale Research.

Temple, Wayne C. 1995. *Abraham Lincoln: From Skeptic to Prophet.* Mahomet, Ill.: Mayhaven.

Wallace, Alfred Russel. 1905. *My Life,* 2 vols. Cited in Shepard 1984.

DOWSING MYSTERIOUS SITES

I AM NOT AN ARCHAEOLOGIST, but as something of a jack-of-all-trades, I have participated in some archaeological investigations and digs, including a forensic one that unearthed hidden skeletal remains and a bullet (Renovation 1981). In short, I know enough to appreciate what a boon psychic power would be to the field—if such power actually existed.

Psychic Archaeology

Certainly, there are many who believe in psychic archaeology—the supposed "application of clairvoyance and other psychic skills to the field of archaeology, especially in the location of dig sites and the identification of artifacts." It may involve psychometry (in which an object is used to obtain psychic "impressions"), dowsing (divination with a device such as a rod or a pendulum to locate things hidden on-site or on a map), automatic writing (in which spirits of the dead supposedly guide the hand to produce messages), or some other alleged psychic mode (Guiley 1991).

What has been termed "perhaps the first, best-known case of deliberate psychic archaeology" was launched in 1907 by Frederick Bligh Bond in excavations at England's Glastonbury Abbey. Unknown to the Church of England officials who appointed him, Bond was an occultist who turned to a friend's automatic writing for help in locating the ruins of two chapels. Soon, Gulielmus Monachus (William the Monk) and other spirits, including "watchers from the other side," were tapping the "universal memory" to provide the necessary site information. Bond's excavations were successful, but when he eventually revealed his methods in 1917, the church was embarrassed and forced him out, ending the work in 1922 (Guiley 1991).

Archaeologist, skeptic, and CSI fellow Kenneth L. Feder, in his *Frauds,*

Myths, and Mysteries (1996, 198), points out the problem of prior knowledge in such cases. "Bond was an expert on medieval churches," notes Feder, "and we know that he had access to and had examined many of the documents, maps, plans, and drawings of the abbey before initiating field research." Moreover, "although much of the abbey was a ruin, some walls and foundations were visible at the surface." The locations of the chapels, supposedly identified for Bond by spirits, had been generally identified in old documents, and previous searches had greatly narrowed the areas left to explore. Feder observes that Bond simply "searched for and found the chapels in the only reasonable places left for them to be." Scientific tests have not proved the efficacy of psychic archaeology (Feder 1980, 1995). Such tests "either are not conducted or are conducted so poorly as to render the results meaningless" (Feder 1996).

Some defenders of dowsing would object to its being categorized as a psychic method, suggesting that it may have a natural explanation. Dowsers often attribute the movement of their rods or pendulums to "earth force fields" that supposedly send out "vibrations," such as electromagnetic or other radiation. Yet many dowsers work from maps, far from the actual locations, and some claim to receive images—including from the past and future—like clairvoyants (Guiley 1991, 155–56). Dowsers have claimed success in locating hidden objects and even missing persons (Nickell 1994). Unfortunately, dowsers fare poorly in properly controlled tests of their abilities, as James Randi (1982, 1991) has repeatedly demonstrated. I once tested some gold dowsers in the Yukon Territory of Canada, site of the famed Klondike gold rush. Alas, they could not differentiate among gold nuggets, fool's gold, chromium nuts and bolts, and empty boxes—although they tried to rationalize their failures (Nickell 1976).

The well-established, scientific explanation for the movement of dowsing rods and pendulums is "the unwitting translation of thoughts into muscular action"—the same force responsible for various other phenomena such as automatic writing, table tipping, and the movement of a Ouija board's planchette (Gardner 1957, 109). Nevertheless, the claims continue. Here are two examples—one from Australia, the other from Germany—that involve dowsing to locate or provide information about alleged archaeological sites.

The Mahogany Ship

Reportedly, a boat carrying three seal hunters capsized off southeastern Australia in 1836, drowning the captain. The two survivors sought safety along this now aptly named "Shipwreck Coast" (where more than eighty shipping disasters occurred between 1836 and 1922). At that site, between present-day Port Fairy and Warrnambool, the two spied a wrecked ship lodged in the hummocks (or sand dunes) (Lindsay 1996, 2). Since then, the legend of the Mahogany Ship has challenged historians and intrigued tourists. It has even been memorialized in these closing verses of an unattributed poem, "The Ancient Ship" (Lindsay 1996):

> An ancient ship—we've heard the tales—
> Was forced ashore by southern gales,
> Nothing left—no masts or sails,
> Just timbers like mahogany.
> Will it be discovered soon
> That ancient ship beneath a dune?
> Only the sun, the stars, the moon
> Are witness to this mystery.

There is also an eye-catching Mahogany Ship replica at the McDonald's restaurant in Warrnambool (figure 14)—dubbed the "McReplica" by a waggish Bob Nixon, Australian Skeptics' chief investigator.

The chronology of events is illuminating. Just after the 1836 sighting by the two sealers, an expedition was mounted by Captain John Mills to recover their capsized boat, along with the drowned captain's body. However, the searchers failed to find the reported shipwreck. Mills searched again in 1843 and did discover a wreck, which he revisited in 1847. There were sightings off and on over subsequent decades, with the ship presumably disappearing and reappearing due to shifting sands, until it was last seen in 1880, leaving only controversy behind. Worse, it was a perambulating wreck. As Nixon (2001a) observed:

> It is variously described as close to Port Fairy, mid-way between Port Fairy and Warrnambool, three miles west of Warrnambool. She is said

Figure 14. Faux "Mahogany Ship" at the McDonald's in Warrnambool, along Australia's "Shipwreck Coast"—dubbed the "McReplica" by Bob Nixon. (Author's photo by Bob Nixon)

to be high in the hummocks, well above the high tide mark, in the water, between two hummocks, at the end of a gap in the hummocks. She is identified to be in various states of decay, in various orientations, bows pointing west and north. In short there is little agreement among the reports.

Some believed that the legendary wreck was Dutch, Spanish, or Portuguese (Loney 1998, 20), possibly offering proof of an early, "secret" discovery of Australia by the Portuguese rather than by Captain Cook (McIntyre 1977). Others were more skeptical, however. In 1896 a local historian expressed doubt about the existence of the wreck, stating that most older residents regarded it as mere fable. He noted that old timbers saturated with whale oil, which had been used for flooring in a house, were mistakenly thought to have been salvaged from the Mahogany Ship, but they had probably come from "an old whaling punt" (Loney 1998, 17–18).

I was fortunate enough to investigate the Mahogany Ship mystery with Bob Nixon and Richard Cadena (Victoria Skeptics vice president). Bob had contacted Peter D'Aloisio, the 1988 Australian "champion" water diviner (dowser) and a professional water driller. After determining the general location of the wreck by means of local landmarks, D'Aloisio had used his divining rods to locate what he believed was a chain and a nine-foot anchor, possibly from the fabled wreck itself. He "found" the alleged relics in December 1992, and between February and June 1993, he drilled two holes at the location. One turned up bits of metal, so he sank a large-diameter pipe to a depth of some thirty-three feet, but unfortunately, the shaft flooded. He and a diver searched the bottom of the flooded pipe shaft but could not ascertain what was there. Since then, the pipe had been sealed with a metal cover. So far, D'Aloisio had spent about $150,000 (Australian) in motel bills and exploration costs (D'Aloisio 2000).

We met Peter, his brother Dominic, and two of their friends in Warrnambool and followed them to the location at Levy's Point Coastal Reserve. Peter demonstrated his dowsing technique for us at the site, and we took photographs (figure 15). Later, we discussed the evidence at the Mahogany Ship Restaurant (where I had a delicious kangaroo steak). Peter showed us some papers related to his project, including a report on the metal traces he had obtained by drilling; the tests, performed by Monash University, determined that the metal had probably come from one of Peter's own broken drill bits (D'Aloisio 2000; Nixon 2001a).

Therefore, the dowsing evidence is unsupported, and a lot of other evidence makes it unlikely that a Mahogany Ship anchor has been found. For example, whereas one possible location for the wreck (shown on a widely published map) is appropriately near the beach, the D'Aloisio site is almost a kilometer inland, which is difficult to reconcile with a beached ship. Actually, there is evidence that casts doubt on the existence of any ancient wreck—Portuguese or otherwise. As it happens, the "original" 1836 sighting was not reported until decades later, and there are conflicting—and apparently even "doctored"—versions of some accounts (McKiggan 1987, 65). Indeed, Hugh Donnelly, who claimed to have participated in the recovery of the capsized whale boat and the drowned captain's body in 1836, did not arrive in Australia until five years later (Nixon 2001a, 33).

Figure 15. Peter D'Aloisio dowsing the site where he believes the anchor of the Mahogany Ship may lie. (In background, left to right, are Bob Nixon, Richard Cadena, Peter's brother, and a friend.) (Photo by Joe Nickell)

In addition to visiting the D'Aloisio site, Richard, Bob, and I explored the area in and around Tower Hill. This ancient, lake-filled volcano crater provided a magnificent view of Armstrong's Bay to the south, the reputed site of the Mahogany Ship. We also did research at the Flagstaff Hill Maritime Museum, where we obtained clippings and learned that an anchor from an ancient Portuguese ship would have been much smaller than the one described by D'Aloisio. We also interviewed a member of the Mahogany Ship Committee, John Lindsay (2000), who told us that extensive searching with a magnetometer had yielded nothing, making it unlikely that an anchor would be found in the area. Finally, we visited the local library, where we stayed until closing time, photocopying material. This included information from a book cited in a Mahogany Ship display at the museum—which turned out to be a novel!

Back in Melbourne, Bob and I visited the state library of Victoria to conduct further research. We searched for early newspaper accounts on microfilm, notably one from the October 29, 1847, edition of the *Portland Guardian* describing a wreck found near Warrnambool. It was "thrown completely into the hummocks, and buried in the sand"; its deck was "completely gone." The account went on to suggest that the wreck had been the source of "a number of articles strewed along the beach" in 1841, and "from several articles of French manufacture that were then found it was deemed that the vessel had been a French whaler."

Bob and I have come to believe that this French whaler is a plausible—I will go so far as to say probable—candidate for the Mahogany Ship. Given the differing descriptions and locations, however, it appears that more than one wreck could be involved. In any case, to date, there is no evidence that dowsing has added anything other than confusion to the shipwreck mystery.

Celtic Sites

During an investigative tour of Germany in the fall of 2002 that included some locales in Franconia (northern Bavaria), I was able to explore three sites associated with the legendary Celtic priesthood of the Druids (Nickell 2003a, 2003b). The expedition, which took place on a bleak, drizzly October 13, was arranged at the request of my excellent German guide, Martin Mahner, executive director of the Center for Inquiry–Europe. Accompanying us were several intrepid members of the Bamberg Skeptics Guild and our distinguished leader, geologist Michael Link from the Paleontological Institute of the University of Erlangen. Michael was kind enough to conduct the three-site tour in English especially for my benefit.

From Bamberg, our little convoy proceeded some fifty kilometers southeast into the area known to tourists as "Franconian Switzerland" because of its mountainous terrain, caves, castle ruins, and other scenic features. It was once inhabited by the Celts, a tribe that extended into central Europe in about 1200 BC. Our first stop took us to a remote wooded hill known as Ringwall. Had we not been with Michael, we would have seen it only as a scenic place with some natural rock outcroppings. However, with his guidance, we could see distinct earthworks covered with thick moss and a stand of trees. They had been added to the limestone formations to create what was, indeed, an ancient Celtic fortress—hence the name Ringwall ("circular rampart"). Michael informed us

Figure 16. Entrance to a German cave with a fifteen-meter-deep pit that yields evidence of apparent Druidic activity. (Photo by Joe Nickell)

that excavations at the site had turned up iron implements and pottery dating to circa 500 BC.

From Ringwall we proceeded to another isolated site, about one and a half kilometers further southeast, known as Espershöhle (*höhle* meaning "cavern").

Cold air emanates from this cave of Jurassic limestone, giving it the popular name Eishölle ("Ice Hell"). It may have had mystical meaning for the Celts. Having been an avid spelunker during my college years, I was an apt pupil when Michael pointed out that the amphitheater-like entranceway was the result of a cave "room" collapsing and, over time, becoming exposed at the surface (figure 16). A passageway (which is home to hibernating bats from October to April) leads to a fifteen-meter-deep pit. An archaeological excavation in 1937–1938 recovered artifacts that identified it as a Celtic site. The presence of skeletal remains—some bones exhibiting knife marks—suggested the practice of sacrifice (Link 2002).

The last of the three sites we visited is known as Druidenhain or "Druid's Grove." Arrangements of giant rocks litter the wooded area, interspersed with passageways to create a labyrinthine effect, thus inspiring the popular belief that it is an ancient Celtic site. Some have called it the "University of the Druids." Supposedly, the Celts subjected the rocks to heating and cooling to produce fracturing and create the monoliths, leading to another sobriquet for the place: the "Franconian Stonehenge" (Link 2002). Imaginative names have been given to the formations, such as "Christening Stone," "Bowl Stone," "Entrance to the Underworld," and "Sacrificial Stone," the last based on the belief that the place was used for sacrifices—an idea that dates from 1863.

Dowsers eventually got into the game and in 1983 determined that the "Altar Stone" was at the intersection of two "earth-ray" lines. These are apparently similar to the earth-energy or "ley" lines that are said to connect mystical sites. The idea of leys was advanced by English beer salesman Alfred Watkins (1925), an amateur antiquarian. Dowsing is often touted as a method of detecting such "earth energies" (Guiley 1991, 157). Dowsing has also been used in other ways at Druidenhain. For example, dowsers employed their witching wands to determine the supposedly true nature of one of the megaliths, giving it the fanciful name "The Grave" (Link 2002).

Alas, Druidenhain has yielded no potsherds, skeletal remains, or other evidence of human habitation, and there is no evidence that the site is Celtic or even man-made. In fact, the array of monoliths is actually a natural formation—the product of geologic forces and erosion. During the formation of the mountain, pressure caused the rock to fracture, producing numerous faults crisscrossing one another. These faults were then attacked preferentially by seeping water, with erosion along the fault lines eventually resulting in a multitude of rocks aligned in rows (Link 2002).

As both the Mahogany Ship and the Druidenhain cases demonstrate, dowsing is not an effective method of archaeological investigation—whether it is considered a psychic means or not. However, science is an ongoing process, and so is popular belief. From either perspective, it is important to continue to look at significant new cases and to rework the "cold" cases—not with the mystery mongers' desire to promote them or the debunkers' hope to dismiss them, but as investigators trying to understand and explain them. In so doing, we can learn more about ourselves and our world—a reward that dogmatists often seem to be unaware of.

References

D'Aloisio, Peter. 2000. Interviews by Joe Nickell, November 19 and 20.

Feder, Kenneth L. 1980. Psychic archaeology: The anatomy of irrationalist prehistoric studies. *Skeptical Inquirer* 4, no. 4 (Summer): 32–43.

———. 1995. Archaeology and the paranormal. In *Encyclopedia of the Paranormal,* ed. Gordon Stein, 32–46. Buffalo, N.Y.: Prometheus Books.

———. 1996. *Frauds, Myths, and Mysteries,* 2nd ed., 194–210. Mountain View, Calif.: Mayfield Publishing.

Gardner, Martin. 1957. *Fads and Fallacies in the Name of Science.* New York: Dover.

Guiley, Rosemary Ellen. 1991. *Harper's Encyclopedia of Mystical and Paranormal Experience,* 470–72. San Francisco: HarperCollins.

Lindsay, John. 1996. *The Legend of the Mahogany Ship.* Warrnambool, Australia: Mahogany Ship Committee.

———. 2000. Interview by Joe Nickell, November 20.

Link, Michael. 2002. Personal communication (and numerous technical handouts), October 13.

Loney, Jack. 1998. *The Mahogany Ship,* 7th ed. N.p.: Marine History Publications.

McIntyre, Kenneth Gordon. 1977. *The Secret Discovery of Australia.* Sydney, Australia: Pan Books.

McKiggan, Ian. 1987. Creation of a legend? A liberal underview. In *The Mahogany Ship: Relic or Legend,* ed. Bill Potter, 61–68. Warrnambool, Australia: Mahogany Ship Committee and Warrnambool Institute Press.

Nickell, Joe. 1976. Not recommended for serious mineral exploration. *Yukon News,* September 1.

———. 2003a. Germany: Monsters, myths, and mysteries. *Skeptical Inquirer* 27, no. 2 (March–April): 24–28.

———. 2003b. Legend of the White Lady. *Skeptical Briefs* 13, no. 1 (March): 10–12.

Nickell, Joe, ed. 1994. *Psychic Sleuths: ESP and Sensational Cases,* 11, 163–64. Buffalo, N.Y.: Prometheus Books.

Nixon, Bob. 2001a. A fresh perspective on the Mahogany Ship. *Skeptic* (Autumn): 31–34.

———. 2001b. The real "secret history." *Skeptic* (Autumn): 35–37.

Randi, James. 1982. *Flim-flam! Psychics, ESP, Unicorns and Other Delusions.* Buffalo, N.Y.: Prometheus Books.

———. 1991. *James Randi: Psychic Investigator.* London: Boxtree.

Renovation work slowed after skull, bones found. 1981. *Georgetown News and Times,* November 5.

Watkins, Alfred. 1925. *The Old Straight Track: Its Mounds, Beacons, Moats, Sites and Mark Stones.* Reprint, London: Abacus, 1974.

THE STIGMATA OF LILIAN BERNAS

CANADIAN LILIAN BERNAS CLAIMS to exhibit—"in a supernatural state"—the wounds of Christ's crucifixion. On March 1, 2002, I observed one of her bleedings (figure 17). It was the eleventh such event that "the Lord allows me to experience on the first Friday of the month," she told the audience, "with one more to come" (Bernas 2002a). But was the event really supernatural, or was it only a magic show?

The History of Stigmata

Popularly associated with saintliness, stigmata are marks resembling the wounds of the crucified Jesus that supposedly appear spontaneously on the body. Following the death of Jesus, in about AD 29 or 30, the phenomenon waited nearly twelve centuries to appear, other than a cryptic biblical reference to St. Paul (Galatians 6:17). St. Francis of Assisi (1182–1226) is credited with being the first "true" stigmatist (after a man with crucifixion wounds was arrested for imposture two years earlier). Since St. Francis, a few hundred people have exhibited stigmata, including several saints—most recently Padre Pio (1887–1968). He was canonized in 2002, although not for his stigmata; the Catholic Church has never declared the alleged phenomenon miraculous (D'Emilio 2002; Tokasz 2003).

In addition to the copycat aspect, stigmata are suspect on other grounds. They appeared mostly in Roman Catholic countries, notably Italy, until the twentieth century. Also, the form and placement of the wounds have evolved. For example, those of St. Francis (except for his side wound) "were not wounds which bled but impressions of the heads of the nails, round and black and standing clear from the flesh" (Harrison 1994, 25). Subsequently, stigmata have typically been bleeding wounds, albeit with "no consistency even remotely suggesting them as replications of one single, original pattern" (Wilson 1988, 63).

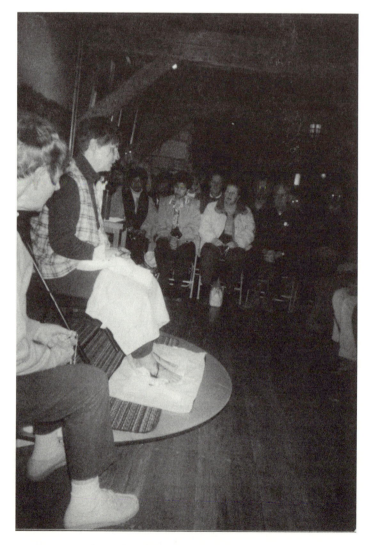

Figure 17. Canadian Lilian Bernas impressed many with her stigmata materializations. (Photo by Joe Nickell)

It is well established that many stigmatics were engaging in trickery. For instance, during a serious illness in 1543, Magdalena de la Cruz confessed that her stigmata had been faked. In 1587 Maria de la Visitacion, known as the "holy nun of Lisbon," was caught painting fake wounds on her hands. Pope

Pius IX privately branded Palma Maria Matarelli (1825–1888) a fraud, stating that "she has befooled a whole crowd of pious and credulous souls." And more recently, in 1984, an Italian court convicted stigmatic Gigliola Giorgini of fraud (Wilson 1988, 26, 42, 147).

The twentieth century's two best-known stigmatics—Theresa Neumann and Padre Pio—were also suspected of deception. Professor Martini, who conducted a surveillance of Neumann, observed that blood would flow from her wounds only when he was persuaded to leave the room, as if something "needed to be hidden from observation" (Wilson 1988, 53, 114–15). And a pathologist who examined Padre Pio concluded that his wounds were superficial at best and that the side "wound" had not penetrated the skin at all (Ruffin 1982, 146–54, 305).

Catholic scholar Herbert Thurston (1952, 100) found "no satisfactory case of stigmatization since St. Francis of Assisi." He believed that the phenomenon was due to suggestion, but attempts to duplicate it experimentally through hypnosis have ranged from doubtful to unsuccessful. As for St. Francis, his extraordinary zeal to imitate Jesus may have led him to engage in a pious deception (Nickell 2000).

A New Stigmatist

Enter Lilian Bernas, a Catholic convert (in 1989) and onetime nursing-home worker. She first exhibited stigmata during Easter of 1992, having previously received visions of Jesus. According to one of her two self-published booklets, Jesus appears frequently to her, addressing her as "My suffering soul," "My sweet petal," and "My child" (Bernas 1999). The Archdiocese of Ottawa, Ontario, where she was then living, established a commission to investigate Bernas's claims. "The inquiry did not make a judgment on the authenticity," stated Gabrielle Tasse, spokeswoman for the archdiocese. Tasse told the *Buffalo News,* "It doesn't really concern the general public. It just creates propaganda." The Catholic Church often resists publicity about supernatural claims, noted the Reverend Thomas Reese, a Jesuit priest who edits the weekly Catholic magazine *America.* "The church is very skeptical of these things," Reese explained (Tokasz 2003).

Bernas now resides in Niagara-on-the-Lake, Ontario, living since 1996 with a retired couple who agreed to take her in, supposedly at Jesus's request. They are impressed with Bernas, whom they regard as a "victim soul" (one who suffers for others). In 2001 the *Ottawa Citizen* published a profile of Bernas (Wake 2001), apparently provoking displeasure from her home archdiocese of Ottawa. Church policy (according to a spokesman for the Buffalo Diocese) is "that she is not to speak publicly because her faith journey is private" (Tokasz 2003).

However, Bernas does speak publicly, addressing the faithful and the curious at various churches. I attended a talk she gave, for example, at Resurrection Church in Cheektowaga, New York, in February 2002. Although she claimed that Jesus guided her in her talks (she sometimes departed from her prepared text), she also said that "the devil" was at her elbow at all times and that she had to struggle with pride and self-will. She spoke of Lent, of praying the Rosary, and of other Catholic topics, and she claimed that Jesus had given her "a vision of aborted babies" (Bernas 2002b). Afterward, she answered questions from those who gathered around her. Asked what Jesus looked like, she said that he appeared as we did, solid; he had shoulder-length hair with a beard and a mustache, and he wore a white robe. In other words, he exhibited the conventional likeness of Jesus as it has evolved in art. Bernas's devotees exhibit a portrait of Jesus "drawn under the inspiration of the Holy Spirit on May 20, 1994, by Lil Bernas."

The Wounds

I asked Bernas about her wounds, noting that there were reddish scars on the backs of her hands. She replied that she also bled from the palms on occasion, but that no marks were left in those instances. She told me that she was "permitted" to retain those on the backs of her hands and also on the tops of her feet. Someone asked about cross-shaped wounds (she has, for example, an apparent cruciform scar on her right jaw near the ear), and she stated that before her genuine stigmata came she had periods of possession, and those stigmata were of the devil (Bernas 2002b).

I found the absence of wounds on the palms and soles highly suspicious. A sham stigmatist might well avoid those areas, which would be painful and difficult to heal. But if a person were truly exhibiting the nail wounds of Jesus, his or her hands and feet would be completely pierced. When I attended another exhibition of Lilian Bernas's stigmata at Niagara-on-the-Lake on March 1, 2002, my suspicions were increased. The bleeding was already in progress when she appeared, and the wounds were only superficial, limited to the backs of the hands and tops of the feet. In addition, there were small wounds on the scalp, supposedly from a crown of thorns (John 19:2), but they were only in the front, as if merely for show.

Significantly, there was no side wound, like that inflicted on Jesus by a Roman soldier's lance (John 19:34; 20:25, 27). Such a large wound would represent a real commitment by a fake stigmatist, so it rarely appears, and then usually in a questionable fashion. Bernas exhibits a photo of an alleged wound in her left side, but it lacks rivulets of blood and—conveniently—she claims that it disappeared without a trace. Bernas did say that she would be receiving a side wound later in the day (Bernas 2002a), but of course, the crowd would not be there to witness it.

The side wound was not the only one of Bernas's stigmata with unique properties that were seemingly best displayed in photographs. Bernas exhibited other photos depicting a squarish nail head emerging from a hand wound (hark back to St. Francis), a thorn in her forehead that supposedly emerged over a week's time, and even an entire crown of thorns that allegedly materialized around her head—believe it or not! As we watched Bernas bleed, I regretted that we were not getting to see such remarkable manifestations. I observed that her wounds soon ceased to flow, consistent with their having been inflicted just before she came out.

After she had spoken to the audience for about an hour, people gathered around to get a closer look at Bernas (figure 18). One man attempted, rather surreptitiously, to obtain a sample of her blood, presumably as a magical "relic." While shaking hands with her, he clasped his other hand, containing a folded handkerchief, against the back of her hand. Unfortunately, the blood had dried, and even rubbing did not yield a visible trace. Although I too shook Bernas's bloody hand, I obtained a better look at the wound shortly before, when she hugged the woman in front of me and thus placed her hand virtually

Figure 18. Although Bernas attracts the credulous, her stigmata do not convincingly replicate the wounds of Christ's Crucifixion. (Photo by Joe Nickell)

under my nose. I noticed that the actual wound looked like a small slit, but surrounding that was a larger red area that appeared to have been deliberately formed with blood to simulate a larger wound, like one made by a Roman nail. (For my demonstration of a similar effect, see Nickell 2000, 27–28.)

Assessment

Bernas makes other supernatural claims as well. For example, she says that towels used during her stigmata sessions, put away in plastic bags, "disappear within 48 hours" (Wake 2001). (I would be willing to wager that they would not vanish while in my custody.) Such outlandish and unsubstantiated claims should provoke skepticism in all but the most gullible, yet a professor of philosophy at a Catholic college took exception to my views. I had told the *Buffalo News* that, based on the evidence, I regarded stigmatics as "pious frauds," and I said of Lilian Bernas's stigmata: "Everything about it was consistent with trickery. Nothing about it was in the slightest way supernatural or intriguing" (Tokasz 2003). Professor John Zeis (2003) replied with the astonishing statement that "trickery is consistent with any reported miracle (including Jesus' resurrection) but that is no reason to reject belief in the miracle." He found more reasonable a priest's statement that "it is up to each person to believe or not." CSI public-relations director Kevin Christopher (2003) responded: "Zeis is suggesting that objective evidence is irrelevant. What, in fact could be a more unreasonable conclusion?" And in reply to Zeis's claim that "the *Skeptical Inquirer* is biased against claims concerning faith in the miraculous," Christopher stated: "The magazine's mission is to inform its readers about the state of the evidence for paranormal and supernatural claims. When the evidence is poor or nonexistent, it is not 'biased' to report that fact. It is, in fact, a moral duty."

References

Bernas, Lilian. 1999. *This Is the Home of the Father.* Privately printed.
———. 2002a. Remarks to audience at Navy Hall, Niagara-on-the-Lake, Ontario, March 1 (transcript by Jenny Everett, *Popular Science* magazine).
———. 2002b. Talk at Resurrection Church, Cheektowaga, N.Y., February 17.
Christopher, Kevin. 2003. Letter to the editor. *Buffalo (N.Y.) News,* July 7.
D'Emilio Frances. 2002. Italian monk and mystic raised to sainthood. *Buffalo (N.Y.) News,* June 17.
Harrison, Ted. 1994. *Stigmata: A Medieval Phenomenon in a Modern Age.* New York: St. Martin's Press.
Nickell, Joe. 1993. *Looking for a Miracle.* Amherst, N.Y.: Prometheus Books.
———. 2000. Stigmata: In imitation of Christ. *Skeptical Inquirer* 24, no. 1 (July–August): 24–28.

Ruffin, C. Bernard. 1982. *Padre Pio: The True Story.* Huntington, Ind.: Our Sunday Visitor.

Thurston, Herbert. 1952. *The Physical Phenomena of Mysticism.* Chicago: H. Regnery.

Tokasz, Jay. 2003. In apparent stigmata, a question of belief. *Buffalo (N.Y.) News,* June 15.

Wake, Ben. 2001. The crucifixion of Lilian Bernas. *Citizen's Weekly* (magazine of the *Ottawa Citizen*), July 8, C7–C9.

Wilson, Ian. 1988. *The Bleeding Mind.* London: Weidenfeld & Nicolson.

Zeis, John. 2003. Letter to the editor. *Buffalo (N.Y.) News,* June 27.

RIDDLE OF THE CRYSTAL SKULLS

HERE AND THERE AROUND THE WORLD, mysterious artifacts are found: crystal skulls that many New Age enthusiasts believe possess mystical powers. Now new claims—and new reviews of the evidence—have sparked further controversy. What is the truth about these remarkable objects?

Skull of Doom

Perhaps the most famous of these artifacts—dubbed "the weirdest gem in the world" (Welfare and Fairley 1980, 51) and "the granddaddy of all crystal balls" (Garvin 1973, 6)—is the one commonly known as the Mitchell-Hedges crystal skull. It is also referred to as the "Skull of Doom" by those who believe that it holds the power of death over those who would mock it (Nickell 1988, 30).

Fashioned from a single block of natural rock crystal (massive clear quartz), although its lower jaw detaches, the Skull of Doom weighs eleven pounds seven ounces (figure 19). It allegedly first came to light in 1927 (or 1926 or 1924, depending on the account) during the excavation of a lost Mayan citadel in Belize (then British Honduras). Adventurer F. A. Mitchell-Hedges participated in the work, and it was supposedly his young adopted daughter, Anna, who found it under an altar of the ruined city of Lubaantun (from the Mayan word for "place of fallen stones").

Mitchell-Hedges mentioned the skull in the first edition of his autobiography, *Danger My Ally* (1954), but he did not specify where or by whom it had been found. He merely published a photograph of what he called "the sinister Skull of Doom," stating in his customarily glib fashion: "It is at least 3,600 years old and according to legend was used by the High Priest of the Maya when performing esoteric rites. It is said that when he willed death with the help of the skull, death invariably followed." Of the skull's provenance, Mitchell-Hedges said only: "How it came into my possession I have reason for not revealing." As

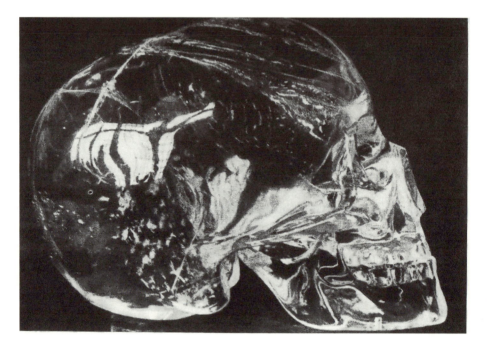

Figure 19. The Mitchell-Hedges Skull of Doom—carved from a block of rock crystal, allegedly by the ancient Mayans—as it appeared in the July 1936 issue of *Man*, at which time it was owned by art dealer Sydney Burney. (Copy of photo by Robert H. van Outer)

if that were not mysterious enough, later editions of *Danger My Ally* omitted all references to the skull, which the publishers disclaimed any knowledge of.

To answer the many questions raised by the crystal skull—Did Anna Mitchell-Hedges indeed find it at Lubaantun? If not, where did it come from? Does the skull actually have the mystical powers ascribed to it?—I conducted an investigation with my forensic colleague John F. Fischer that ran from 1982 to 1984. We obtained as much data on the skull as possible—combing through old newspaper records; corresponding with major museums and laboratories; consulting distinguished experts; amassing information on the Maya, on rock crystal, and on the skull motif in art; and seeking out those who had examined the skull, as well as Anna Mitchell-Hedges herself.

As far as we know, F. A. Mitchell-Hedges—a habitual liar and faker (Nickell 1988, 38; McConnell 1996)—made no reference to the skull at the time of his return from Lubaantun or in the years immediately following. In the 1930s he wrote newspaper articles and a book that discussed Lubaantun at length, but he omitted the Skull of Doom in favor of relatively humble figurines. In fact, as we discovered, the earliest published reference to the celebrated skull—the July 1936 issue of *Man* (a British anthropological journal)—makes no reference to the adventurer. Instead, the skull was described as "in the possession of Mr. Sydney Burney," a London art dealer (Morant 1936, 105). Moreover, there is documentary evidence that Mitchell-Hedges bought the skull in 1944 from Burney, who had apparently owned it for ten years (Morrill 1972, 28; Welfare and Fairley 1980, 53).

Anna Mitchell-Hedges has attempted to rationalize this damning evidence by claiming, in a letter to me, that her father had left the skull with Burney "as security for a loan to finance an expedition" (Mitchell-Hedges 1983). Asked if she had any proof—such as a letter or a newspaper clipping—that might help establish her father's prior ownership of the skull, Anna Mitchell-Hedges (1983) replied that she had "no documentary evidence" and added, "all my father's papers were lost in Hatteras during a cyclone—photographs and all—also a trunk of his belongings was lost in Plymouth." Be that as it may, no one who was actually at Lubaantun ever mentioned Anna being at the site or the skull being discovered there (Nickell 1988, 35–36). Subsequently, evidence surfaced that further discredits Anna's claim that she discovered the crystal skull at Lubaantun. A letter written by Sydney Burney to George Vaillant of the American Museum of Natural History makes it clear that Burney had the skull at that time (March 21, 1933) and that he had indeed "bought it" from an unnamed collector (Burney 1933).

Clearly, the Mitchell-Hedges crystal skull did not come from Lubaantun; it was acquired later from Burney. This might explain why references to the skull were deleted from subsequent editions of *Danger My Ally*. No doubt in 1954 (some three years after Burney's death) there were persons who could recall Burney's prior ownership of the skull and its sale to Mitchell-Hedges. Might not such a person have threatened to expose the deceiver?

We had hoped to examine the skull and thus learn more about its origins, and we had contacted various experts—including famed microanalyst Walter C. McCrone—about what tests might be performed. Disappointingly, however, Anna Mitchell-Hedges refused to allow us access to the skull. Nevertheless, we learned that, contrary to assertions that the skull lacked any evidence of modern workmanship, there were "traces of mechanical grinding" on the teeth (Garvin 1973, 84), as well as holes, intended for support pegs, that had been drilled by metal (Hammond 1983).

Many other fanciful assertions about the skull remained. In his autobiography, Mitchell-Hedges (1954) wrote of the skull: "It is stated in legend that it was used by a high priest of the Maya to concentrate on and will death. It is said to be the embodiment of all evil; several people who have cynically laughed at it have died, others have been stricken and become seriously ill"—or so "it is said." Richard M. Garvin, author of *The Crystal Skull* (1973, 100), concluded, "the claims that the crystal skull has caused or can cause death should most likely be filed right next to the curses of old King Tut."

Other claims about the skull have also failed to survive scrutiny. For instance, it was said that the skull remained at a constant temperature of seventy degrees Fahrenheit, regardless of the temperature it was subjected to. In fact, the skull's physical properties are no different from those of other natural quartz crystals, according to California art expert Frank Dorland (1983). Mystical properties of the skull—the sound of silver bells and perceived images, such as faces—are probably "the result of intense concentration and meditation" (Garvin 1973, 100).

Less in touch with reality is the approach of Joshua Shapiro, who, along with others, has had channeling sessions to seek psychic impressions from the crystal artifact. These led him to opine that it was an "ancient computer" storing messages for humanity. Instead of a Mayan origin, he posits that the skull could be from a lost civilization or even from some extraterrestrial site (Hunter 2005).

Closer to earth, at age ninety-eight, Anna Mitchell-Hedges told Canadian reporter Colin Hunter (2005) that the skull was the secret to her longevity. When Hunter traveled to Indiana to visit Anna at a friend's home, she stuck to her story about having found the skull at Lubaantun, although she continued to give conflicting versions of the facts. Hunter's investigative report reviewed my findings and essentially substantiated and augmented them.

As to the true origin of the Mitchell-Hedges crystal skull, there is little evidence beyond the object itself, the meager historical record, and some similar rock crystal skulls in museums and private collections.

Other Skulls

Various other crystal skulls exist, ranging from as small as an inch in width to half-life-size and life-size specimens in the Musée de l'Homme (Museum of Man) in Paris and the British Museum, respectively. They are generally classified as Aztec, but there are doubts that any of them are pre-Columbian, according to Gordon F. Ekholm (1983), an anthropologist from the American Museum of Natural History.

At least one such skull, the one at the British Museum, has been scientifi-cally examined. Although it is fashioned in a single piece and has more stylized, circular eye sockets than the Mitchell-Hedges skull, the two look remarkably alike (Nickell 1988). Ian Freestone, former head of the museum's scientific research and now a professor at the University of Wales, led the museum team that conducted the examination. The scientists used dental resin to obtain casts of the skull's surface and then studied them with a scanning electron microscope. According to Freestone: "It does appear that in some areas of the skull they have used a rotary tool, and as far as we know that sort of technique was only introduced after the Europeans came to the Americas, so it's post-Columbus." He also observed that the type of rock crystal used has never been found in Mexico, the domain of the Aztecs. All the evidence led Freestone to conclude that the skull was likely a fake, apparently fashioned from a lump of rather poor-quality Brazilian crystal. The great gem's cutting and polishing was probably done by a lapidary in nineteenth-century Europe, perhaps Germany, who used a rotating wheel like those common to jewelry houses of that place and time (Pennink 2005; Connor 2005).

In recent years, yet another skull—dubbed "Max," the Texas crystal skull—has surfaced. It is billed as the "largest ancient crystal skull" and is reputed to be up to 36,000 years old. It was allegedly "found in a tomb in Guatemala between 1924 and 1926" (Max 2005), but there appears to be no documentation of that claim. The skull's owner, JoAnn Parks of Houston, reportedly received the skull from Norbu Chen, a Tibetan healer she met in 1973. Before his death, he gave Parks and her husband the artifact, which they kept in a closet from 1980 to June 1987, when they saw a television program on UFOs that featured the Mitchell-Hedges crystal skull, at which time they began to publicize Max. According to Parks, Max talks to her in her dreams and says that he comes from both the Pleiades (a group of stars in the constellation Taurus) and Atlantis (the mythical continent). Parks adds: "He is a gift to mankind. He's here as a teacher, and as a tool, to bring people together as a Oneness. . . . He seems to open up an energy in the mind. . . . People pick up visions of the past, of other planets and some are creatively inspired. They feel healing" (Max 2005).

Toward a Solution of the Riddle

Interestingly, Jane Walsh, an archivist at the Smithsonian Institution, has uncovered documents showing that at least two of the crystal skulls were sold by the same man, a French collector of pre-Columbian artifacts named Eugene Boban. The British Museum purchased its skull in 1897 from Tiffany's, the New York jeweler, which in turn had bought it from Boban (who had earlier attempted to sell it to the Smithsonian). And the skull at the Musée de l'Homme in Paris was donated by a collector who likewise had purchased it from Boban (Connor 2005).

From what we know, it is conceivable that the Mitchell-Hedges skull was also sold by Boban. Putting aside the discredited claim that it was discovered at Lubaantun, the skull can be traced back to Sydney Burney, who owned it as early as 1933. He wrote that "for several years [the skull was] in the possession of the collector from whom I bought it and he in his turn had it from an Englishman in whose collection it had been also for several years" (Burney 1933). But where did the English collector get it?

One possible source for many of the crystal skulls was the renowned gemstone center of Idar and Oberstein in Germany. The area underwent a resurgence in the 1870s with the shipment of quartz crystals from Brazil that were carved into various objects—including a few crystal skulls—by the region's skilled artisans. (See Max 2005, which displays a modern example; see also Kunz 1913, 54.)

New Agers assert that, according to "prophecy," thirteen authentic ancient crystal skulls—all reputedly from Mexico or Central America—will be brought together one day, uniting people of all races and healing the earth (Max 2001;

Smoker 1995). Yet none of the famous skulls appears to be pre-Columbian; in fact, all of them may be European forgeries.

The chief power of the skulls seems to be that of attracting the credulous, including those with fantasy-prone personalities, and transporting them to a mystical realm from which they return with addled senses. It seems likely that further revelations about the crystal skulls will come not from channeling sessions but from science and scholarship.

References

Burney, Sydney. 1933. Letter to George Vaillant, March 21. Copy obtained from Gordon F. Ekholm, American Museum of Natural History.

Connor, Steve. 2005. The mystery of the British Museum's crystal skull is solved. It's a fake. *Independent News* (U.K.), January 7.

Dorland, Frank. 1983. Letter to Joe Nickell, May 20.

Ekholm, Gordon F. 1983. Letters to Joe Nickell, January 5, February 1.

Garvin, Richard M. 1973. *The Crystal Skull.* Garden City, N.Y.: Doubleday.

Hammond, Norman. 1983. Letter to Joe Nickell, May 27.

Hunter, Colin. 2005. Caretaker to a mystery. *Kitchener, Ontario, Record,* August 20.

Kunz, George Frederick. 1913. *The Curious Lore of Precious Stones.* Reprint, New York: Dover, 1971.

Max, the crystal skull. 2001. Ad for an "Evening Circle with JoAnn Parks." *Learning Light* 7, no. 3 (December): 3 (Learning Light Foundation newsletter, Anaheim, Calif.).

Max: The Texas crystal skull. 2005. www.v-j-enterprises.com/maxcs.html (accessed December 22).

McConnell, Rob. [1996]. The Mitchell-Hedges crystal skull. www.crystallinks.com/crystalskulls.html (accessed January 3, 2005).

Mitchell-Hedges, Anna. 1983. Letters to Joe Nickell, March 1, April 25.

Mitchell-Hedges, F. A. 1954. *Danger My Ally,* 240–43. London: Elek Books.

Morant, G. M. 1936. A morphological comparison of two crystal skulls. *Man* 36 (July): 105–7.

Morrill, Sibley S. 1972. *Ambrose Bierce, F. A. Mitchell-Hedges and the Crystal Skull.* San Francisco: Caledon Press.

Nickell, Joe. 1988. Gem of death. In *Secrets of the Supernatural,* 29–46. Buffalo, N.Y.: Prometheus Books.

Pennink, Emily. 2005. "Aztec" crystal skull "likely to be fake." http://icwales.icnetwork .co.uk/printable_version.cfm?objectid=15050983&siteid=50082 (accessed January 7).

Smoker, Debbie. 1995. Max, the crystal skull. *New Avenues,* June–July. Reprinted at Max 2005.

Welfare, Simon, and John Fairley. 1980. *Arthur C. Clarke's Mysterious World.* New York: A&W Publishers.

PHANTOM HITCHHIKERS:
THUMB MYSTERY!

LABELED "UNQUESTIONABLY THE MOST POPULAR and widespread ghostly legend in the United States" (Cohen 1984, 291), the "vanishing hitchhiker" is a spine-tingling tale that is told in other countries as well, from Italy to Pakistan (Goss 1984, 12). Having come across two roadside phantom cases myself—one reported by an alleged eyewitness—I wondered whether there was more to the phenomenon than meets the eye.

Folklore at Work

In its basic form, the vanishing hitchhiker is an urban legend about a young woman who asks for a ride but then disappears from the closed automobile without the driver's knowledge. When he reaches her destination, he is told by someone there, perhaps the young lady's mother, that his passenger had actually died some time before. The driver may be told that the hitchhiker has made other attempts to return, typically on the anniversary of her death in an auto accident.

There are countless variants of the story. These variants are a "defining characteristic of folklore," since oral transmission naturally produces differing versions of the same story (Brunvand 1978, 7). One version of the vanishing hitchhiker may feature a taxi, for example; in another, the passenger may be a nun (possibly delivering a prophecy), and so on. Frequently, the hitchhiking phantom leaves an item, such as a traveling bag or a scarf, behind in the backseat. In some versions, because the weather is cold, the passenger borrows a coat or a sweater, which is later discovered draped over her tombstone. Such a motif, or story element, is obviously provided to add verisimilitude to the tale; that is, it is supposed to confirm that the incident actually happened and is not just the product of someone's imagination (Thompson 1955; Brunvand 1981, 24–46). Another touch of verisimilitude comes from the source supposedly being one of the narrator's friends or a friend of a friend (called a "foaf" by folklorists). Nevertheless, despite its alleged provenance, a given tale typically cannot be verified. Indeed, that is not surprising, since—as noted American folklorist Jan Harold Brunvand (1981, 21) observes—multiple versions of a tale provide "good evidence against credibility." The prototypical story has antecedents from as far back as 1876, wherein the automobile is replaced with a horse-drawn vehicle (Brunvand 1981, 32).[1]

Knoche Road Hitchhiker

One such hand-me-down tale comes from the town of Tonawanda in the Greater Buffalo, New York, area. The story of the ghost of Knoche Road reportedly dates from the time of the earliest settlers. Joan Gerstman (2003)—a museum volunteer at the Tonawanda-Kenmore Historical Society (which is actually located on Knoche Road)—told me that she had heard a version in which the ghost girl was killed by a carriage at the time of her wedding in the very church building that now houses the museum. However, Gerstman stated that no such wedding had ever been held in the little church (which later became a school).

Another version of the Knoche Road story, according to local historian John Percy (2003), supposedly dates from the 1880s. In that tale, the ghost of a girl, buried in one of the nearby cemeteries, was apparently trying to return to her parents. Wearing a "diaphanous" outfit, she would hail the driver of a horse-drawn buggy, giving an address about a mile away. When the buggy arrived at the destination, the young miss was nowhere to be seen.

Whatever the true vintage of such tales, a version of the story has definitely been around since at least 1937. As Brunvand (1981, 25) observes, the basic elements of the vanishing hitchhiker legend were "well known in oral tradition and occasionally reported in newspapers since the early 1930s." Buffalo newspapers included articles headlined "Town of Tonawanda Shivers at Motorist's 'Ghost Story'" (Ford 1937) and "Town Police Deny Rumors of 'Ghost Girl' on Knoche Road" (Town 1937).

In 1968 a young Tonawanda man wrote this version (published in Ainsworth 1978, 88):

I heard this legend when I was about twelve years old. It told of a girl who walked Knoche Road in the Town of Tonawanda in a wedding gown. Whenever men would stop to give her a ride, she would enter the car, but when they went to drop her off at her destination, she had mysteriously gone already. This story was told by many men who experienced the plight of the disappearing woman, and it has been said to this day that this woman was believed to be a ghost from the cemetery along side Knoche Road.

Sometimes she is said to be a "shivering, weeping young girl on a bench near the cemeteries at Delaware Avenue and Knoche Road" (Ghost 2003).

In one version, told by a detective, a policeman had stopped his patrol car to pick up a hitchhiking woman and take her to police headquarters. But when he arrived, she had vanished. Reportedly, the officer refused to write up the incident (Percy 2003), thus rendering the alleged occurrence unverifiable.

As with other versions of the vanishing hitchhiker legend, the story of the Knoche Road ghost is a proliferating, metamorphosing tale. Local residents I spoke with—including one who has lived in the area since 1928 (Stewart 2003) and another who has resided there since 1946 (Heyer 2003)—had never seen the phantom lady and were skeptical of her existence. The president of the Tonawanda-Kenmore Historical Society, James M. Rapp (2003), stated that he had never seen the ghostly hitchhiker himself, and he knew of no one who had. As the historical society's Halloween museum display pointed out, "Though no one claims to believe in such a ghost, it is remarkable how persistent this story has remained in the history of Tonawanda folklore" (Ghost 2003). The same is true for other hitchhiking ghost tales, but what do we make of an account by an actual eyewitness?

Cold Springs Witch

A stretch of highway at Lockport, New York, known as Cold Springs Road, has a cemetery on either side. The road is reputedly haunted by a phantom that—in contrast to the typical vanishing hitchhiker—often takes the form of "an old lady" (Stutz 1978). Significantly, the ghost of an old woman haunted Lockport in 1900, not long after Halloween. Actually, some thought that it was not a ghost at all but "merely a poor demented woman from the south side who enjoys nocturnal rambles." That could explain an incident in which the figure spooked a young couple and, as the man ungallantly fled, approached the girl, "jammed her hat over her eyes, and pulled her hair." In any case, the newspaper account of the event (Lockport's 1900) made no mention of a hitchhiking ghost legend or the haunting of Cold Springs Road, which might indicate that those elements were of later vintage. In time, however, that 1900 story was cited as early evidence of "Lockport's ghostly hitchhiker" (1984). It thus appears that the vanishing hitchhiker legend became grafted onto the earlier ghost story. As reported in *Legends of New York State* (Ainsworth 1978, 57), circa 1965:

> The Cold Springs Bridge is where several motorists have encountered an old woman standing directly in the center preventing their passage. The drivers were forced to stop, giving the old woman the opportunity to enter their cars. This old woman, or witch, as many believed her to be, horrified the drivers so badly that one car crashed into the nearby cemetery wall, while another hit the side of the bridge. Several other motorists also reported seeing the witch, but as they approached she vanished. Still another motorist claims to have driven right over the witch without doing her any harm. The two accidents which occurred only days apart from one another, in addition to the other reports, resulted in a further investigation. The Cold Springs Bridge was kept under surveillance by the police. The witch was reportedly apprehended and was being taken to Lockport Police Station for further questioning when she completely vanished from the patrol car.

In other versions (Stutz 1978; Kerrison 2003), the unnamed officer is a deputy sheriff, but a Niagara County Sheriff's Department spokesperson was unable to confirm the account (Stutz 1978).

In one 1973 incident, a man claimed that he and a friend had picked up an old woman, taken her to "an unidentified house," and then, "while the headlights were still on her," watched as she vanished. Raising questions about the event was the fact that it occurred during "a rash of ghost reports in the area," and when the men stopped for the woman, they had actually joked that she might be the local ghost. Also, the men equivocated, admitting that rather than vanishing she might have just plunged into the bushes (Stutz 1978).

The story continued to evolve, and by 1977, it had become a Halloween tale involving a "lady in black" (Ainsworth 1978, 57):

> One Halloween night a man was driving down Cold Springs Road. He stopped for a red light and heard his car door open. He looked in his rear view mirror and he saw a lady sitting in his back seat. She was dressed all in black. He just sat still and waited for the light to change. When it turned green, he started going and the lady in black got out. The next night he and some of his friends walked down Cold Springs Road to see if they could see her again. Soon a lot of people heard about the lady in black. Every night there would be more and more people looking for her. They looked in Cold Springs Cemetery, but no one ever saw her again. It is still believed by many people that she is still there and many people of Lockport are still afraid to drive on Cold Springs Road at night.

By the following decade, a version appeared in which the specter was called the "gray lady," the spirit of a woman who had allegedly been killed by a car as she crossed Cold Springs Road near the bridge. Former Lockport resident Ginger Burg (2003) told me that the story had been a "big deal" when she was in her early teens in the mid-1980s, and young people would visit the location at night to look for the ghostly figure.

In still other versions, the wandering, sometimes hitchhiking spirit is said to be that of a "young woman who once lived in a nearby house." She supposedly "met an untimely and horrible death and stalks the street and bridge in search of her murderer." One reporter writing about the Cold Springs ghost claimed—incorrectly—that witnesses always described her as "a young woman" (Salamone 1982).

I investigated the Cold Springs Road case in 2003, making several trips to the area. I conducted research at the local library and historical society, interviewed area residents, repeatedly drove the stretch of roadway (often at night), and visited the two proximate graveyards (figure 20). At Cold Springs

Figure 20. Cold Springs Road, Lockport, New York—flanked by cemeteries—is reputedly haunted by a hitchhiking phantom. (Photo by Joe Nickell)

Cemetery, the caretaker, Dean Kerrison (2003), told me that he had heard the stories in the 1960s but believed that they were actually much older. He recalled that the phantom woman was supposedly searching for her daughter.

Kerrison gave me the name of an eyewitness, Rod McKeown (b. 1961), the proprietor of a business on the haunted road. McKeown (2003) told me that in November 2000, at about 6:30 P.M., he was driving back to his workplace after running an errand. It was getting dark at the end of a long day, and it was cold and raining. As he came over a rise on Cold Springs Road, a woman suddenly appeared, walking on the opposite side of the road but going in the same direction as he was. She was perhaps in her twenties, had long blonde hair, and was wearing a black sweatshirt and pants but no shoes. "I can still see her, plain as day," he told me.

I rode with McKeown as we retraced the route. He said that the woman appeared to be a real person, except that she seemed very bright, as if from an inner light. As he passed her, she turned as if to look at him, but *she had no face.* Startled, he hit his brakes and looked in the rearview mirror but could not see her—either because of the rain on the rear window or because she had disappeared. He turned around at his place of business and drove back, but she was gone. He insisted that she was clearly otherworldly, not a jogger or someone just walking along the road.

I was able to discuss this case with Jan Brunvand (2003), over dinner at a CSI conference in Albuquerque. He pointed out that the incident was only superficially related to the vanishing hitchhiker legend because the figure was not actually hitchhiking and, as he sagely observed, what had been related to me was "an experience, not a folktale."

But what was the nature of that experience? If it was not a made-up story (McKeown seemed sincere) or a prank (it would have been an apparently isolated, pointless one), then it might best be explained as an apparitional experience. This can occur when a mental image wells up from the subconscious and is momentarily superimposed on the visual scene—analogous to a photographic double exposure. The possibility gains credence, I think, when one considers the power of suggestion: the location was associated with many such incidents, and the sighting occurred not long after Halloween. Significantly, it also took place at the end of a long day. Apparitional sightings are more likely to occur when one is tired, in a relaxed state, or doing something routine, and they often derive from daydreams or other altered states of consciousness (Nickell 2001, 290–92).

In his book *The Evidence for Phantom Hitch-Hikers,* Michael Goss writes: "Regardless of how many times the Phantom Hitch-Hiker is presented as fact, there will be little resistance from researchers to the evidence that most stories featuring the itinerant ghost are fabricated, folklore creations retold in new settings." Very few cases that Goss researched had alleged eyewitnesses (like the Cold Springs case), and even his strongest case, he conceded, was far from solid—no more credible than many other ghost anecdotes (Goss 1984, 32, 90–99). The possibility that any of the roadside ghost tales is true is diminished by the sheer volume of the variants. The tale persists, I think, because it is memorable, moving from the mundane to the supernatural in a brief narrative that is easily adapted to various places and times. In any event, perhaps everyone—skeptic and paranormal believer alike—can at least appreciate the sentiment of one alleged witness (quoted in Brunvand 1981, 40): "I just hope that poor girl gets wherever it is she's going."

Note

1. One source (Bennett 1998) cautions that the legend is more complex and diffuse than previously thought and that "the search for its origins has long since been abandoned as futile."

References

Ainsworth, Catherine Harris. 1978. *Legends of New York State,* 2nd ed. Buffalo, N.Y.: Clyde Press.

Bennett, Gillian. 1998. The vanishing hitchhiker at fifty-five. *Western Folklore* 57, no. 1 (Winter): 1–17.

Brunvand, Jan Harold. 1978. *The Study of American Folklore.* New York: W. W. Norton.

———. 1981. *The Vanishing Hitchhiker: American Urban Legends and Their Meanings.* New York: W. W. Norton.

———. 2003. Interview by Joe Nickell, October 24.

Burg, Ginger. 2003. Interview by Joe Nickell, September 17.

Cohen, Daniel. 1984. *The Encyclopedia of Ghosts.* New York: Dorset Press.

Ford, Leslie N. 1937. Town of Tonawanda shivers at motorist's "ghost story." *Buffalo (N.Y.) Courier Express,* March 2.

Gerstman, Joan. 2003. Interview by Joe Nickell, September 21.

Ghost story. 2003. Museum Halloween display text. Tonawanda-Kenmore Historical Society.

Goss, Michael. 1984. *The Evidence for Phantom Hitch-Hikers.* Wellingborough, U.K: Aquarian Press.

Heyer, Jane. 2003. Interview by Joe Nickell, September 21.

Kerrison, Dean. 2003. Interview by Joe Nickell, September 24.

Lockport's annual ghost story again. 1900. *Niagara Gazette,* November 19.

Lockport's ghostly hitchhiker. 1984. *Niagara Gazette,* October 31.

McKeown, Rod. 2003. Interview by Joe Nickell, September 24.

Nickell, Joe. 2001. *Real-Life X-Files.* Lexington: University Press of Kentucky.

Percy, John. 2003. Telephone interview by Joe Nickell, September 27.

Rapp, James M. 2003. Interview by Joe Nickell, September 21.

Salamone, Chris. 1982. The Cold Springs ghost. *Lockport (N.Y.) Union-Sun,* October 30.

Stewart, Margaret. 2003. Interview by Joe Nickell, September 21.

Stutz, Eric. 1978. Mysterious "hauntings" from Youngstown to Appleton. *Niagara Gazette,* October 29.

Thompson, Stith. 1955. *Motif-Index of Folk Literature,* vol. 2. Reprint, Bloomington: Indiana University Press, 1989. (The vanishing hitchhiker is motif no. E332. 3.3.1.)

Town police deny rumors of "ghost girl" on Knoche Road. 1937. *Buffalo (N.Y.) Evening News,* March 5.

THE CASE OF THE ALIEN HAND

IT WAS MONDAY, MARCH 24, 2003, when the voice of CSI executive director Barry Karr came over my intercom: "How would you like to travel to Wyoming County to examine an 'alien hand'?" (Barry knew that I was familiar with the area from my investigation of the fabled Silver Lake serpent a few years earlier [Nickell 1999].) Barry put me in touch with Jane Monaghan, an assistant county attorney, who described the unusual object to me. Whatever it was, she assured me, it was not from an animal. It had pea-green "skin" over what looked like bone. I then contacted Deputy Sheriff Susan Omans, whose daughter had found the object lying in the hay outside their horse barn the previous Saturday, and we agreed to meet at her office in the Wyoming County courthouse in Warsaw, New York. I packed a few items I thought I might need—camera, close-up lenses, scale, stereomicroscope, evidence-collection materials, notebook—and was soon on the road.

By shortly after two in the afternoon, I was looking at the strange object (figure 21), and I spent the next two hours photographing, examining, and discussing it with a number of local folks, including deputies, a district attorney, and courthouse staff, as well as Jane Monaghan and Sue Omans. A photographer from the local newspaper had already been by. Having grown up in a small town myself, I knew how quickly word of something unusual could spread.

The object was clearly not a human hand, since it lacked an opposable thumb, and it did not look like an animal paw or a bird claw; nor did it have the characteristics of a plant root. In short, it did not appear to be any of the things people had suggested or I had envisioned—except, of course, a genuine or simulated "alien hand." I told Deputy Omans that she had acted commendably, securing the unusual object, handling it cautiously, and seeking to have it identified.

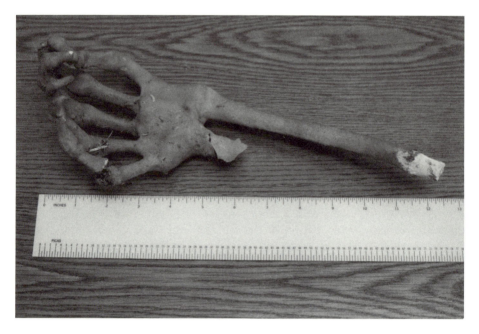

Figure 21. Mysterious object, resembling an "alien hand," provoked curiosity in Wyoming County, New York. (Photo by Joe Nickell)

One of the first things I did after removing the curious object from its zipper-lock plastic bag was to photograph it and then examine it with various lighted magnifiers, including a Bausch & Lomb 10× illuminated loupe. It did not look like diseased or decomposed material, and I decided to risk the often instructive sniff test. To me, the "skin" smelled exactly like latex. I coaxed a dozen or so curiosity seekers to take a whiff, and each agreed that it smelled like latex. I found that the material did indeed stretch with the elasticity of a balloon or a rubber band.

The underlying structure resembled bone and even had recognizable knuckles and other joints. Close inspection, however, also revealed an unmistakable seam mark on either side of the long "bone" (figure 22)—evidence of a casting process that utilized a two-piece mold. The "skin" was torn here and there, and I discovered underneath, at the tip of the "little finger," a silver metal ring, which further indicated manufacture (figure 23). I suspected that it might have been a means of suspending the figure's articulated skeleton for dipping

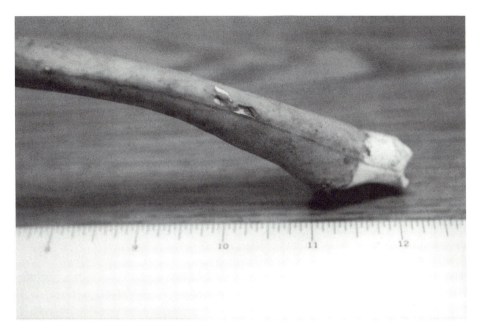

Figure 22. Long "bone" exhibits a telltale seam mark on either side. (Photo by Joe Nickell)

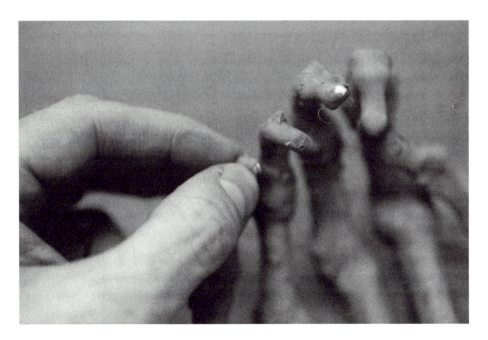

Figure 23. Metal ring at the tip, or "finger," indicates a manufactured object. (Photo by Joe Nickell)

in a solution of green, liquid rubber. With the stereomicroscope, I even examined a fiber embedded in the "skin" on the back of the hand, its ends sticking out—an indication that it had been trapped in the rubber before it solidified.

With Sue Omans's permission, I took small scrapings of the "bone" and removed a little piece of green "skin" for further examination. At my lab the next day, I subjected a bit of each to a flame test, using tweezers to hold it in the flame of an alcohol lamp. The "bone" flamed readily, unlike actual bone (or at least actual terrestrial bone), but consistent with plastic. The "skin" was also readily flammable and produced black smoke, just like rubber. The mystery object had obviously been broken from a larger piece, which I suspect was an entire figure. Although it might have been a ghoul or a leprechaun, the structure of the hand indicates an "alien"—probably the stereotypical little humanoid extraterrestrial with a big head and wraparound eyes (Nickell 1997).

One possibility is that it was a lawn figure displayed at Halloween that somehow ended up in a field, perhaps tossed by the wind. If it was not already broken, a mowing or bailing machine probably did the damage, and the hand found its way into a hay bale, thus explaining its presence in the hay outside the Omans' barn. If the figure was manufactured in some quantity, perhaps an entire specimen will eventually surface for comparison and final identification. Until then, I am telling anyone who asks that it is a real alien hand—not *genuine* but *real* (a distinction often made by carnival showmen). It appears to have come from the remote realm I can only name Planet Latex.

References

Nickell, Joe. 1997. Extraterrestrial iconography. *Skeptical Inquirer* 21, no. 5 (September–October): 18–19.

———. 1999. The Silver Lake serpent: Inflated monster or inflated tale? *Skeptical Inquirer* 23, no. 2 (March–April): 18–21.

HUSTLING HEAVEN

ON-AIR SÉANCES ARE NOTHING NEW. In 1969 I arranged one in a dimly lit radio studio in Toronto for a CBC documentary *Houdini in Canada.* (Despite the spiritualist's pronouncements, Houdini was a no-show—as far as I could discern.) However, the *Larry King Live* presentation of alleged psychic medium James Van Praagh on February 26, 1999 (one of several such appearances, before and since), was a study in crassness. The purpose of Van Praagh's appearance was to pitch the sequel to his best seller *Talking to Heaven.* Titled *Reaching to Heaven,* it elaborates on his professed belief that, as he told King, "There is no such thing as death." *Reaching to Heaven* is a touted elixir composed of such metaphysical ingredients as auras, the astral world, and reincarnation, all stirred into a syrupy pabulum about the "Higher Life" (Van Praagh 1999). Even for New Age snake oil, however, *Reaching to Heaven* is quite a stretch.

For his part, the famous talk-show host took a critical tone, asking Van Praagh how much of his apparent success was due to people's strong desire to believe him. "So when there are all the skeptics who accuse you of being a charlatan, one of the edges any charlatan has is, they want to believe." The accused charlatan scarcely missed a beat, replying glibly:

That's right. That's right. Well, it all comes down to a matter of belief, and everyone's truth, because skeptics have their truth. They have their right to express themselves the way they choose. And everyone has an awareness; that's their awareness. And my work isn't necessarily for everyone, and it's not meant to be. It resonates with those who it's meant to resonate with. And thousands of people that it's helped and transformed their lives, that's what it's about. It's not about the skeptics.

Skeptics, however, rightly observe that the burden is on Van Praagh and his fellow spiritualists to prove that they can genuinely talk with the dead. It is a significant burden, made all the more imperative by the fact that the history of spiritualism is one of charlatanism (Keene 1997, 115–29).

Of course, the spirit contacts by "mediums" such as Van Praagh and John Edward (who has also been promoted on *Larry King Live*) have been streamlined for the modern media. Largely gone is the necessity of turning out the lights—once a common practice so that mediums could perform "levitations," spirit "materializations," and other trickery. Gone too are the feigned trance states, spirit writing, and other trappings of old-fashioned mediumistic phenomena (Nickell 1998). Instead, the modern celebrity spiritualist opts for purely "mental" mediumship—one advantage being a lower risk of being proved a charlatan. Who can say, lacking evidence of trick devices or overt acts of legerdemain, whether any given medium is sincere?

It is possible, however, to carefully analyze recorded readings and assess their credibility. In no instance on the *Larry King Live* show did Van Praagh reveal anything of a substantive, convincing nature. Instead, he appeared to be practicing "cold reading"—a fortune-teller's technique of cleverly fishing for information while giving the subject the impression that it is coming from a mystical source (Hyman 1977; Gresham 1953). Here is a look at some of the stock techniques employed by James Van Praagh.

1. He asks questions.

In twelve of fifteen readings, Van Praagh led off with a query and continued asking questions throughout (figure 24). With this ploy, it is the subject (called the sitter), not the reader, who actually supplies the information.

> VAN PRAAGH: OK, who was the drinker, or someone with alcohol, please?
> CALLER [No. 5]: It was my father.

2. He follows up by treating a positive response to a question as verification of a statement that was made.

> VAN PRAAGH [continuing with caller 5]: Because I feel like it was something he had to get over, the alcohol condition, when he passed over.

Figure 24. James Van Praagh uses the "psychic" technique of asking questions. (Cartoon by Joe Nickell)

3. *In case of a negative response, he avoids admitting error, instead persisting in an attempt to redeem his point.*

> VAN PRAAGH: OK. Was there a problem in his head area as well?
> CALLER [No. 1]: Pardon?
> VAN PRAAGH: I feel like there's some problem with headaches with this man, too.
> CALLER: No.
> VAN PRAAGH: No? I feel he had head problems with him. Who's having headaches? Because I'm feeling a head problem here, too.

Unfortunately for Van Praagh, the caller still responded, "No, no, I've no idea."

4. *When completely on the wrong track, he may shift the focus to the future.*

> VAN PRAAGH [continuing with caller 1]: OK. Well, I keep on getting head stuff, so be careful of that. I just see it.
> CALLER: Right. Thank you.

Again (in the case of caller 10):

> VAN PRAAGH: She's also giving me a number of twenty-nine. I don't know why she's giving me twenty-nine, but she is.
> CALLER: Twenty-nine.
> VAN PRAAGH: So see with twenty-nine. It's like a date for a month.
> CALLER: OK, the twenty-ninth. I don't know.
> VAN PRAAGH: It's the twenty-ninth. So keep that; that's later [shifting to a question].

In another case (with caller 11):

> VAN PRAAGH: I also am being told that someone has been looking at a map.
> CALLER: I don't know. It could be my mother-in-law.
> VAN PRAAGH: Well, ask her, would you please?
> CALLER: Yes.

5. He makes widely applicable statements.

Nearly everyone has some connection to pets, photographs, antiques, or other familiar imagery.

> VAN PRAAGH: I'm also picking up something on a dog. So, I don't know why, but I'm picking up a dog around you.
> CALLER [No. 1]: Oh, my dog died two years ago.

6. He often employs a scattershot technique, with multiple variables that enhance the opportunity for a "hit."

> VAN PRAAGH: Also, does your mother have any trouble with her lungs or does Velma [the caller's grandmother] have trouble with her lungs, breathing?
> CALLER [No. 10]: I think she did have trouble breathing at the very end.

Again (to caller 12):

> VAN PRAAGH: She's talking about the family reunion, so I don't know if

she was talking in spirit, or she was talking here on the earth—but a family reunion.

7. *He draws additional, obvious inferences once a fact is known.*

For example, after caller 11 confirms that her father-in-law was working on the house and doing other construction projects (in response to Van Praagh's mention of "seeing a ladder for some strange reason"), there is this revelation:

VAN PRAAGH: OK, I see calloused hands, also.
CALLER: Yes.

As another example, after caller 3 tells him that her daughter had had a lengthy illness, the medium extrapolates:

VAN PRAAGH: . . . I want to tell you, did they give her IVs?
CALLER: Yes.
VAN PRAAGH: Because I'm being shown IVs a lot, with this girl. I'm also shown a lot of medication, and I'm feeling very ill with medication, a lot of drug medication.
CALLER: Right.

Now on a roll, he continues. But when he apparently goes too far, he quickly cuts off a negative response:

VAN PRAAGH: OK, I also feel, before this girl passes over, there's a fogginess in her head, and she doesn't know what's going on. A little bit of—she's out of it. Do you understand?
CALLER: Yes, but . . .
VAN PRAAGH: She's kind of conscious. She's out of it. I also want to ask you. . . .

As another example of expounding on the obvious, after caller 5 has confirmed that her father had a drinking problem, there is this offering:

VAN PRAAGH: . . . And I feel this man was very saddened. The impression I get is he was very saddened.
CALLER: Right.
VAN PRAAGH: And he was saddened with life at the end, OK?
CALLER: Right.
VAN PRAAGH: I also feel like he was in a situation, maybe it was the mar-

riage, or a family situation he did not want to be in. Do you understand that?

CALLER: Right.

8. He takes advantage of the caller's hesitation or negative feedback to adjust course.

For example, he may broaden the possibilities:

> VAN PRAAGH: OK, who had the heart trouble? [Caller hesitates.] There's something with the chest I am picking up very strong here.
> CALLER [No. 2]: Lung cancer, my father.

Or he may subtly alter the focus, as in this reading for caller 8, who had lost her best friend:

> VAN PRAAGH: Don't you have multiple pictures of this lady?
> CALLER: Yes I do.
> VAN PRAAGH: In a scrapbook or a photograph album, and then elsewhere?
> CALLER: Just several pictures [negating the album].
> VAN PRAAGH: OK, and I'm also being shown an envelope with pictures in it.
> CALLER: Yes, that's right.

9. He invites the caller to interpret vague offerings.

> VAN PRAAGH: I feel someone—here, again, I'm getting something with cancer; I don't know why.
> CALLER [No. 5]: My brother died of lung cancer.

He uses words like some, someone, or something no fewer than sixty-five times, and on at least twenty-seven occasions he says, "I don't know why" or "I don't know what that means" or a similar statement, thus inviting the caller to make a connection, offer some interpretation, or simply accept the vague pronouncement. Over and over—at least twenty-one times—he asks the caller to acknowledge a possible interpretation by saying, "Do you understand?" or "OK?" or a similar query.

10. He uses "weasel" words and phrases to provide extra wiggle room.

> VAN PRAAGH [to caller 7]: . . . I feel he was a loner too, in certain ways . . . [emphasis added].

He frequently says, "I'm feeling," "the impression I get," "it feels like," "I get a sense," and so on. He often adds a fuzzy phrase such as "in certain ways," "this sort of thing," "something to do with," "a little bit," and similar ambiguities.

11. He benefits from many sitters' helpfulness in converting a "miss" to a "hit."

> VAN PRAAGH: Was she [the deceased] found in bed?
> CALLER [No. 8]: Yes. She was found in the bathroom floor; [but] she had been sick in the bed.

Again:

> VAN PRAAGH: OK, was this a quick passing with her?
> CALLER [No. 3]: Yes. I mean, she had a long illness but it went quickly.

Still again:

> VAN PRAAGH: OK, is there an anniversary of a birthday coming up?
> CALLER: Yes, it was just his birthday.

Such techniques and maneuvers by Van Praagh do not inspire confidence in the genuineness of his readings. Nor did his refusal—when we appeared together on a San Diego radio program—to contact a deceased relative I had named. He said he had nothing to prove to skeptics (Nickell 1998), but I got the impression that he feared a trap.

During the televised readings, Larry King provided an occasional skeptical note, once querying Van Praagh why a spirit—a nonphysical entity—would continue to have a leg problem or chest pains, as Van Praagh represented to callers. But King did not challenge the spiritualist's nimble response: "It's a memory—it's a memory, but that might seem very real, because they're in the earthly mind-set, again. They re-experience that earthly mind-set." Indeed, King showed his approval on one occasion by exclaiming, "Wow!" and on another by boasting of Van Praagh, "We brought him to the world."

I am often asked, even if spirit communications are not genuine, what harm is there in the pretense, in giving people the solace of apparent contact with their deceased loved ones? My short answer is that the truth should matter. Not only is it unethical to perpetrate a falsehood for personal gain, but falsehoods have consequences. Houdini (1924, 180) cataloged many of these consequences—"the suffering, losses, misfortunes, crimes and atrocities"—of spiritualistic fraud. I have personally counseled victims of phony spiritualism who were bilked not only of their money but also of their self-respect. I saw a marriage severely strained when one spouse awoke to the deception while the other continued to be beguiled. Even apart from these demonstrable harms, as reformed spiritualistic con man M. Lamar Keene observes in his classic exposé *The Psychic Mafia* (1997, 140), "The services of the phony medium do not help the sitter—they hinder him or her in developing the inner resources to face life realistically." If spiritualists and their media front men really want to help the grieving, they will quit preying on their vulnerabilities and instead allow them to find a measure of honest acceptance.

References

Gresham, William Lindsay. 1953. *Monster Midway,* 113–36. New York: Rinehart & Co.

Houdini, Harry. 1924. *A Magician among the Spirits.* New York: Harper & Brothers.

Hyman, Ray. 1977. Cold reading: How to convince strangers that you know all about them. *Skeptical Inquirer 1,* no. 2 (Spring–Summer): 18–37.

Keene, M. Lamar (as told to Allen Spraggett). 1997. *The Psychic Mafia* [1976]. Amherst, N.Y.: Prometheus Books.

Nickell, Joe. 1998. Investigating spirit communications. *Skeptical Briefs,* September, 5–6.

Van Praagh, James. 1999. *Reaching to Heaven: A Spiritual Journey through Life and Death.* New York: Dutton.

PETER POPOFF'S
"GIFT OF KNOWLEDGE"

IN CASE YOU HAD NOT HEARD, God is still talking to Peter Popoff. But Mrs. Popoff is no longer the one secretly broadcasting the "word of knowledge" whispered into the TV evangelist's ear. I wondered what the good reverend had been doing since his 1986 exposure as a fraud, so when he brought his act to Toronto on Sunday, June 2, 2002, I was there, posing as a working man afflicted with a bad back.

Out with the Old

Peter Popoff is the director of a religious empire based in Upland, California. It once raked in an estimated 10 million to 20 million tax-free dollars annually. Popoff is a Pentecostal, and he claims that as a child he witnessed his father transform water into wine during a wartime communion service in Berlin. As an "anointed minister of God," the evangelist supposedly exhibits several "gifts of the spirit" that are central to Pentecostalism. The apostle Paul (1 Corinthians 12:7–11) enumerated nine gifts that are manifestations of the Holy Spirit: the word of wisdom, the word of knowledge, faith, healing, the working of miracles, prophecy, discernment of spirits, speaking in unknown tongues, and the ability to interpret tongues. Pentecostals place a special emphasis on such gifts, whereas many other fundamentalists believe that they were intended only for the early disciples who were specifically anointed by Jesus (Nickell 1993, 101–2). These Christians believe that between Jesus's resurrection and his ascension to heaven, he promised his disciples that they would be "baptized with the Holy Ghost" (Acts 1:5), which occurred when the apostles gathered for Pentecost and were struck with religious ecstasy (Asimov 1969).

Peter Popoff combines his gift of healing with the word of knowledge, which, Pentecostals believe, consists of receiving supernatural revelations. According to *Christian Online Magazine* (Kazenske 2003), this is "the God-given ability to receive from God, by revelation, the facts concerning something that is humanly impossible for us to know anything about"—a sort of holy clairvoyance. Popoff's gift was openly demonstrated when he "called out" audience members for healing, revealing his knowledge of their diseases, their addresses, and similar personal information, including the names of their doctors—all promptly verified by the astonished individuals. For example, at a service in Anaheim, California, on March 16, 1986, Popoff called out: "Virgil. Is it Jorgenson? Who is Virgil?"—whereupon a man in the audience identified himself as that person. Popoff continued, "Are you ready for God to overhaul those knees?" As Jorgenson reacted to Popoff's amazing knowledge about him, the evangelist continued: "Oh, glory to God. I'll tell you, God's going to touch that sister of yours all the way over in Sweden." Popoff then took the "healed" man's cane, broke it over his knee, and stood by as the man walked about unaided, giving praise to both Popoff and God (Steiner 1989).

Soon, however, Popoff's apparent gift was exposed as blatant trickery. Famed magician and paranormal investigator James Randi was curious about the alleged healer's wearing of an apparent hearing aid. He began to suspect that the device might actually be a tiny radio receiver and that someone was secretly broadcasting the information that had allegedly come from God. In what would become a classic in the history of paranormal investigation, Randi smuggled in an electronics expert with computerized scanning equipment and discovered that the words of knowledge came not from heaven but much closer: the ministry's trailer parked just outside. The evangelist's wife, Elizabeth, was obtaining the relevant information from the so-called prayer cards the attendees filled out before the service and then broadcasting the information to Popoff's "hearing aid." The first message at the service was a test: "Hello, Petey. I love you. I'm talking to you. Can you hear me? If you can't you're in trouble" (Steiner 1986, 1989; Randi 1987, 141–49). The session with the ailing Mr. Jorgenson—actually, investigator Don Henvick—sounded like this when Mrs. Popoff's secret broadcasts were included (Steiner 1989, 126):

ELIZABETH [transmitting to Peter]: Virgil Jorgenson. Virgil.
PETER [calling out]: Virgil.
ELIZABETH: Jorgenson.
PETER [inquiringly]: Is it Jorgenson?

ELIZABETH: Way back in the back somewhere. Arthritis in knees. He's got a cane.

PETER: Who is Virgil?

ELIZABETH: He's got a cane.

PETER: Are you ready for God to overhaul those knees?

ELIZABETH: He's got arthritis. He's praying for his sister in Sweden, too.

PETER: Oh, glory to God. I'll tell you, God's going to touch that sister of yours all the way over in Sweden.

Subsequently, on Johnny Carson's *Tonight Show,* Randi played a videotape of one of several recorded "calling out" sessions that he had intercepted. Randi presented it in before-and-after fashion, so viewers could appreciate the original effect of Popoff's apparent gift of knowledge and then see the true situation involving the secret broadcast. Popoff's initial reaction was to deny everything; his ministry later charged that the videotapes had been "doctored" by NBC. Finally, Popoff admitted to use of the "communicator" device (the radio receiver) but denied any intention to deceive. Randi, however, had videotaped documentation to the contrary (Randi 1987, 149–50, 291; Garrison 1991).

The callousness of Popoff and his organization was deep. A former aide revealed that when Popoff sent out "personal" special-appeal letters to top donors, he had the aide sign most of the letters for him. Donors who responded to these appeals would send in money, but most of the special projects did not even exist; according to an ex-controller of the Peter Popoff Evangelical Association, "the money would just go into the daily deposit." Popoff also promised those who wrote him letters (with expected donations enclosed) that he would pray over them, but, says the aide, he never did. Instead, the letters would "sit there in a big pile for a month, then they'd be shredded." Also, Elizabeth Popoff (who, unbeknownst to the faithful, was not even a Pentecostal but a Roman Catholic) "laughed and joked at the 'boobs' and 'big butts' of terminally ill women who were there giving their money and their confidence to the Popoffs" (Randi 1987, 152, 158, 298).

Randi's effective exposé of Popoff was carried by the national media, dealing the evangelist a body blow. In just four months, he was unable to draw the large crowds he was accustomed to. Worse, public outrage and diminishing donations eventually forced him off television entirely (Alexander 1987). He even changed the organization's name from the Peter Popoff Evangelical

Association to People United for Christ and relocated to a shopping-center storefront (Randi 1987, 156).

Resurrecting the Word of Knowledge

Despite all this, Popoff managed to rebound, eventually returning to the airways —and his old ways—albeit without his "hearing aid" (Stein 1993). Now he depends on other means to seemingly receive words of knowledge. One method is the old generalization technique, a mainstay of fortune-tellers and spiritualists. Consider this letter of July 26, 2001, written by Popoff—or one of the professional letter writers he employs (Randi 1987, 140)—and sent to me, *personally* (and no doubt to thousands upon thousands of others):

> Dear Joe,
>
> In prayer for you this morning . . . God showed me that I must come to Toronto, Ontario. We are in the 7th month of the year and still you are feeling crushed by an onslaught of excessive worry in and around your home. During this time of prayer . . . I felt an unusual "BONDING" between us. I feel now as if I am speaking to you face to face.
>
> There is something I just can't quite put my finger on . . . it has been troubling you, and it seems it keeps interfering with your day to day life.
>
> GOD DID SHOW ME . . . that you need Him to move in the lives of your loved ones. I SEE through the eyes of the spirit . . . you also need a touch in your life, your finances are not the way you want them. . . . If it seems I'm reading you like a book . . . I sense it's happening because of this "BONDING" between us in the spirit.

Now, if this isn't holy clairvoyance—a true word of knowledge—I don't know what is. A second technique for appearing to receive words of knowledge before an audience of believers is a version of the "shotgun" technique. As typically practiced by evangelists such as Pat Robertson and Benny Hinn, this involves stating that certain healings are taking place without specifying who is being favored (Randi 1987, 228–29; Nickell 2002). Popoff also uses it as a means of calling someone out for a healing. For example, during a televised "Miracle Crusade" on November 11, 2002, Popoff received the word of knowledge that someone was afflicted with a ringing in the ears; a woman with that condition identified herself and came forward. Popoff does not limit the shotgun technique to illnesses but applies it to other problems as well. On television, he can even direct the method to the home audience. On an April 10, 2003, broadcast, he stated, without fear of contradiction, "I feel there's a mother out there whose son is in jail." In this way, many are led to believe that Popoff is speaking directly and individually to them.

In his live crusades, Popoff uses the shotgun technique extensively. At the service I attended in 2002—after Popoff had written to me, saying, "Joe, you are going to see some awesome things happen in your life"—many people vied to be the one who fit the illness Popoff mentioned. A woman in front of me seemed to have several conditions—or perhaps she was just anxious to be videotaped by the ministry's TV crew and thus achieve her moment of fame.

Peter Popoff Packs a Punch of Pentecostal Power

Another aspect of Popoff's performance is called "going under the power." In the caption to a publicity photo showing a woman falling backward at his touch, Popoff terms this "Pentecostal Power" (figure 25). Pentecostals and others of the charismatic movement (after the Greek *charisma,* or "gift") refer to this effect as being "slain in the Spirit." Even many Christians regard the phenomenon skeptically, however. As might be surmised, the persons involved are merely engaging in role-playing as a result of suggestion and are "predisposed to fall" (Hinn 2002; Nickell 2002).

During the performance I attended, one woman who was called to come forward to receive Popoff's "laying on of hands" started toward the stage without her cane (clearly indicating that she could walk without it). Popoff had her go back and fetch it and made a big production of tossing it away. She and others were treated to Popoff's touch—actually, more of a push—and reacted accordingly. A few merely staggered or trembled, while others promptly fell into the arms of one of Popoff's catchers who had moved into position behind them. They collapsed in a variety of styles: some slumping, others reeling, still others stiffening and falling straight back. Once down, many seemed to be knocked out, while others writhed as if possessed.

I want to meet YOU... and personally minister to the needs in your life.

PENTECOSTAL POWER FLOWS

AS PETER POPOFF MINISTERS UNDER THE MIGHTY ANOINTING OF THE HOLY SPIRIT

In the early morning hours I was awakened by the Holy Spirit, you were on my mind. God said, "This is your hour to experience GROWTH"... get this, GROWTH TOWARD fulfilling your vision, future, destiny and all of your dreams. However, you must exercise the faith that activates the invisible potential available in the Christ. IF YOU DO NOT, YOUR DREAMS CANNOT GROW AND BECOME A REALITY, and they will die in the wasteland of frustration and disappointment.

Encoded in your genes is your predetermined eye color, shape and a divine destiny that you must fulfill. This same God also created you to bring about the fulfillment of SPECIFIED works and dreams from the foundation of the world. **You are God's Child and He has placed specified boundaries of blessing, health, and prosperity around you for you to enjoy and walk in. I sense in my spirit, at this moment, satan is doing all he can to STOP THIS FULFILLMENT.**

Figure 25. Excerpt from Popoff promotional mailing received by the author. (Author's collection)

I did not get to experience Popoff's powerful touch personally. Only a few of the audience of perhaps 1,500 could be singled out for the "power" treatment. I almost got lucky when he called out a woman with back trouble and then mentioned a man who was also afflicted. I stood up, but since I was a distance away, Popoff gestured for me to stay there, saying that when the woman received her anointing, I would receive mine too. Apparently, his gift of the word of knowledge failed to tell him that I was malingering—just as it often did during Randi's extensive investigation.

I had two more opportunities to be healed, though not by touch. After many individual callings out, Popoff tried a group approach. The audience had been given packets of anointing oil, and we were told to place the oil on our afflicted spots (or on our foreheads) while the evangelist beseeched, entreated, gesticulated, and spoke in tongues. (Known as *glossolalia,* this is the babbling of nonsense syllables that pass as an unknown language but are actually pseu-

Figure 26. Peter Popoff works the crowd at a performance in Toronto, Canada. (Photo by Joe Nickell)

dolanguage [Nickell 1993].) Finally, Popoff prayed over several people, including me (figure 26).

Meanwhile, Popoff's helpers were collecting wastebaskets full of envelopes bearing offerings. People were supposed to exchange their offering envelopes for some sort of mystico-magico wristband, but they ran out of those and substituted small packets of "Miracle Spring Water," which a helper tossed out by the handful. (I still have mine, giving it all the reverence it is due.) Great efforts were made to collect every offering, and one helper who ended up with a handful of stragglers' envelopes but no wastebasket to deposit them in simply stuffed them in his coat pocket.

Many were supposedly healed at the service. One attention-seeking woman put on a big show of running around the congregation, although there was no reason to believe that she had previously been unable to do that. Several gave testimonials, a common response to a healing session. Due to the power of suggestion and the excitement of the event, which can release endorphins that reduce pain temporarily, people believed that they had been healed and so convinced others. According to psychologist Terence Hines, "One can find testimonials attesting to the effectiveness of almost anything." Regarding faith-healing testimonials like those cited by Popoff, Hines states: "It is safe to say that if testimonials play a major part in the 'come on' for a cure or therapy, the cure or therapy is almost certainly worthless. If the promoters of the therapy had actual evidence for its effectiveness, they would cite it and not have to rely on testimonials" (Hines 1988, 236–37).

Like the touted successes of Benny Hinn and other faith healers, those of Peter Popoff do not withstand scrutiny. In one case, for example, a girl's "inoperable, malignant brain-stem tumor" had supposedly been confirmed by two computerized tomography (CT) scans and attested to by doctors at Johns Hopkins University. In fact, medical investigator and CSI consultant Dr. Gary P. Posner discovered that the "dark mass" on the CT scan was only an imperfection in the scanning process. The girl's physicians had never suspected a tumor at all. The "miracle" was an invented one, and the girl continued to suffer from the migraine headaches that had prompted the CT scan (Randi 1987, 291–92).

Although many may have left Popoff's "Miracle Crusade" falsely believing themselves healed, some knew better, such as the woman I photographed exiting the service in the wheelchair she had arrived in. Randi (1987, 305) calls attention to an appropriate passage—yea, a word of knowledge—in Matthew (7:15–16):

> Beware of false prophets, which come to you in sheep's clothing, but inwardly they are ravening wolves.
>
> Ye shall know them by their fruits.

References

Alexander, David. 1987. Peter Popoff's broken window. *Free Inquiry* 7, no. 4 (Fall): 47–49.

Asimov, Isaac. 1969. *Asimov's Guide to the Bible,* vol. 2, *The New Testament,* 337–39. New York: Avon Books.

Garrison, Greg. 1991. Unmasking fake miracles. *Birmingham (Ala.) News,* January 11.

Hines, Terence. 1988. *Pseudoscience and the Paranormal.* Amherst, N.Y.: Prometheus Books.

Hinn, Benny. 2002. Pros and cons. www.rapidnet.com/~jbeard/bdm/exposes/hinn/general.htm.

Kazenske, Donna. 2003. Spiritual gifts: The gift of the word of knowledge. *Christian Online Magazine.* http://www.christianity.com.

Nickell, Joe. 1993. *Looking for a Miracle: Weeping Icons, Relics, Stigmata, Visions and Healing Cures.* Buffalo, N.Y.: Prometheus Books.

———. 2002. Benny Hinn: Healer or Hypnotist? *Skeptical Inquirer* 26, no. 3 (May–June): 14–17.

Randi, James. 1987. *The Faith Healers.* Buffalo, N.Y.: Prometheus Books.

Stein, Gordon. 1993. *Encyclopedia of Hoaxes,* 219–20. Detroit: Gale Research.

Steiner, Robert A. 1986. Exposing the faith-healers. *Skeptical Inquirer* 11, no. 1 (Fall): 28–31.

———. 1989. *Don't Get Taken!* 124–26. El Cerrito, Calif.: Wide-Awake Books.

HAUNTED GAS CHAMBER

ALTHOUGH IT CLOSED MORE THAN half a century ago, the name Dachau still evokes horror. After Adolf Hitler and his National Socialists seized control of Germany on January 30, 1933, they began to inflict their Nazi ideology of racism and state supremacy on targeted groups: especially Jews, but also Gypsies, homosexuals, the mentally ill, dissenting clergymen, and many others. These people began to fill Dachau, the first concentration camp, which was established March 20. The camp also became the site of horrific medical experiments and executions. So many prisoners died or were killed there that a crematorium was built to dispose of the corpses. When it proved inadequate in 1942, a new building—dubbed Barracks X—was constructed with four double-chamber ovens (Distel 1972; Marcuse 2001; Memorial 2002). The presence of a gas chamber at that facility is still the subject of controversy.

Holocaust "revisionists" such as David Irving have denied the existence of a gas chamber at Dachau. Irving has declared that the gas chambers at Auschwitz and elsewhere were fakes, "just as the Americans built the dummies in Dachau" (quoted in Evans 2001). The official view of the Dachau memorial itself is expressed by a sign on site, rendered in five languages: "Gas chamber[:] disguised as a 'shower room'—never used as a gas chamber." Others have stated that the chamber was indeed used.

The issue impacts the paranormal when ghostmonger Dennis William Hauck (2000) reports ghost sightings associated with the gas chambers at Dachau. "German historians insist these were used for disinfectant purposes," he writes, "but the paranormal evidence seems to contradict these claims" (more on this presently). "Several reports," he continues, "of disembodied screaming, voices shouting 'gas,' and naked running apparitions originate from these shower stalls." He cites no source for these reports, other than appending a general bibliography of ghost-promoting books and Internet sources. In any event, there is considerable evidence that apparitions are a product of the experiencers' own psychological and cultural expectations (Nickell 2001), which means that people—not places—are "haunted." If ghosts did exist, however, Dachau would probably be crowded with them, because gas chambers or not, huge numbers perished there under horrendous conditions (Distel 1972).

Hauck (2000) also reproduces a photo taken by an American tourist that, he states, "appears to show a ghostly figure running out of the showers." Actually, all I can see is a fuzzy, light area that could be the result of several mundane causes (Nickell 1994). Indeed, elsewhere in his book, Hauck exhibits photos that, in my opinion, result not from ghosts but from glitches. These include some attributable to the camera's wrist strap (in one case, the telltale loop is visible [p. 110]) or an encroaching fingertip (p. 130); in each instance, the result is flash bounce-back, creating a white, ghostlike form. Even when such anecdotal and photographic "evidence" is not immediately explainable, it still represents the logical fallacy called "arguing from ignorance," since a conclusion cannot be drawn from an unknown.

The presence and use of gas chambers are matters best left to real evidence. For instance, on exhibit at Dachau is a copy of a letter, dated August 9, 1942, from Dr. Sigmund Rascher to the Reichsführer (Hitler). Translated, it reads in part: "As you know, in the concentration camp Dachau the same facilities are being built as in Linz [Austria]. Since the 'invalid transports' end up in certain chambers anyway, I am asking whether in these chambers the effect of our various war gasses couldn't be tested on the persons to be destined for such purpose anyway?"

In fact, there was a single gas chamber at Dachau, built in 1942 as part of the new crematorium (Barracks X). The confusion of Hauck and others as to there being several such facilities results from the presence of a number of nearby disinfection chambers that were used to fumigate clothing to kill lice (Marcuse 2001). Martin Mahner and I visited Dachau, and over the gas chamber entranceway is the old lettering, BRAUSEBAD ("shower bath"). As shown in figure 27, the door has heavy steel construction, a flange for airtightness, and external locking handles—all unnecessary for a mere shower. A similar door is on the opposite side, leading to another room that in turn leads to the ovens. According to Harold Marcuse in his *Legacies of Dachau* (2001), the

Figure 27. Gas chamber (labeled "shower bath") at Dachau.
(Photo by Joe Nickell)

gas chamber was indeed made functional, although only "trial gassings" were actually conducted there. Until Dachau was liberated by American soldiers on April 29, 1945, large-scale exterminations continued to be carried out at the Vernichtungslager (extermination camps) such as Treblinka.

Nevertheless, many of Dachau's dead were cremated at Barracks X. Paul Kurtz (1988), CSICOP's chairman, was a barely eighteen-year-old American

106

GI during World War II, and he arrived at Dachau just days after it was liberated. "When I first visited Dachau, I stood in the pit where the ashes and bones of thousands of victims were strewn," he writes. "I saw the high piles of clothing and shoes that had been seized from the victims." There, and later at Buchenwald and elsewhere, he spoke with "victims of the Nazi scourge, who had suffered the torments of the extermination camps, and who with muted whispers recounted the tales of horror: men, women, and children herded into cattle cars, starved and beaten, driven into gas chambers, and then reduced to ashes."

Although I did not see, hear, or photograph any apparitions at the crematorium or anywhere else at Dachau, I am not surprised that others believe they have. Knowledge of the horrors that took place there can easily inspire images of the past—or "ghosts." To many, these are merely deeply poignant metaphors, but to others, they may actually seem to erupt into reality.

References

Distel, Barbara. 1972. *Dachau Concentration Camp.* N.p.: Comité International de Dachau.

Evans, Richard J. 2001. *Lying about Hitler,* 124–25. New York: Basic Books.

Hauck, Dennis William. 2000. *The International Directory of Haunted Places.* New York: Penguin.

Kurtz, Paul. 1988. *Forbidden Fruit: The Ethics of Humanism,* 249. Buffalo, N.Y.: Prometheus Books.

Marcuse, Harold. 2001. *Legacies of Dachau,* 37–46, 185. Cambridge: Cambridge University Press.

Memorial site concentration camp Dachau. [2002]. Dachau brochure.

Nickell, Joe. 1994. *Camera Clues: A Handbook for Photographic Investigation,* 146–59. Lexington: University Press of Kentucky.

———. 2001. Phantoms, frauds, or fantasies? In *Hauntings and Poltergeists,* ed. James Houran and Rense Lange, 214–23. Jefferson, N.C.: McFarland.

THE CASE OF
THE PSYCHIC DETECTIVES

ALTHOUGH MAINSTREAM SCIENCE HAS never validated any psychic ability, self-styled clairvoyants, diviners, spirit mediums, and soothsayers continue to sell their fantasies—and, in some cases, to shrewdly purvey their cons—to a credulous public. Particularly disturbing is a resurgence of alleged psychic crime solving. In fact, the media—especially Court TV's *Psychic Detectives,* NBC's *Medium,* and various segments of *Larry King Live*—have shamelessly touted several self-claimed psychic shamuses as if they could actually identify murderers and kidnappers or locate missing persons. Here is an investigative look at five such claimants. (Another, Phil Jordan, is featured in a later chapter.)

Allison DuBois

Allison DuBois is the real-life Phoenix-area clairvoyant and spiritualist whose alleged assistance to law enforcement is the basis for NBC's drama series *Medium* (featuring Patricia Arquette as DuBois). Executive producer Glenn Gordon Caron (creator of *Moonlighting*) says of DuBois: "I was amazed by her tale. She has this radio in her head that she has no control over. Wherever she looked, she saw dead people. It was a tremendous albatross in terms of having a family life. And I thought, 'I've never heard that story before, certainly not from the point of view of a soccer mom'" (Hiltbrand 2005).

But Caron has been snookered. The *Medium* Web site (www.nbc.com/Medium/) boasts that "DuBois has consulted on a variety of murders or missing persons cases while working with various law enforcement agencies including the Glendale Arizona Police Department, the Texas Rangers, and a County Attorney's office in the Homicide Bureau." In fact, both the Glendale police and the Texas Rangers deny that DuBois ever worked with them. Glendale police spokesperson Michael Pena told *Skeptical Inquirer* managing editor Benjamin Radford that the detective who investigates missing persons cases "does not recall using DuBois at all in [one specific] case, or in any other cases." And Texas Rangers spokesperson Tom Vinger stated flatly to Radford, "The Texas Rangers have not worked with Allison DuBois or any other psychics" (Radford 2005, 7).

In any event, I find it curious that the show's Web site claims only that DuBois "consulted" on cases—not that she solved a single one. The site also mentions that DuBois is "the youngest member of the elite medium 'Dream Team' studied by Dr. Gary Schwartz at the University of Arizona in Tucson." That is not much to boast of: Schwartz, a professor of psychology and psychiatry at Arizona, is credulous about the paranormal, and in his book *The Afterlife Experiments* (2002), he claims to have provided scientific evidence for the survival of consciousness and the reality of spirit communication. However, noted parapsychology critic Ray Hyman (2003, 22) observes that Schwartz is "badly mistaken," adding: "The research he presents is flawed. Probably no other extended program in psychical research deviates so much from accepted norms of scientific methodology as this one does."

Nevertheless, the publicity DuBois receives "appears to have been good for business," according to one reporter (Hiltbrand 2005). He notes that DuBois now has a "backlog of murder cases," for which she does not charge a fee, and years of bookings for personal readings, for which she does. She also acts as a jury consultant for prosecutors (Bloom 2005). DuBois thus follows the approach of the late Illinois psychic Greta Alexander, who worked for free with police departments at every opportunity, which brought her publicity and bolstered her business of offering palm readings, operating a 900-number telephone inspiration line, selling astrology and numerology charts, and other endeavors (Nickell 1994, 12; Lucas 1994, 134).

Noreen Renier

High-profile psychic Noreen Renier employs an old divination technique called psychometry, by which she claims to get psychic impressions and visions from objects connected with particular people. Actually, the claim of psychometric power is testable, but Renier has not been willing to accept the challenge of psychic investigator James Randi, who has offered $1 million to anyone who can exhibit such a power under scientifically controlled conditions. Indeed, like many alleged psychics, Renier prefers to avoid skeptics, offering her alleged paranormal abilities only to the credulous.

She claims to have had a vision of President Reagan's attempted assassination, but there are varying accounts of what Renier actually said. When asked under oath about predicting that Reagan would be shot, she answered: "Some of those predictions were not mine. The newspaper put in three or four jazzy ones without my—I didn't do two or three of those predictions" (Posner 1994, 65). Regarding Reagan, on various occasions Renier apparently referred to chest "problems," possibly a heart attack or at least chest pain. Then she converted that to a gunshot, finally stating, according to FBI agent Robert Ressler (1986, 12, 13), that the president "would be killed in a machine gun assault on a parade stand by many in foreign uniforms." Renier was then in a position to use a technique called *retrofitting* (after-the-fact matching). She could score if Reagan had a coronary or other chest-related problems; if there was an attack on his life, with or without a bullet to the chest, and whether he survived or not; and if he died in a hail of gunfire. In fact, Renier's error regarding the machine-gunning was later shifted to claim the successful prediction of the assassination of President Anwar Sadat of Egypt. Renier shrewdly observed that she had not specified "*which* president" (Posner 1994, 64). Renier is reported to have a history of inaccurate predictions, such as forecasting that after his reelection in 1980 President Jimmy Carter would be assassinated on the lawn of the White House; she also saw Vice President Walter Mondale committing suicide (Posner 1994, 66).

One of Renier's most celebrated cases is that of seventy-six-year-old Norman Lewis, a resident of Williston, Florida, who vanished on March 24, 1994, and remained missing for two years. The police supposedly had no leads or suspects, but when Renier was consulted, she immediately "saw" Lewis in his red truck. She also visualized the numbers 45 and 21 and other "clues," including a cliff wall, loose bricks, a bridge, and railroad tracks. This led police to a rock quarry, and navy divers soon located Lewis's truck containing his skeletal remains. Or so the case is typically presented in the media, citing Renier and the Williston police. On September 22, 2004, Court TV featured a slanted treatment of the case that omitted crucial information and offered a highly dubious re-creation of events. Like so many psychic sleuth success tales, this one seems to get better with each retelling.

In this case, however, the Williston story was thoroughly investigated by Dr. Gary Posner (1997, 2005), with revealing results. Williston police actually knew that Lewis had been "despondent" and had confided to a friend that if his situation deteriorated "he would find a river or pit"—that is, where he would end his life—and "made some reference to knowing every rock pit in the county." Significantly, Lewis had left behind both his wallet and his respiratory inhaler (he had emphysema), suggesting that he did not intend to return.

Renier knew that Lewis's truck had not been found, despite intensive searching. Thus, as Posner (1997, 3) notes, if it was anywhere in the vicinity, the logical assumption would be that it was "submerged in a body of water." If Renier had looked at a map—something she appears to do quite often (e.g., Voyles 1999)—she would have observed that the Williston area is dotted with limestone quarries and crisscrossed with railroad tracks, as well as highways 45 and 121. In fact, the police had looked into several bodies of water before searching the Whitehurst pit, where Lewis's truck and remains were finally found. Brian Hewitt, the lead detective on the case, admitted that he had "walked around probably thirty quarries" before finally deciding to search Whitehurst. Actually, a different pit that was nearer to Lewis's home best matched the psychic's so-called clues (Posner 1997, 2, 6–7). But if Lewis had traveled north on the main road from his home (Route 45), Whitehurst was the first large quarry he would have come to.

The "clues" Renier provided were either obvious for the area or the result of retrofitting. After the fact, for example, abandoned railroad tracks were belatedly uncovered, and an old truck scale was interpreted as resembling a bridge to fit Renier's statements.

Carla Baron

Yet another would-be clairvoyant is psychic profiler Carla Baron of Los Angeles. She makes grand claims—such as having solved fifty cases during the last two decades—but there is little to substantiate them. That is the conclusion of the Independent Investigations Group (IIG), which examines paranormal claims. The group looked into fourteen cases that Baron claimed involvement with, concluding that "every case we investigated was either solved without Baron's involvement or remains unsolved" (IIG 2004).

As an example, Baron's publicity materials assert that she worked on the O. J. Simpson case and did "some channeling work" with the Brown family. The IIG, however, contacted Nicole Simpson's sister, Denise Brown, who was the primary spokesperson for the family during the Simpson trials and is now an advocate for victims of violent crime. She responded, "I've never heard of this person," and neither had any of her family members. Concludes the IIG (2004), "It seems clear that Baron's claim that she worked on the 'O. J. Simpson case' is baseless."

Carla Baron also claimed on a Los Angeles radio program that she had predicted correctly that fourteen-year-old kidnap victim Elizabeth Smart would be found alive. (Alive or dead is a fifty-fifty proposition.) When the teenager was found in the custody of a cult leader calling himself "Emmanuel," Baron claimed that she had provided information to Ed Smart, Elizabeth's father, through a tip hotline operator named "Melinda." However, Ed Smart was quoted as saying that "the family didn't get any valuable information from psychics" (IIG 2004).

Baron has reportedly stated: "I don't think it's about the accuracy. I think it's about the assistance that I give." The IIG (2004) responds:

> But how can you assist people with inaccurate information? Doesn't providing the missing piece of the puzzle, or insight and information, connecting the dots usually lead to a solution? Implicit in the claim of being a "psychic detective" is the claim that you provide accurate information that leads to the successful resolution of a mystery. Imagine if a police detective said, "police detectives don't actually solve the case, they just come up with ideas and hope for the best." Such a statement would not generate much confidence in police procedure, and rightly so.

Carol Pate

We hear a lot about psychics' alleged successes, but less about their much more frequent and notable failures. Take two cases of Little Rock, Arkansas, psychic Carol Pate, for example. The first is claimed as a success.

Pate appeared on Court TV's *Psychic Detectives* and *Larry King Live* regarding her alleged assistance in the case of a missing Arkansas teenager. Although it was claimed that Pate had "helped find" the boy, she did nothing of the sort. He was released after being repeatedly raped by his kidnapper. So when the announcer for *Larry King Live* asked, before a commercial break, "Can detectives use a psychic's vision to catch a kidnapper?" the answer is no. After the fact, Pate could only try to match up her stated "clues" using the police psychic's stock-in-trade, retrofitting. For instance, the word *ridge* "came into my head," says Pate, and Ridge Road was the name of the main route leading away from the kidnap site (Psychics 2004). But Pate could have learned that when she visited the location or consulted a map.

Another case involving Carol Pate was that of Dr. Xu "Sue" Wang of Darien, Illinois, who disappeared in 1999 after she left for work at a medical center. Just over a year later, Pate claimed that, based on some photos mailed to her by the Darien police, she had a psychic vision. She said that she had visualized the scene where Wang had been buried in a previously dug grave (Zorn 2000b). Subsequently, the police, acting on Pate's advice, announced plans to conduct an aerial search and to use dogs to look for the missing physician's burial site (Police 2000). *Chicago Tribune* columnist Eric Zorn was skeptical. He quoted me as stating, "They count their lucky guesses and ignore all their misses. . . . I have just one question for all of them: Where's Jimmy Hoffa?" Zorn (2000b) gave odds that the police would not "find anything" and concluded that Pate was merely "guessing." Subsequently, Zorn sent an e-mail to *Skeptical Inquirer,* quoting Darien's deputy police chief Ron Campo, who said of Pate's psychic input, "It didn't pan out." Concluded Zorn (2000a): "Turns out the woman was just guessing, like every other phony who claims to have such powers—exactly, eerily as I predicted. Hey, d'ya suppose . . . ?"

Etta Louise Smith

One of the most unusual psychic cases I ever investigated was that of Etta Louise Smith. Actually, Smith never claimed to be a psychic sleuth. She allegedly had a one-time "vision" of a murder victim's body that was so accurate that it led to her arrest by Los Angeles police, although she was subsequently "vindicated" by a Los Angeles Superior Court jury. The case occurred in 1980 but was featured on a *Larry King Live* program in 2004, hosted by Nancy Grace.

Smith's alleged vision was of the location of the body of a missing nurse, Melanie Uribe, in rural Lopez Canyon. After Smith went to the police and pinpointed the location on a map, she decided to drive to the site with two of her children. They had located the body and were en route to a telephone when they met the arriving police. Smith was later questioned about her precise knowledge and was given a lie detector test, which she failed. According to a detective's sworn testimony, "the polygraphist indicated that she was being deceptive," even "trying to control her breathing" (Guarino 1987, 5, 10). She was jailed for four days on suspicion of having some connection with the crime or the criminals.

Smith subsequently sued the police for the trauma she had suffered, asking $750,000 in damages. She won her case, but the jury, some of whom were apparently suspicious of Smith's psychic vision, awarded her a mere $26,184—sufficient to reimburse her for lost wages and attorney's fees, but providing little for pain and suffering (Varenchik 1987).

Forensic analyst John F. Fischer and I looked into the intriguing case, obtaining court transcripts and other materials, and concluded that it was possible to be skeptical of Smith's psychic powers without suspecting her of being an accessory (Nickell 1994, 161–62). We recalled an earlier case in which the police had concealed an informant's identity by means of a cover story attributing the information to a psychic. Was it possible that an acquaintance of Smith's, privy to information about the crime, had sought her help? Might Smith merely be protecting her source? The possibility gains credence when it is revealed that the killers were eventually caught because one of them had boasted about the crime to people in his Pacoima neighborhood, and at the time, Smith lived in Pacoima. Interestingly, as Smith went searching for the nurse's body, her psychic powers seemed to wane, because it was one of her children who actually spied the white-clad corpse (Klunder 1987; Varenchik 1987, 44–45).

That Smith could locate the canyon site on a map is revealing. She was clearly not employing a technique of divination (such as map dowsing, which usually involves the use of a pendulum) to locate something hidden (Guiley 1991; Nickell 1994, 163–64). Instead, she seemed to already know the location and was merely pointing it out on a map for the police. Apparently, Smith also gave conflicting accounts of her "vision." She said on a television program, "It was as if someone had put a picture right in front of me" (*Sightings* 1992). Yet the book *Psychic Murder Hunters* assures us, "Strangely Etta didn't have a vision of any kind—she described it as a feeling rather than a vision" (Boot 1994, 348).

That her alleged vision was a one-time occurrence appears to support police suspicions, as does the failed polygraph test, especially the allegation that she was trying to control her breathing. Revealingly, the National Center for Missing and Exploited Children cautions against completely ignoring such psychic tips, since the purported visions may be a cover for someone who is afraid or unwilling to become directly involved (Henetz 2002).

As these cases and profiles indicate, psychics do not solve crimes or locate missing persons unless they employ the same nonmystical techniques as real detectives: obtaining and assessing factual information, receiving tips, and, sometimes, just getting lucky. In addition to the technique of retrofitting, psychics may shrewdly study local newspaper files and area maps, glean information from family members or others associated with a tragedy, and even impersonate police and attempt to bribe detectives (Nickell 1994; 2004). It is bad enough that they are often able to fool the media; detectives should know better and should, well, *investigate* their alleged psychic counterparts.

References

Bloom, Rhonda Bodfield. 2005. Medium awareness. *Arizona Daily Star,* January 17.

Boot, Andrew. 1994. *Psychic Murder Hunters,* 343–61. London: Headline Book Publishing.

Guarino, Anthony. 1987. Testimony in Superior Court (Los Angeles, Calif.), *Etta L. Smith v. City of Los Angeles et al.,* March 25, 1–50.

Guiley, Rosemary Ellen. 1991. *Harper's Encyclopedia of Mystical and Paranormal Experience,* 155–57. New York: HarperCollins.

Henetz, Patty. 2002. For kidnapped girl's family, "every day is a struggle" of not knowing. *Buffalo (N.Y.) News,* November 29.

Hiltbrand, David. 2005. Destined to succeed. *Sydney Morning Herald,* April 13. www .smh.com.au.

Hyman, Ray. 2003. How not to test mediums: Critiquing the afterlife experiments. *Skeptical Inquirer* 27, no. 1 (January–February): 20–30.

IIG special investigation: Carla Baron, psychic detective (?). 2004. www.iigwest.com/ carla_report.html (accessed May 3, 2005).

Klunder, Jan. 1987. Woman whose "vision" led to murder victim sues over arrest. *Los Angeles Times,* March 19.

Lucas, Ward. 1994. A product of the media: Greta Alexander. In Nickell 1994, 130–55.

Nickell, Joe. 1994. *Psychic Sleuths: ESP and Sensational Cases.* Buffalo, N.Y.: Prometheus Books.

———. 2004. Psychic sleuth without a clue. *Skeptical Inquirer* 28, no. 3 (May–June): 19–21.

Police search ANL-E area for missing doctor. 2000. *Argonne (Ill.) News,* September 5. www.anl.gov/Media_Center/Argonne_News/news00/an000905.html (accessed April 27, 2005).

Posner, Gary. 1994. The media's rising star psychic sleuth: Noreen Renier. In Nickell 1994, 60–85.

———. 1997. A not-so-psychic detective. *Skeptic* 5, no. 4, 2–7.

———. 2005. Noreen Renier and the Williston case on Court TV's *Psychic Detectives. Skeptic* 11, no. 3, 16–17.

Psychics helping police solve crimes. 2004. *Larry King Live,* April 29. www.cnn.com/ TRANSCRIPTS/0404/29/lkl.oo.html (accessed May 25, 2004).

Radford, Benjamin. 2005. Psychic detectives fail in the real world but succeed on TV. *Skeptical Inquirer* 29, no. 2 (March–April): 6–7.

Ressler, Robert. 1986. Deposition in the Circuit Court of Jackson County, Oregon, September 5. Cited in Posner 1994, 63–65.

Schwartz, Gary E. and William L. Simon. 2002. *The Afterlife Experiments: Breakthrough Scientific Evidence of Life After Death.* New York: Pocket Books.

Sightings. 1992. Fox network, September 4.

Varenchik, Richard. 1987. L.A. court vindicates psychic vision. *Fate,* August, 42–48.

Voyles, Karen. 1999. Psychic discovery: Levy woman claims she solves cases. *Gainesville (Fla.) Sun,* June 8.

Zorn, Eric. 2000a. E-mail to Kevin Christopher, October 5.

———. 2000b. Psychic's guess is as good as no guess at all. *Chicago Tribune,* August 31.

ITALY'S MIRACLE RELICS

IN OCTOBER 2004, AFTER PARTICIPATING IN the Fifth World Skeptics Congress in Abano Terme, Italy—near Padua, where Galileo discovered Jupiter's moons (Frazier 2005)—I remained in the beautiful country for some investigative work. Here are some of my findings.

Relics of the Saints

I visited a number of churches containing alleged relics—objects associated with a saint or martyr. These may consist of all or part of a holy person's body (in Catholicism, a first-class relic) or some item associated with him or her, such as an article of clothing (a second-class relic). Venerated since the first century AD, relics were thought to be imbued with special qualities or powers —such as healing—that could be tapped into by those who touched or even viewed them (Pick 1979, 101).

Relic veneration had become so prevalent in St. Augustine's time (about AD 400) that he deplored "hypocrites in the garb of monks" for hawking the bones of martyrs, adding with due skepticism, "if indeed of martyrs" (*Encyclopaedia Britannica* 1973, s.v. "Relics"). In about 403, Vigilantius of Toulouse condemned the veneration of relics as nothing more than a form of idolatry, but St. Jerome defended the cult of relics, on the basis of miracles that God reputedly worked through them (*New Catholic Encyclopedia* 1967, s.v. "Relics"). Such relics included the fingers of St. Paul, St. Andrew, and Doubting Thomas, as well as multiple heads of John the Baptist. Especially prolific were relics associated with Jesus, whose foreskin was enshrined at no fewer than six churches. His swaddling clothes, hay from the manger, and vials of his mother's breast milk were also preserved. A tear that he shed at Lazarus's tomb was collected and saved, along with countless relics of his crucifixion and burial (Nickell 1993, 75–76).

Italy is especially rich with relics. With the generous assistance of my

Italian friends, who relayed me from city to city by train across the northern part of the country, I witnessed reputed holy relics in Vienna, Milan, and Turin (before flying to Naples). In Venice, beneath the high altar of the Basilica di San Marco (St. Mark's Basilica), supposedly lies the body of the author of the Gospel of Mark, martyred in Alexandria and later brought to the city by Venetian merchants. Some Italian colleagues and I visited the cavernous Byzantine basilica on October 11, first paying a fee to see a collection of relics that included an alleged piece of the stone column of Jesus's flagellation, then paying again to pass by St. Mark's reputed remains. Unfortunately, since the remains did not come to Venice until AD 829 (whereupon construction of the basilica was immediately begun to enshrine them), there is a serious question as to their provenance. Even accepting the substance of the story about their acquisition, one source notes, "the identity of the piously stolen body depends on the solidarity of the Alexandrine tradition" (Coulson 1958, 302). Moreover, according to a National Geographic Society travel guide (Jepson 2001, 143), "many claim the saint's relics were destroyed in a fire in 976."

In Milan, I visited the Basilica of St. Eustorgio, guided by noted writer (and fellow *Skeptical Inquirer* columnist) Massimo Polidoro. In a dark recess of the church we read the inscription, SEPVLCRVM TRIVM MAGORVM (Sepulcher of the Three Magi). A carved stone slab nearby was accompanied by a sign that informed us, "According to tradition this stone slab with the comet was on top of the Magi's tomb and was brought to Italy along with their relics." Actually, the story is a bit more complicated. Legendarily, the relics were discovered by St. Helena (248–328), mother of Constantine the Great. They were supposedly transferred to Milan by St. Eustorgio (d. 518), who carried them by oxcart. After Milan fell to Frederick Barbarossa in 1162, they were transported to Cologne two years later (Cruz 1984, 154; Lowenthal 1998). According to an article by David Lowenthal (1998), however, it appears that the relics were never in Milan at all. It seems that the whole tale was made up by Reinald, the archbishop of Cologne. In any event, in 1909, some fragments of the alleged Magi bones were "returned" to Milan and enshrined in the church named for their legendary transporter, the sixth-century bishop of Milan.

In Turin, I visited the Cathedral of St. John the Baptist, which houses the notorious Shroud of Turin. This supposed burial cloth of Christ is actually

Figure 28. A lighted-cross reliquary in a Turin church purportedly contains a piece of the True Cross and some of the Holy Blood of Christ. (Photo by Joe Nickell)

a tempera-painted forgery, radiocarbon-dated to the time of the confessed fourteenth-century artist. With a small group of Turin skeptics, I also studied the latest shroud developments at the Museo della Sindone (Holy Shroud Museum), along with many items associated with the cloth, including the mammoth camera with which it was first photographed in 1898. (For more on the shroud, see Nickell 1998; McCrone 1996).

Elsewhere in Turin, I visited the Church of Maria Ausiliatrice, whose crypt is a relic's chapel containing a fabulous collection of an estimated five thousand relics of saints. There are endless panels and display cases along the walls, including relics alleged to be from Mary Magdalene and, more credibly, St. Francis of Assisi. The focal point of the chapel is a lighted cross containing, purportedly, a small amount of the Holy Blood of Christ (figure 28). As with other blood relics, however, there is no credible evidence to link it with Jesus or even with his time. Along with the blood is an alleged piece of the True Cross, discovered thanks to a vision St. Helena had in 326. Protestant reformer John Calvin, in his *Treatise on Relics* (1543, 61), stated that there were enough alleged fragments of the cross to "form a whole ship's cargo."

Because such relics were eagerly sought by noblemen and churches alike to enhance their influence, there were always people willing to supply them—even by unholy means. The Catholic Church addressed the question of the authenticity of relics in something less than a head-on-fashion. It often sidestepped the issue, declining to take a position regarding the genuineness of a particular relic. The veneration of certain doubtful relics was permitted to continue on the grounds that, even if a relic was in fact spurious, God was not dishonored by an error that had been made in good faith. In addition, it was thought that a final verdict could not easily be pronounced in the case of many relics. Besides, it was argued, the devotions "deeply rooted in the heart of peasantry" could not be dismissed lightly (Christian relics 2004). Thus, an end-justifies-the-means attitude—which helped create and promote fake relics in the first place—prevailed.

Holy Grail, Holy Hoax

In Milan and Turin I visited sites that have gained new popularity due to Dan Brown's best-selling novel *The Da Vinci Code* (2004). The novel presents a modern-day quest for the Holy Grail, the legendary cup that Jesus and his disciples drank from at the Last Supper and was subsequently used to catch and preserve his blood at the Crucifixion (figure 29)—an act that is usually attributed to Mary Magdalene or Joseph of Arimathea.

The original grail story is the French romance *Le Conte du Graal* (The Story of the Grail), written in about 1190 by Chrétien de Troyes (Barber 2004, 17–19). Brown's novel is predicated on a conspiracy theory involving Jesus and Mary Magdalene. Supposedly, the Old French word *sangreal* is interpreted not as *san greal* ("holy grail") but as *sang real* ("royal blood"). Although the concept was not current before the late Middle Ages, a source that Brown drew heavily on, *Holy Blood, Holy Grail,* argues that Jesus was married to Mary Magdalene,

Figure 29. Statue of Faith holding the Holy Grail stands before the Gran Madre di Dio church in Turin. According to legend, this is the site where the Holy Grail is hidden. (Photo by Joe Nickell)

that they had a child, and that Jesus might have survived the Crucifixion. Jesus's child, or so the "nonfiction" book claims, thus began a bloodline that led to the Merovingian dynasty, a succession of kings who ruled from 481 to 751 in present-day France (Baigent, Leigh, and Lincoln 1996). Evidence of the holy bloodline was supposedly contained in a trove of parchment documents discovered by Bérenger Saunière, the priest of Rennes-le-Château in the Pyrenees. The secret had supposedly been kept by a shadowy society known as the Priory of Sion, which harked back to the era of the Knights Templar and claimed among its past Grand Masters Leonardo da Vinci, Isaac Newton, and Victor Hugo.

Brown's novel seizes on Leonardo—borrowing from "The Secret Code of Leonardo Da Vinci," the first chapter of another work of pseudohistory titled *The Templar Revelation* coauthored by "researchers" Lynn Picknett and Clive Prince (1998). Their previous foray into nonsense was their claim that Leonardo had created the Shroud of Turin—even though that forgery appeared nearly a century before the great artist and inventive genius was born. Among the "revelations" of Picknett and Prince (1998, 19–21) adopted by Brown in *The Da Vinci Code* is a claim regarding Leonardo's fresco *The Last Supper,* which I viewed in Milan with Massimo Polidoro. Supposedly, the painting contains hidden symbolism relating to the *sang real* secret. Picknett and Prince claim, for instance, that St. John (seated at the right of Jesus) is actually a woman—Mary Magdalene—and that the shape made by "Mary" and Jesus is "a giant, spread-eagled 'M,'" allegedly confirming the interpretation. By repeating this silliness, Brown provoked critics to note that his characterizations revealed a certain ignorance about his subject (Bernstein 2004, 12).

Alas, the whole basis of *The Da Vinci Code*—the "discovered" parchments of Rennes-le-Château relating to the alleged Priory of Sion—was part of a hoax perpetrated by a man named Pierre Plantard. Plantard commissioned a friend to create the fake parchments, which he then used to concoct the bogus priory story in 1956 (Olson and Miesel 2004, 223–39). Of course, Brown—along with the authors of *Holy Blood, Holy Grail* and *The Templar Revelation*—was also duped by the Priory of Sion hoax, which he in turn foisted onto his readers. He is apparently unrepentant, however, and his apologists point out that *The Da Vinci Code* is, after all, fiction, although at the beginning of the novel, Brown claims that it is based on certain facts. Meanwhile, despite the devastatingly negative evidence, *The Da Vinci Code* mania continues, along with the quest for the fictitious Holy Grail.

Blood of St. Januarius

Joined by paranormal investigator Luigi Garlaschelli (from the Department of Organic Chemistry at the University of Pavia), I flew from Turin to Naples to further investigate a miracle claim I had already spent a lot of time on. It concerned the "blood" of the legendary martyr San Gennaro—St. Januarius—who was supposedly bishop of Benevento, Italy, in AD 305 when he was beheaded during Diocletian's persecution of Christians. Eyewitnesses dating back to at least the fourteenth century reported that the substance purported to be the martyred saint's congealed blood periodically liquefies, reddens, and froths—in apparent contravention of natural laws. The ritual takes place several times annually. According to tradition, if the phenomenon fails to occur, disaster is imminent (Nickell and Fischer 1992, 145–51).

Reasons for suspicions abound. First, the Catholic Church has never been able to verify the historical existence of San Gennaro. Moreover, there is absolutely no record of the saint's blood relics prior to 1389 (when an unknown traveler reported his astonishment at witnessing the liquefaction). Another reason for suspicion is that there are other examples of saints' blood that liquefies—some twenty in all—and virtually every one of them is found in the Naples area. Such proliferation seems less suggestive of the miraculous and more indicative of some regional secret.

It is important to note that no sustained scientific scrutiny of the blood relics has ever been permitted. Also, descriptions of the liquefaction vary, and it is not always easy to separate what may be permutations in the phenomenon's occurrence from differences attributable to individual perceptions. Assertions that the substance in the vials is genuine blood are based solely on spectroscopic analyses that employed antiquated equipment and were done under such poor conditions as to cast grave doubt on the results. (For a full discussion of the Januarian legend and phenomenon, see Nickell and Fischer 1992, 145–64.)

Forensic analyst John F. Fischer and I offered a solution to the phenomenon that involved a mixture of olive oil, a small amount of melted beeswax, and pigment. When the mixture is cool, it is solid, but when it is slightly warmed (by body heat, nearby candles, and the like), the trace of congealing substance melts, and the mixture liquefies—whether slowly or quite suddenly. As one authority states: "A very important fact is that liquefaction has occurred during repair of the casket, a circumstance in which it seems highly unlikely that God would work a miracle" (Coulson 1958, 239).

In 1991, before we could publish our research, a team of Italian scientists made international headlines with their own solution to the Januarian mystery. Writing in the journal *Nature*, Professor Garlaschelli and two colleagues from Milan, Franco Ramaccini and Sergio Della Sala, proposed "that thixotropy may furnish an explanation." A thixotropic gel is one capable of liquefying when agitated and resolidifying when allowed to stand. The Italian scientists created such a gel by mixing chalk and hydrated iron chloride with a small amount of salt water, resulting in a convincing replication of the Januarian phenomenon (Garlaschelli et al. 1991).

Figure 30. Luigi Garlaschelli, intrepid Italian paranormal investigator, poses with the Pozzuoli Stone on which St. Januarius was
legendarily beheaded. (Photo by Joe Nickell)

In 1996 Garlaschelli was able to examine a similarly liquefying blood relic,
that of St. Lorenzo at the Church of St. Maria in Arnaseno, Italy. Using a test-
tube mixer, he whirled the ampoule containing the "blood" to test the thixotropic gel hypothesis, but there was no effect. He then immersed the ampoule
in warm water to test the melting hypothesis, whereupon a "miracle" occurred:

the contents liquefied and turned red—just like the Januarian phenomenon (Polidoro 2004).

In 2004, accompanied by Luigi Garlaschelli himself, I visited the Italian sites that hold the reputed relics of San Gennaro, and we discussed all the evidence. One of these sites is the Chapel of the Treasury, situated inside the Cathedral of Naples. This baroque chapel—rich in frescoes and marbles—holds the gilded silver bust of the saint and the ampoule of "blood" that periodically liquefies and then coagulates again. Garlaschelli (2004) cautions that the St. Januarius and St. Lorenzo "blood" relics do not necessarily work on the same principle, and he still believes that the former may be a thixotropic substance.

We also visited the Church of Capuchin Monks at Pozzuoli, Italy, a short train ride from Naples. A marble slab in the church wall is reputed to be the stone on which Januarius was beheaded (figure 30). In the late 1980s, however, the stone was examined and determined to be a Paleo-Christian altar, possibly dating from the seventh century (hundreds of years after the martyrdom). The red spots that were supposed to be the blood of the saint are believed to be traces from an old painting along with some candle drippings. According to Garlaschelli (2004), the church itself now discourages the cult of the Pozzuoli Stone "as a superstition originating from the wishful thinking and self-delusion of the worshippers." That could apply to many other miracle claims—throughout Italy and beyond.

References

Baigent, Michael, Richard Leigh, and Henry Lincoln. 1996. *Holy Blood, Holy Grail*. London: Arrow.

Barber, Richard. 2004. *The Holy Grail*. Cambridge, Mass.: Harvard University Press.

Bernstein, Amy D. 2004. Decoding the Da Vinci phenomenon. In *Secrets of the Da Vinci Code* 2004, 7–15.

Brown, Dan. 2004. *The Da Vinci Code*. New York: Doubleday.

Calvin, John. 1543. *Traité des Reliques* [Treatise on Relics]. Reprinted in *Jean Calvin: Three French Treatises*, ed. Francis M. Higman, 47–97. London: Athlone, 1970.

Christian relics. 2004. http://www.religionfacts.com/christianity/things/relics.htm (accessed February 28, 2005).

Coulson, John, ed. 1958. *The Saints: A Concise Biographical Dictionary*. New York: Hawthorn.

Cruz, Joan Carroll. 1984. *Relics*. Huntington, Ind.: Our Sunday Visitor.

Encyclopaedia Britannica. 1973. Chicago: Encyclopaedia Britannica.

Frazier, Kendrick. 2005. In the land of Galileo, Fifth World's Skeptics Congress solves mysteries, champions scientific outlook. *Skeptical Inquirer* 29, no. 1 (January–February): 5–9.

Garlaschelli, Luigi. 2004. Personal communications, October 15–16, and typescript, "Miraculous Italian Blood Relics."

Garlaschelli, Luigi, et al. 1991. Letter to *Nature* 353 (October 10): 507.

Jepson, Tim. 2001. *National Geographic Traveler: Italy*. Washington, D.C.: National Geographic Society.

Lowenthal, David. 1998. Fabricating heritage. *History and Memory* 10, no. 1 (Spring). http://iupjournals.org.history/ham10–1.html (accessed March 7, 2005).

McCrone, Walter. 1996. *Judgement Day for the Turin "Shroud."* Chicago: Microscope Publications.

New Catholic Encyclopedia. 1967. New York: McGraw-Hill.

Nickell, Joe. 1993. *Looking for a Miracle*. Amherst, N.Y.: Prometheus Books.

———. 1998. *Inquest on the Shroud of Turin*. Amherst, N.Y.: Prometheus Books.

Nickell, Joe, and John F. Fischer. 1992. *Mysterious Realms*, 145–64. Buffalo, N.Y.: Prometheus Books.

Olson, Carl E., and Sandra Miesel. 2004. *The Da Vinci Hoax*. San Francisco: Ignatius Press.

Pick, Christopher, ed. 1979. *Mysteries of the World*. Secaucus, N.J.: Chartwell Books.

Picknett, Lynn, and Clive Prince. 1998. *The Templar Revelation*. New York: Touchstone.

Polidoro, Massimo. 2004. What a bloody miracle! *Skeptical Inquirer* 28, no. 1 (January–February): 18–20.

Secrets of the Da Vinci Code. 2004. Collector's edition, *U.S. News and World Report*.

DAY OF THE DEAD

The northernmost country of Latin America, Estados Unidos Mexicanos (United States of Mexico) is rich in prehistoric and historic culture; it is a land of legend, lore, and struggle. Home to various indigenous peoples since around 2600 BC, Mexico was seized by the Spanish in 1519–1521, when Hernán Cortés conquered the Aztec empire. The population was subsequently decimated by Old World diseases. Spanish Catholic culture was established, and the country was exploited for its natural resources. Following a struggle for independence that began in 1810, Spanish rule ceased in 1821. The nineteenth and early twentieth centuries saw a series of revolts, revolutions, and wars, one of the consequences of which was the loss of Texas, New Mexico, and California to the United States. A new constitution in 1917 helped ensure democracy, although not without continued economic crises and political strife.

In the fall of 2003, following a CSI (at the time, still CSICOP) conference in Albuquerque, New Mexico, colleague Vaughn Rees and I made an investigative trip across northern Mexico from Ciudad Juárez to Tijuana, where we observed the cultural festivity known as the Day of the Dead (see also "Fortune-telling, Mexican Style" and "Undercover in Tijuana"). In ancient Mesoamerica, the *indigenistas* used music and dance in festivities presided over by the Aztec deities *Mictlantecuhtli* and *Mictecacihuatl* (Lord and Lady of the Dead) to celebrate the spirits of the deceased (*Huey* n.d.). The indigenous mythology clashed with Catholic teachings about heaven and hell, and as a result, the native customs were suppressed and overlaid with Christian ones. Spanish priests moved the time of the festivities to coincide with All Hallows' Day, so Mexicans now celebrate November 1 and 2 as, respectively, *Día de Todos Santos* (All Saints' Day) and *Día de Muertos* (Day of the Dead) (Andrade 2002, 9, 22; Salvador 2001). Concludes one writer, "Remember the dead they still do, and the modern festivity is characterized by the traditional Mexican

127

blend of ancient aboriginal and introduced Christian features" (Salvador 2001).

Despite some seepage of customs from north of the border, the Day of the Dead is not Mexico's Halloween. Whereas the All Hallows concept stems from medieval European notions of death that involve punishment and gratuitously sinister imagery, the Day of the Dead incorporates more playful and celebratory features. People honor their deceased loved ones and await some signal or manifestation from them (Joseph 2003). Customs (including the date of observance) vary from region to region, but cemeteries as well as many Mexican homes are typically readied for the occasion. At noon on the first day, the home's patio may be swept and the house decorated with white flowers. Offerings consisting of small jugs of cream, fruit, candies, and toys are set out for the spirits of deceased children. These child spirits are believed to join in the celebration and to consume the "essence" of the offerings. The next day, the home is prepared anew for the spirits of deceased adults, who may be honored with sugar skulls bearing their names. Other offerings may include tortillas, cigarettes, tequila, fruit, and *pan de muerto* (bread of death), all placed on the home's dinner table (*Huey* n.d.).

In Mexicali, on November 1, Vaughn and I stopped at a large cemetery where we watched the locals sprucing up and decorating their family plots. They washed gravestones, swept graves, painted fences, placed flowers, and fastened crepe streamers—all as part of an expressly festive occasion. Music blared, and a mariachi band roved in search of pesos. Vendors were in profusion, selling everything from brooms and flowers to burritos, soft drinks, and cotton candy. It was part picnic, part religious observance, and part family reunion—intended for the living *and* the dead.

The following day we were in Tijuana—Mexico's fourth largest city—for the Day of the Dead festivities held in El Centro (downtown). A Mexican-Aztec warrior dance group entertained with their expressive folk dancing as part of *Huey Mikailhuitl* (Great Celebration of the Dead). Services were being held in the cathedral while, outside, vendors sold devotional and other items. Along the streets, shop owners had their Day of the Dead wares prominently displayed, including little costumed skeletal figures, articulated skeletons of

Figure 31. Investigator Vaughn Rees surveys Day of the Dead
sugar skulls. (Photo by Joe Nickell)

wood and string, and the popular confectionary skulls made of hard sugar
with touches of color added (figure 31).

Despite its superstitious basis, the Day of the Dead is a colorful and enjoy-
able occasion, as well as a poignant one—a time to remember those no longer
among the living.

References

Andrade, Mary J. 2002. Day of the Dead in Mexico. San Jose, Calif.: La Oferta Review.

Huey Mikailhuitl (Great celebration of the dead). N.d. [ca. 2003]. Brochure of Mexican-Aztec Warrior Dance Group.

Joseph, Dana. 2003. Life in death. *Southwest Airlines Spirit,* October, 87–90.

Salvador, Ricardo J. 2001. What do Mexicans celebrate on the "Day of the Dead"? www.public.iastate.edu/rjsalvad/scmfaq/muertos.html (accessed May 14).

JACK THE RIPPER—IDENTIFIED?

THE GRUESOME MURDERS BY JACK THE RIPPER—history's most notorious serial slasher—continue to inspire horror. And the question of his identity continues to attract theorists, most recently popular crime novelist Patricia Cornwell (2002). But is she really justified in pronouncing the mystery solved (figure 32)? Did her touted $6 million, thirteen-month search actually lead her along a trail of evidence that finally uncovered the maniacal culprit? Or did she begin with an improbable suspect and work backward through myriad, often conflicting details, picking and choosing those that incriminated him? To answer these questions, some background is in order.

The Ripper Case

Sometimes called the Whitechapel murders, the series of slayings attributed to Jack the Ripper occurred in 1888 in or near the Whitechapel district of London's squalid East End. The victims were all prostitutes: Mary Ann "Polly" Nichols (August 31), Annie Chapman (September 8), Elizabeth Stride and Catharine Eddowes (September 30, only some forty minutes apart), and Mary Jane Kelly (November 9). All had their throats cut, and most were mutilated in other ways, except for Stride; her attack was apparently interrupted, prompting the killer to seek another victim. Nichols's abdomen was only slashed open, but Chapman, Eddowes, and Kelly were disemboweled; Eddowes's uterus and left kidney were taken, as was Kelly's heart. Kelly, whose body was grossly mutilated, was the only victim found indoors (see Begg, Fido, and Skinner 1994).

According to an 1894 memorandum by M. L. Macnaghten, chief constable, Criminal Investigation Department, Scotland Yard, there were at least three prominent Ripper suspects: M. J. Druitt, who was "sexually insane" and committed suicide (by drowning) after the Ripper murders; "Kosminski" (apparently Aaron Kosminski), a Polish Jew who resided in Whitechapel, hated

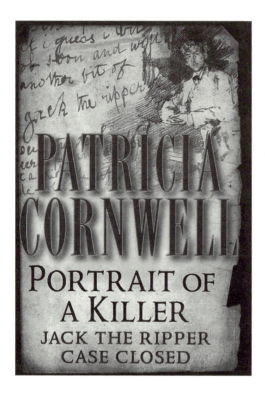

Figure 32. Patricia Cornwell's *Portrait of a Killer* leaves much to be desired. (Courtesy of *Skeptical Inquirer* magazine)

prostitutes, and was subsequently imprisoned in an asylum for the insane; and Michael Ostrog, allegedly a Russian doctor and a "homicidal maniac," whose "whereabouts at the time of the murders could never be ascertained" (Begg et al. 1994, 116–21, 241–45, 279–90, 340–45).

In the midst of the attacks, after the death of Annie Chapman, letters were sent to the Central News Agency and the Metropolitan Police signed "Jack the Ripper" (Evans and Skinner 2001). The earliest one, which was only recently rediscovered (Cornwell 2002, 211), was received on September 17. Most "Ripperologists" today accept the mounting evidence that these were the work of one or more journalists (Begg et al. 1994, 209–11). Nevertheless, the sobriquet "Jack the Ripper" stuck.

As the horrible crimes remained unsolved, popular writers began to propose suspects. Over the years, something of a Ripper industry has grown up, with authors proposing first one candidate and then another. Ripperologist Martin Fido (2001) took the words out of my mouth when he said of some of the books, "The common reader like myself found each identification quite convincing as he read it, and kept changing his mind about which was the Ripper." There is a formula to such "identifications." The author starts with someone who lived in Whitechapel (or elsewhere in London, or at least in England) and proceeds to build a case against him. Maybe he showed an interest in the Ripper crimes (who didn't?) or exhibited some odd behavior; perhaps he owned a knife. Such elements can be built up with speculation and innuendo, while any contrary facts can be ignored, swept aside, or rationalized. Voilà! To the unsuspecting reader, the real Jack the Ripper has emerged from the shadows.

Various suspects have come and—often mercifully—gone, including assorted lunatics and doctors. The latter were postulated based on the notion, probably mistaken, that the Ripper's handiwork showed surgical skill. Along similar lines, Sir Arthur Conan Doyle—creator of the world's most famous fictional sleuth, Sherlock Holmes—opined that the murderer was a woman. He surmised that the killer would have been heavily stained with blood, but that a midwife wearing a bloodstained apron could pass without suspicion (Begg et al. 1994, 207).

An alleged diary of Jack the Ripper brought me into the case in 1993. Surfacing two years earlier in the possession of a Liverpool scrap-metal dealer named Mike Barrett, the "diary" was ostensibly written by James Maybrick, a Liverpool cotton merchant who died of poison in 1889. According to the entries, Maybrick sought revenge on his philandering wife, perpetrating the Ripper murders in drug-induced frenzies. Warner Books intended to publish the text if it proved to be authentic, so manuscript authority Kenneth Rendell and I, together with a team of forensic experts, examined the diary. Conclusive handwriting evidence, in addition to a number of other suspicious features, revealed it to be an obvious forgery. Eventually, Barrett confessed that he had faked the diary using an old photo album. He had removed the used pages and then transcribed the text (which he had composed over ten days' time on a word processor) using a reproduction Victorian ink purchased at an art store. Although Barrett soon retracted his confession, ink analysis (performed on our team's samples at the instigation of friend and fellow investigator Melvin Harris) confirmed the presence of a modern preservative (Nickell 1995, 1997).

Another Suspect

Enter mystery writer Patricia Cornwell. Like others who proclaimed that their books represented "the final solution," "the mystery solved," and so on (Begg et al. 1994, 216, 217), Cornwell gave her *Portrait of a Killer* the subtitle *Jack the Ripper, Case Closed*. Actually, as a *New York Times* reviewer correctly characterizes it, "this book is a prosecution, not an investigation" (Carr 2002). Cornwell begins with her suspect—artist Walter Sickert (1860–1942)—without ever explaining how she chose him. She does state, however, "I began to wonder about Sickert when I was flipping through a book of his art" (2002, 12). Elsewhere, she "has repeatedly said that she doesn't like the look of the painter's face in his self-portraits, or the subject matter and tone of his paintings generally" (Carr 2002).

Having targeted her suspect, Cornwell then begins to hack and slash at poor Sickert's life and reputation, like a veritable Pat the Ripper. Sickert, a major British postimpressionist, was a leader of a school of painting that focused on gloomy urban interiors. One such Sickert work, titled *Jack the Ripper's Bedroom* (1908), is treated as an *aha!* by Cornwell. Actually, it is simply an interior of a bedroom at 6 Mornington Crescent, Camden Town, part of the upper two floors that Sickert rented in 1906 after returning to London from France. He believed that a man suspected of having been Jack the Ripper—a veterinary student whose name Sickert eventually forgot—had lodged there in the 1880s (Cornwell 2002, 60–61; Begg et al. 1994, 214, 426–29). Elsewhere, Cornwell notes that—to her, at least—most of Sickert's "sprawling nudes" look dead and that faces in a 1903 sketch and a 1906 painting "resemble" the face of Mary Ann Nichols (2002, 121–22). Subjectivity and innuendo are ever present, and Cornwell continually speaks of Sickert as Jack the Ripper and vice versa, as if her imaginings were fact.

Learning from a nephew that Sickert had had operations to correct a fistula of the penis, Cornwell admits that, lacking medical records, she "can't say exactly what Sickert's penile anomaly was," but she concludes, after pages devoted to the topic, that the operations "would have resulted in strictures and scarring that could have made erections painful or impossible." She adds, "He may have suffered partial amputation." Cornwell believes that her speculations establish a "possible motive" for Sickert to mutilate prostitutes, "but," she concedes, "I needed more" (*Ripper* 2002).

Of course, as Cornwell seems to know, intuition and imagination can take one only so far. "I'm not just a fiction writer," she said on a television documentary (*Ripper* 2002); indeed, she once worked in a coroner's office, "helping out" around the corpses (Cornwell 2002, 10). She insists that she is "100 percent sure" that Walter Sickert was Jack the Ripper—"absolutely positive," she says (*Ripper* 2002). But we should recall Ambrose Bierce's definition of *positive*: "Mistaken at the top of one's voice" (Bierce 1911).

"Ripper" Letters

In presenting her case in her book as well as on television, Cornwell says that she took a forensic approach, observing that previous Ripper identifications were "based on theories, not evidence" (*Ripper* 2002). Actually, Cornwell did employ forensic techniques such as DNA testing and watermark identification. Unfortunately, the results were far less meaningful than some people believe, and the procedures were flawed by being predicated on intuition and pseudoscience.

Cornwell believes that the hundreds of letters supposedly written by Jack the Ripper were not mostly hoaxes, as Ripperologists generally conclude. She states: "It is obvious that the actual Ripper wrote far more of the Ripper letters than he has ever been credited with. In fact, I believe he wrote most of them. In fact, Walter Sickert wrote most of them." She also states, "I have no doubt that Sickert had an amazing ability to write in many different hands" (Cornwell 2002, 14, 181). She repeatedly states what she *believes*—not what she can *prove*.

Cornwell states, "Using chemicals and highly sensitive instruments to analyze inks, paints, and paper is scientific," but "handwriting comparison is not. It is an investigative tool that can be powerful and convincing, especially in detecting forgeries. But," she continues, "if a suspect is adept in disguising his handwriting, comparison can be frustrating or impossible" (Cornwell 2002, 167). Certainly, handwriting comparison is not an exact science, but it is more scientific than Cornwell seems to think, and qualified document examiners have made serious studies of the traits of natural, imitated, and disguised handwriting; they can often demonstrate individual identifying characteristics even in disguised handwriting and hand printing (O'Hara 1973; Nickell 1996). As one expert notes, "the task of maintaining an effective disguise grows more difficult with each additional word" (Hilton 1982, 169).

Even so, the problem with Cornwell is not her skepticism of handwriting evidence; it is the fact that, having dismissed the opinions of professional handwriting experts, she feels free to replace them with the findings of a "letterer," which she defines as someone "who designs and draws lettering"—in other words, a calligrapher or graphic artist. When Cornwell's letterer perused the so-called Ripper letters, she "connected" a number of them, says Cornwell, "through quirks and how the hand made the writing." She states, "These same quirks and hand positions lurk in Sickert's erratic handwriting as well" (Cornwell 2002, 14, 181).

In addition to the letterer, Cornwell (2002, 187–88) states, "It has required intellectual sleuths such as these [an art historian, paper experts, and an archivist] to discover that many of the Ripper letters contain telltale signs of Sickert's handwriting." Oh really? Do any of these opiners know that distinct similarities between two writings may be nothing more than *class* characteristics (i.e., those common to the same writing system)? Mistaking these for *individual* characteristics is, according to a distinguished expert, "the most common error of the unqualified examiner" (Hilton 1982, 209).

There is more. Cornwell, playing linguist, also links many of the Ripper letters together and connects them to Sickert through certain words and phrases. This seems particularly ludicrous, since many of the phrases—including "ha ha," "catch me," "little games," and others—were in an early "Jack the Ripper" letter and postcard (believed to be journalistic hoaxes, as mentioned earlier). Facsimiles of these were pictured on a Metropolitan Police flyer and reproduced and quoted in newspapers (Evans and Skinner 2001, 29–44). It seems quite probable that copycat hoaxers—at least three of whom were actually caught (Evans and Skinner 2001, 72–80)—were prompted to imitate those communications. What is the connection to Sickert? Cornwell points out that the artist James McNeill Whistler, for whom Sickert had apprenticed, was fond of using the word *games* and of cackling, "ha! ha!" Need more proof? Both Sickert and some of the Ripper letters used the word *fools* (Cornwell 2002, 54–58).

Cornwell also engages in psychobabble. Stating that many Ripper letters "show the skilled hand of a highly trained or professional artist," she adds: "More than a dozen include phallic drawings of knives—all long, dagger-like instruments—except for two strange, short truncated blades in brazenly taunting letters." Apparently, the "short" phallic blades are cited to evoke the "partial amputation" of Sickert's penis that she has fantasized (Cornwell 2002, 65–66). As to the "professional" nature of the drawings, one is more so than Cornwell realizes. Reproduced in *Portrait of a Killer,* it depicts the head of a rough-looking fellow, with surrounding text stating: "This is my Photo of Jack the Ripper. 10 more and up goes the Sponge. Sig [i.e., signed] Jack the Ripper." Cornwell thinks the illustration is a drawing, but a color photograph (Evans and Skinner 2001, xii) shows that whereas the script is brownish, like most aged writing ink of the period, the image is jet black, like printing ink. More significantly, whereas the writing has the line quality of a "dip" pen, the image does not; instead, it exhibits characteristics of a common wood engraving (a variety of woodcut), with its graver-scooped lines and "negative" crosshatching (Gascoigne 1986). Since wood engravings were used in newspapers during the Ripper period, this could be evidence of a simple and obvious hoax, and possibly a journalistic one as well.

Cornwell tries to boost the evidence from the letters by matching watermarks in the paper. Much effort was expended in determining that some of the Ripper letters and some of Sickert's bore "A Pirie & Sons" and "Joynson Superfine" watermarks. Sums up a critic, the situation is "roughly analogous to what we would have faced in 1977 if one of David Berkowitz's famous 'Son of Sam' letters to Jimmy Breslin had been written on a Hallmark card" (Carr 2002). Here, Cornwell's reportage is not always accurate. For instance, in a photo caption she states that a certain Ripper letter has a watermark that matches one on a letter Sickert wrote to Whistler, but in fact, a close look at the photographs shows that they are merely from the same company (A. Pirie & Sons). They are *date* watermarks, with the Sickert letter showing an "86" and the Ripper letter an "87."

DNA Evidence

Cornwell knows the effect that the mention of DNA testing can have on laypeople. A *Publishers Weekly* review of *Portrait of a Killer* (Editorial 2002) gushes, "The book is filled with newsworthy revelations, including the successful use of DNA analysis to establish a link between an envelope mailed by the Ripper and two envelopes used by Sickert."

In fact, nuclear DNA could not be obtained from any of the fifty-five samples in which DNA was sought (from traces of saliva that had moistened envelope flaps or stamps). Therefore, the experts switched to mitochondrial DNA, a much less specific indicator, and an expert concluded that any matching sequences could well be a coincidence. As one reviewer concluded, "it might have been Sickert who licked the stamps on the alleged Ripper letter, or it might have been any one of several hundred thousand other people" (Carr 2002). As it happened, most of the fifty-five samples were apparently contaminated by the DNA of other persons. Cornwell (2002, 168–72) also concedes, "A drawback to our testing is that the ever-elusive Walter Sickert has yet to offer us his DNA profile." (Sickert was cremated.)

Not Guilty

One wonders how far into her research Cornwell was when she realized that Walter Sickert appeared to have an alibi for some of the Ripper crimes. On September 21, 1888, Sickert's wife, Ellen, wrote to her brother-in-law that Walter had gone to Normandy to see "his people" (artist friends) and would be away for weeks. If true, that means he was not in London at the time of the double murder of Elizabeth Stride and Catharine Eddowes on September 30. But Cornwell is committed to what she calls her "crusade" against Sickert (*Ripper* 2002) and sniffs, "Sickert may have left, but, not necessarily for France." In fact, a note that Sickert wrote to a friend, though undated, indicates that he was in a French fishing village, Saint-Valery-en-Caux, in the fall of 1888 (Cornwell 2002, 214–16). Sickert's being in France might explain another of Cornwell's concerns: that his "artistic productivity wasn't at its usual high from August through the rest of the year" (2002, 217). Although she seems to attribute his lack of productivity to the commission of multiple murders, being away from one's studio can have the same effect.

According to the *New York Times,* Cornwell's refusal to concede that Sickert had a credible alibi is yet another example of how she eventually "dispenses with even weak attempts at logical persuasion and begins to simply state possibilities as facts on the basis of nothing more than her intuition" (Carr 2002). When something conflicts with her scenario, she even manages to convert a liability into an asset. For instance, eyewitnesses described certain Ripper suspects as dark, foreign-looking men with black beards or mustaches (Sugden 2002), and Cornwell suggests a possible solution: Sickert, an erstwhile actor, could have used dark grease paint, hair dye, and false whiskers to disguise himself (Cornwell 2002, 245–46).

I think what we have in Patricia Cornwell is a classic example of the difference between a writer of detective fiction and a real detective. The former is in control of the evidence, creating and manipulating it to incriminate the imaginary perpetrator, who has been decided on beforehand (Day 1996). The actual detective, in contrast, may be bereft of obvious clues, confronted with a bewildering array of "facts," and required to uncover evidence to help identify not a storybook culprit but a real one.

Cornwell is well known as a writer of entertaining fiction. She continues that tradition with *Portrait of a Killer.*

References

Begg, Paul, Martin Fido, and Keith Skinner. 1994. *The Jack the Ripper A to Z,* rev. ed. London: Headline Book Publishing.

Bierce, Ambrose. 1911. *The Devil's Dictionary,* facsimile ed. New York: Castle Books, 1967.

Carr, Caleb. 2002. "Portrait of a Killer": Investigating a historical whodunnit. *New York Times,* December 15.

Cornwell, Patricia. 2002. *Portrait of a Killer: Jack the Ripper—Case Closed.* New York: G. P. Putnam's Sons.

Day, Marele, ed. 1996. *How to Write Crime.* St. Leonards, Australia: Allen & Unwin.

Editorial reviews. 2002. www.amazon.com.

Evans, Stewart P., and Keith Skinner. 2001. *Jack the Ripper: Letters from Hell.* Stroud, England: Sutton Publishing.

Fido, Martin. 2001. Foreword to Evans and Skinner 2001, vii–x.

Gascoigne, Bamber. 1986. *How to Identify Prints.* N.p. [New York]: Thames & Hudson.

Hilton, Ordway. 1982. *Scientific Examination of Questioned Documents,* rev. ed. Amsterdam: Elsevier.

Nickell, Joe. 1995. Who was Jack the Ripper? In *Who Was Jack the Ripper?* comp. Camille Wolff, 59–60. London: Grey House Books.

———. 1996. *Detecting Forgery: Forensic Investigation of Documents.* Lexington: University Press of Kentucky.

————. 1997. The "Jack the Ripper diary": History or hoax? *International Journal of Forensic Document Examiners* 3, no. 1 (January–March): 59–63.

O'Hara, Charles E. 1973. *Fundamentals of Criminal Investigation,* 3rd ed. Springfield, Ill.: Charles C. Thomas.

Ripper Murders: Case Closed. 2002. Learning Channel documentary, December 9.

Sugden, Philip. 2002. *The Complete History of Jack the Ripper,* rev. paperback ed. New York: Carroll & Graf.

GHOST-TOWN CURSE

TODAY, THE GHOST TOWN OF Bodie, California, is one of the most authentic abandoned gold-mining towns of the Old West (figure 33). It is also reputed to be a "ghost" town in another sense: according to a TV documentary, some claim that Bodie is inhabited by ghosts who guard the town against pilferers (*Beyond* 2000). Supposedly, a visitor who dares to remove any artifact will be plagued by the dreaded "curse of Bodie."

Boom Town

The 1849 discovery of gold at Sutter's Mill in the western Sierra foothills lured men and women to California from across the United States and elsewhere. Prospectors equipped with picks, shovels, and the ubiquitous gold pans searched for placer deposits—loose flakes and nuggets that had eroded and washed into streams. These deposits were searched for by "panning" (an art I learned in the Yukon), whereby the lighter dirt is deftly washed out, leaving behind the flakes of "color" that are collectively called "gold dust." The discovery of sufficient placer deposits would spark a quest for the "mother lode," involving hard-rock mines laboriously dug, blasted, and shored up with timber (Williams 1992, 5; Smith 1925).

A decade after the gold rush began at Sutter's Mill, four prospectors made a rich strike on the opposite side of the Sierras, in the eastern foothills. They agreed to keep the discovery a secret until the following spring, but one of them, W. S. Bodey, returned with another man, a half-Cherokee named "Black" Taylor. Having traveled to Monoville for supplies, the pair were returning to their cabin when they were caught in a blizzard, and Bodey perished.

Named for its discoverer, camp Bodey was soon rechristened "Bodie" when (according to local lore) a sign painter misspelled the word and the new version was preferred (Bodie 2001; Misspelling 2003). At first, Bodie was

Figure 33. This California ghost town is allegedly haunted by spirits who wield the "curse of Bodie."

largely neglected due to other strikes in the area. Mark Twain was among the gold seekers who rushed to nearby Aurora, Nevada, for instance. However, Bodie eventually boomed. In 1876 a freak mine cave-in exposed a valuable deposit of gold, and the Standard Consolidated Mining Company responded with a large investment in equipment and lumber. Another rich strike followed in 1878 in the Bodie Mine, which in just six weeks shipped gold bullion worth $1 million. Meanwhile, Bodie grew rapidly, with boardinghouses, restaurants, saloons, and other enterprises springing up (Williams 1992, 9–10).

Camps like Bodie attracted an adventurous breed:

Besides the business and professional men, mine-operators, miners, etc., there were hundreds of saloon-keepers, hundreds of gamblers, hundreds of prostitutes, many Chinese, a considerable number of Mexicans, and an unusual number of what we used to call "Bad men"—desperate, violent characters from everywhere, who lived by gambling, gun-fighting, stage robbing, and other questionable means.

The "Bad man from Bodie" was a current phrase of the time throughout the west. In its day, Bodie was more widely known for its lawlessness than for its riches. (Smith 1925)

There were other perils and hardships, including the savage winter of 1878–1879, when hundreds died of exposure and disease, and mining accidents claimed victims by falling timber, exploding powder magazines, and other means (Smith 1925; *Bodie Cemetery* n.d.). Given Bodie's reputation, it is not surprising that one little girl, whose family was moving to the mining town, reportedly prayed: "Goodbye God! We are going to Bodie" (Smith 1925).

Decline

Hardships and violence aside, Bodie was a thriving, bustling place, containing some 600 to 800 buildings and a population that reached more than 10,000 (Williams 1992, 10; Johnson and Johnson 1967, 20). It was described in about 1880 as follows:

> The traffic in the streets was continuous and enlivening. There were trains of huge, white-topped "prairie-schooners," bringing freight from the railroad, each drawn by twenty or more horses or mules, and pulling one or two large, four-wheeled "trailers"; ore wagons, hauling ore down the canyon to the mills; wood wagons bringing huge loads of pine-nut from long distances, for the mines and mills and for general use; hay wagons, lumber wagons, prospecting outfits, nondescript teams of all descriptions, spanking teams driven by mine superintendents' horses ridden by everybody, and most exciting of all, the daily stages that came tearing into town and went rushing out; the outgoing stages often carrying bars of bullion, guarded by stern, silent men, armed with sawed-off shotguns loaded with buckshot. (Smith 1925)

However, like other boom towns, Bodie's period of glory was brief, lasting from 1879 to 1882. The decline was slow, with the two major mines—the Bodie and the Standard—merging in 1887 and operating successfully for the next two decades. One disastrous fire struck in 1892, and another in 1932 destroyed much of the town; in the interim, the town continued to decline, with additional mine closings and abandonment of the Bodie Railway in 1917 (Johnson and Johnson 1967, 20–21).

Although Bodie was already dying, hastened by Prohibition and the Great Depression, some mining continued. However, there were no new strikes, and companies eked out only minor profits, largely by using a cyanide process to extract gold from old tailings (i.e., mine refuse). By the 1950s, even this recovery operation ceased, and Bodie became a ghost town. Explains one writer: "When people were leaving Bodie, there were no moving companies in the area. People simply packed what they could on one wagon or truck and left the rest behind." He adds, "That is why many of Bodie's buildings still contain belongings that were left here years ago" (Williams 1992, 36).

In 1962, after years of neglect, Bodie became a state historic park. Two years later the ghost town of Bodie was dedicated as a California historic site; it has also been designated a national historic site. Bodie is maintained in a state of what is termed "arrested decay," which means that the buildings are protected but not restored (Johnson and Johnson 1967, 21; Bodie 2001, 3).

Ghost-Town Ghosts

Old, deserted places inspire the romantic and the superstitious to think of ghosts, and Bodie is no exception. It represents an entire town full of potentially haunted houses and other premises—168 remaining structures—as well as the Bodie cemetery. It is, gushes one ghost-hustling writer, "A ghost town that is *really* a ghost town" (Myers 1990).

However, the reports of ghostly activity tend to be explainable by familiar, well-understood phenomena. Consider, for example, occurrences at the J. S. Cain House at the corner of Green and Park streets. Once the home of a prominent businessman and then the residence of caretakers' families, it is supposedly haunted by the specter of a Chinese woman, possibly a maid who worked for the Cains (Hauck 1996). Reportedly, this "heavy set" Chinese lady has appeared to children in the second-floor bedroom. Also, a ranger's wife stated:

> I was lying in bed with my husband in the lower bedroom and I felt a
> pressure on me, as though someone was on top of me. I began fight-

ing. I fought so hard I ended up on the floor. It really frightened me. Another ranger who had lived there, Gary Walters, had the same experience, in the same room, except that he also saw the door open and felt a presence and a kind of suffocation. (Myers 1990)

All these effects are well known and may occur when one's consciousness shifts into a state between sleep and wakefulness. In this condition, seemingly realistic "waking dreams" often occur, involving ghosts, aliens, or other beings. Also in this in-between state one may experience "sleep paralysis," in which the mind is awake but the body is still in the sleep mode. The sensation of being held or strapped down is a typical consequence (Nickell 2001).

Some apparitional or auditory experiences reported at Bodie—for example, "a woman peering from an upstairs window in the Dechambeau House" or "the sound of children's laughter . . . heard outside the Mendocini House" (Myers 1990)—can be similarly explained. These experiences typically occur when a person is relaxed or performing routine work. Such a mental state may allow images or sounds to spring up from the subconscious and be superimposed on the consciousness (Nickell 2001).

One man visiting the Bodie cemetery with his little girl noticed her giggling and apparently playing with an unseen entity. This was supposedly the "Angel of Bodie," a child who died when she was accidentally hit in the head by a miner's pick (Myers 1990). Actually, the dead child was Evelyn, the three-year-old daughter of Albert and Fannie Myers, who died in 1897. Her grave is surmounted by the figure of an angel child sculpted of white marble (*Bodie Cemetery* n.d., 5)—an ideal model for a little girl's imaginary playmate (figure 34).

I have found that some people are more likely than others to see ghosts—either because they are more inclined to believe or because they are especially imaginative. I use a questionnaire that helps me analyze reported ghost encounters, and I have found a good correlation between such experiences and the number of traits associated with fantasy proneness (Nickell 2001). This correlation was borne out in my research at Bodie, although colleague Vaughn Rees and I obtained only four completed questionnaires there. (A ranger stopped the project because I had not obtained official permission—something I usually try to avoid to keep employees from being told what to say.) Nevertheless, even

Figure 34. Investigator Vaughn Rees examines the tombstone of the "Angel of Bodie," reportedly one of the resident ghosts. (Photo by Joe Nickell)

with this limited sample, the highest ghostly experiences score was matched by a high fantasy score; similar results were obtained with six questionnaires we obtained at another California ghost town, Calico.

In addition to perceived phenomena, photographs are another form of "evidence" of alleged ghosts at Bodie. Again, however, there are familiar patterns. For example, streaks of light in some photos (Lundegaard 2002) are consistent with the camera's flash rebounding from something—such as the wrist strap—in front of the lens (Nickell 2001).

Bodie Curse

If some people are to be believed, there are not only ghosts in the windswept town but also spirits who are responsible for protecting its treasures by implementing the "curse of Bodie." Explains the narrator of one television documentary:

> Bodie's inhabitants were of hardy stock, fiercely possessive of what they had built in this barren desert, and it is said that the long-dead spirits want to ensure that what they left behind remains intact. According to legend, anyone who removes anything—large or small—from the town is cursed with a string of bad luck. Misfortune and tragedy are heaped upon the victim until the stolen item is returned. Some claim that the ghosts of Bodie patrol the crumbling ruins to guard against thieves. (*Beyond* 2000)

According to park ranger J. Brad Sturdivant, "The curse still exists today." Visitors often take old nails and other souvenirs from Bodie, but "most of it comes back in an unmarked box" from the spooked tourists, said the ranger. "We still get letters . . . from people saying, 'I'm sorry I took this, hoping my luck will change'" (*Beyond* 2000).

The earliest use of the phrase "the curse of Bodie" that I could find appears in the 1925 reminiscences of a former resident. However, he was speaking of something entirely different—namely, what had befallen Bodie and caused its decline. As he wrote: "the curse of Bodie, as it was of 'The Comstock,' was the stock market, which was manipulated by stock gamblers in San Francisco for their own profit, regardless of the merits of the mines, and without thought for the thousands that found their ruin in the unholy game" (Smith 1925).

The notion of a quite different Bodie curse—one that does not harm the town but instead defends it from pillagers—is of much more recent vintage. Not surprisingly, it appears to be connected to efforts to preserve Bodie as a historic site. Obviously, the "curse" is being officially promoted today when a ranger encourages the idea on a television program and the museum/gift shop displays an album of letters from those believing themselves accursed.

Although these letters may be only a selection, and three are undated, the earliest of the remaining twelve was sent in 1992. The writer, who had taken a nail from Bodie, states: "Life since then has been a steady downward slide. It's possible that all the unpleasant events of the past nine months are a coincidence, but just in case the Bodie curse is real I am returning the nail." Another letter from 1994 is addressed, "Dear Bodie Spirits":

> I am SORRY! One year ago around the 4th of July I was visiting the Ghost Town. I had been there many times before but had always followed the regulations about collecting. This trip was different; I collected some items here and there and brought them home. I was a visitor again this year, and while I was in the museum I read the letters of others who had collected things and had "bad luck." I started to think about the car accident, the lost [*sic*] of my job, my continuing illness and other bad things that have "haunted" me for the past year since my visit and violation. I am generally not superstitious but . . . Please find enclosed the collectibles I "just couldn't live without," and ask the spirits to see my regret.

It was signed, "One with a very guilty conscience."

On the TV series *Beyond Bizarre* (2000), a German man related how his uncle had removed a small bottle from Bodie and two days later had a car accident on the Autobahn. The next day his son took the bottle to school to show classmates and on the way home had a bicycle accident. Said the man, "Yes, I do believe in the curse of Bodie."

Belief aside, such anecdotal evidence does not prove the existence of a "curse" (or "hex" or "jinx"), or an alleged paranormal attack. Indeed, belief in curses is merely a superstition, a form of magical thinking. Once the idea takes hold, there is a tendency for any harmful occurrence to be counted as evidence supporting the belief, while beneficial events are ignored. Through the power of suggestion, the magical conviction spreads from person to superstitious person, until many believe in, for example, a King Tut's curse, a Hope diamond jinx, or the Kennedy family's propensity for misfortune (Nickell 1999). A different mind-set allows one to shrug off such nonsense. Skeptics

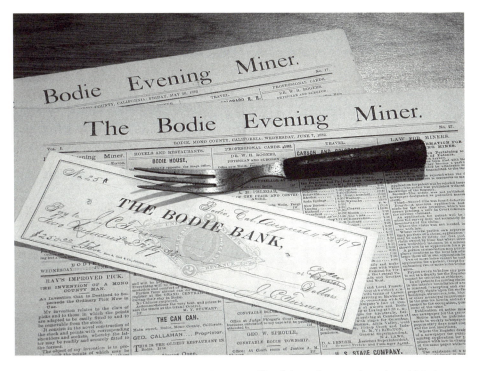

Figure 35. Artifacts from Bodie—especially ones pilfered from there, such as this old fork—supposedly attract the fearsome "curse." (Photo by Joe Nickell, from his collection)

sometimes hold "Superstition Bashes" during which they break mirrors and challenge other superstitions without fear of consequences. In attendance may be a resident spokesperson (such as myself) identified as a friggatriskaidekaphobiologist—that is, one who studies the fear of Friday the thirteenth and, by extension, other supposed causes of bad luck.

I have specifically challenged the curse of Bodie—not by pilfering items from the site, which is appropriately illegal, but by collecting artifacts that have come from there. As shown in figure 35, these include an 1879 check drawn on the Bodie Bank and two 1882 issues of the newspaper the *Bodie Evening Miner*. It might be argued that these were not *pilfered* from Bodie, but the other item shown, an old fork, reportedly was: I bought it from an antiques dealer who said that she had picked it up herself at Bodie several years ago, without apparent consequence. I would like to donate these items to Bodie. I am only waiting for the town's custodians to officially cease promoting superstition and disclaim the existence of any Bodie curse.

References

Beyond Bizarre. 2000. Travel Channel documentary, September 24.

Bodie Cemetery: The Lives Within. N.d. Bridgefort, Calif.: Friends of Bodie.

Bodie State Historic Park. 2001. Guide booklet. Sacramento: California State Parks.

Hauck, Dennis William. 1996. *Haunted Places: The National Directory,* 36–37. New York: Penguin Books.

Johnson, Russ, and Anne Johnson. 1967. *The Ghost Town of Bodie.* Bishop, Calif.: Sierra Media.

Lundegaard, Karen. 2002. Identifying spirit photos. www.karenlundegaard.com/Spirit_Photos/SPhoto16.html.

Misspelling of Bodie. 2003. www.bodie.net/st/Bodey.asp.

Myers, Arthur. 1990. *The Ghostly Gazetteer,* 40–48. Lincolnwood, Ill.: Contemporary Books.

Nickell, Joe. 1999. Curses: Foiled again. *Skeptical Inquirer* 23, no. 6 (November–December): 16–19.

———. 2001. Phantoms, frauds, or fantasies? In *Hauntings and Poltergeists,* ed. James Houran and Rense Lange, 214–23. Jefferson, N.C.: McFarland.

Smith, Grant H. 1925. Bodie: The last of the old-time mining camps. *California Historical Society Quarterly* 4, no. 1. Reprinted in Williams 1992, 11–24.

Williams, George III. 1992. *The Guide to Bodie and Eastern Sierra Historic Sites.* Carson City, Nev.: Tree by the River Publishing.

NASCA: LABYRINTHS
IN THE DESERT

It has been called many things: a giant drawing board, an astronomical calendar, a landing pad for extraterrestrials, and the eighth wonder of the world. "It" is a thirty-mile section of desert near Peru's southern coast covered with giant drawings, designs, and crisscrossing lines etched into the gravel-covered pampa.

Ancient Astronauts?

The Nasca (formerly Nazca) geoglyphs achieved worldwide prominence when they were featured in Erich von Däniken's pseudoscientific classic *Chariots of the Gods?*—a book that consistently underestimates the abilities of ancient "primitive" peoples and assigns many of their works to extraterrestrial visitors. Von Däniken (1970) envisions flying saucers hovering above the desert floor and beaming down instructions for the markings—many so large that they can indeed be viewed properly only from the sky. To him, the large drawings (figure 36) represent "signals," and the longer and wider of the lines are "landing strips" (von Däniken 1970, 1972). However, it is doubtful that alien beings would create signals for themselves in the shape of spiders and monkeys. Moreover, the ground is quite soft, according to the late Maria Reiche, the German-born mathematician who devoted her life to mapping and preserving the markings. "I'm afraid the spacemen would have gotten stuck," she quipped (McIntyre 1975).

Although the markings represent a genuine mystery, we do know who produced them. Their resemblance to the characteristic, stylized art of the Nasca, and the evidence from the carbon dating of wooden stakes marking the termination of some long lines (one dated to AD 525, give or take eighty years), are consistent with the Nasca culture. The Nasca flourished in the area from 200 BC to about AD 600. Their graves and the ruins of their settlements lie near

Figure 36. Etched on the Nasca plains in Peru are giant drawings like these. Their large size has fueled misguided speculation that they were drawn with the aid of "ancient astronauts" or by sophisticated surveying techniques, the secrets of which have been lost. (Graphic by Joe Nickell)

the drawings, and Nasca pottery shards are intermingled with the desert gravel (Isbell 1978, 1980; Aveni 2000, 56–57).

In considering the how and why of the Nasca lines, it is important to note the existence of other giant ground markings elsewhere: at other locales in Peru, for example, and in the Atacama Desert (Welfare and Fairley 1980). Moreover, the plan of Cuzco, the Incan city, was laid out in the configuration of a puma, and its residents were "members of the body of the puma" (Isbell 1978, 1980). In North America, there is Ohio's Great Serpent Mound as well as giant effigies in the Mojave Desert near Blythe, California (Setzler 1952). In 1978 I was taken to see the latter by a Native American guide. However, the human figures and horselike creatures are much smaller and cruder than their Nasca counterparts, typically having solid bodies and sticklike appendages. The similarities and dissimilarities among the various ground drawings complicate our attempt to understand them. Certainly those at the Blythe and elsewhere have no attendant "runways" or other features suggesting that they were drawn by or for extraterrestrials.

Using Sticks and Cord

I thought that an inquiry into how the lines were planned and formed might shed some light on the Nasca riddle. One researcher demonstrated that, by using a series of ranging poles, straight lines could be constructed over many miles. Indeed, the remains of wooden posts have been discovered at roughly one-mile intervals along some of the long lines (Welfare and Fairley 1980; McIntyre 1975).

Maria Reiche's extensive work at Nasca revealed that there were six-foot-square plots near many of the larger figures. She believed that the preliminary drawings were prepared on these small plots and then scaled up as enlargements. She observed that straight lines could be formed by stretching a rope between two stakes, and circles and arcs could be scribed by means of a rope anchored to a stake or a rock. However, she concluded—too fancifully, I think—that "ancient Peruvians must have had instruments and equipment which we ignore and which together with ancient knowledge were buried and hidden from the eyes of the conquerors as the one treasure which was not to be surrendered" (Reiche 1976).

William H. Isbell (1978) suggested that the Nasca used the grid method, in which a small drawing is converted to a larger one square by square. Isbell believed that the Nasca might have gotten the idea from their experience with weaving. However, a characteristic of the grid method is that distortions and errors are effectively confined to individual squares—a fact difficult to reconcile with the poor symmetry of some figures, such as the "condor" shown in figure 36. The plotting of points by a traverse surveying technique that depends on the accurate measurement of angles is similarly unlikely. There is no evidence that the Nasca possessed such a capability.

I tried to duplicate one of the large Nasca drawings, the 440-foot-long condor (see figure 36). Using a large landfill area in eastern Kentucky, and assisted by family and friends,[1] I made the enlargement from a small drawing using only a pair of crossed sticks for sighting and two lengths of knotted cord for measuring. The approach was to establish a centerline and plot the coordinates of points (such as the wing tip). That is, we measured down the centerline on the small drawing until we were directly opposite (at a right angle to) a desired point, then measured from there to the point itself. We repeated the process on the ground, using the same number of larger units. Finally, we connected the points to complete the drawing. (For more details, see Nickell 1983.)

We subsequently flew over our drawing at about a thousand feet and photographed it (figures 37 and 38). *Scientific American* (June 1983) later termed our reproduction "remarkable in its exactness" to the Nasca original. I concluded that the Nasca probably used an even simpler version of this technique, with a significant amount of the work being done freehand (Nickell 1983).

Sacred Paths?

Having answered the important questions of who, when, and how, the mystery of why the Nasca geoglyphs were created remains. One hypothesis is that they represent some form of offering to the Indian gods (McIntyre 1975). Another is that they constitute a giant astronomical calendar or "star chart." Still another stems from the observation that each figure is rendered with a continuous line that does not cross itself—possibly the path of a "ritual maze" (or, more correctly, a labyrinth).[2] The intention may have been for people to walk the drawings and thus gain the essence of the figures represented (Kosok and Reiche 1949; McIntyre 1975).

In 1991 anthropologists Anthony F. Aveni (also a professor of astronomy) and Helaine Silverman reported the results of extensive studies of the Nasca lines. Sightings along some 700 radiating lines showed a near randomness with regard to astronomical significance. Rather, the lines correlated with geographic features, suggesting to the researchers that the line makers were driven by "an inescapable concern about water" and that they might have walked or danced along the lines as part of "irrigation ceremonies."

Aveni (2000, 212–22) elaborates on this possibility in his admirable book *Nasca: Eighth Wonder of the World?* Noting the labyrinthine appearance of many of the designs, he observes that most of the figures were created "from a single line wide enough for only one person to tread," giving credence to the

(Left) Figure 37. The author's duplication of the giant "condor" drawing made full size by using only sticks and cord, such as the Nasca might have employed. (Aerial photo by John May) (Below) Figure 38. Detail showing the author standing in one of the giant bird's claws. (Photo by Wendell Nickell)

idea that individuals walked the lines as part of sacred rituals (Aveni 2000, 221). The idea gains support from the fact that labyrinth designs have been found among the New World's native peoples, including the Hopi Indians of Arizona (Candolini 2003, 16, 80–81). Also, an excavated Peruvian site—Pacatnamú, once the pilgrimage center of a moon cult—has a labyrinthine form. Reports Aveni (2000, 220–21):

> Pacatnamú's principal structure is an adobe-walled square about the size of four football pitches. It consists of several open courtyards and elevated platforms accessible from a single entrance through corridors with walls above eye level that run back and forth in a confused manner. One of the chambers is barely large enough to hold two or three people. One can reach it only via a square spiral that winds ever more tightly through 360 degrees about it. At its centre lies a tiny room, from which archaeologists excavated a small textile showing the design of the labyrinth.

The Evidence

Inspired by the labyrinth hypothesis, I took a new look at the drawings and observed several characteristics that, taken together, clearly suggest that they did function as labyrinths—or, I should say, labyrinth-like designs. They lack some of the significant features of true or classical labyrinths, such as symmetry; although some of the Nasca drawings are approximately symmetrical, many others, such as the monkey, are asymmetrical. Also, unlike labyrinths, the Nasca figures do not have a definite center point; nor do their paths of egress constitute a retracing of the entrance route. (For a discussion of labyrinths, see Candolini 2003.) Nevertheless, they share with labyrinths the characteristics of a winding, universal path and an apparently mystical purpose. Perhaps they could be called *processional geoglyphs*—if indeed they were intended to be trod in ritualistic fashion. The evidence of such a purpose includes the following points.

First, the lines of the drawings are made like paths, with the surface gravel being cleared away to expose the earth beneath. The width of the lines—most of them approximately two feet across—is consistent with a footpath (Kosok and Reiche 1949, 207–8).

Second, the continuous-line construction—which itself invites a comparison to labyrinths—is not characteristic of ordinary Nasca artistic renderings (on pottery, for instance). This indicates that there was some other, specific reason for the distinctive linear technique.

Third, some of the figures contain internal zigzagging lines (see the intricate pelican in figure 36, upper right). These suggest mazes or labyrinths, which those particular Nasca figures obviously resemble.

Fourth, some figures have inherent spiral or zigzag elements as part of their anatomy. These forms may have prompted either the use of a particular figure, such as the spider monkey for its spiral tail (see figure 36), or the fanciful rendering of a figure, such as the sinuous, winding neck of a "snake-bird" (Kosok and Reiche 1949, 208).

Fifth, there are zigzag designs and spirals that are not part of the pictures. Indeed, Aveni notes that the "zigzag motif" is "spread all over the pampa," and he shows, for example, an aerial photograph of "a box labyrinth sandwiched between zigzags." Another photo depicts a spiral unwinding into a zigzag (Aveni 2000, 36). Indeed, one flowerlike Nasca design may be a true labyrinth, according to the curator of a British labyrinth museum, but with a unique feature: whereas classical labyrinths have a four-point construction (based on the intersection of two lines), the Nasca one has five points and is said to be the only such labyrinth in the world (Candolini 2003, 32–33).

Finally, several of the Nasca effigies (e.g., the spiral-tailed monkey; see figure 36) have a definite feature that invites the eye—and probably the feet—into the winding configurations. This consists of an otherwise extraneous appendage consisting of a pair of parallel lines—as if one is meant to lead into the figure and one out of it. To me, this feature strongly corroborates the hypothesis that the Nasca lines were meant to be walked.

Although, technically, the Nasca effigies may not be labyrinths per se, they seem to have functioned in a similar fashion. Recognizing this brings us a step closer to understanding what the lines were—and what they were not. They have no role in the pseudoscientific concept of "ancient astronauts" having visited Earth, but they do represent a wonderful legacy of an indigenous and still largely mysterious people.

Notes

1. I was assisted in my Nasca re-creation project by three cousins, Sid Haney, John May, and Jim Mathis; my father, Wendell Nickell; my nephew, Con Nickell; and pilot Jerry Mays. Benjamin Radford provided essential information about labyrinths.

2. Although *maze* and *labyrinth* are sometimes used synonymously, the former is usually understood to consist of multiple confusing routes, only one of which correctly leads to the goal.

References

Aveni, Anthony F. 2000. *Nasca: Eighth Wonder of the World?* London: British Museum Press.

Aveni, Anthony F., and Helaine Silverman. 1991. Between the lines: Reading the Nazca markings as rituals writ large. *Sciences,* July–August, 36–42.

Candolini, Gernot. 2003. *Labyrinths: Walking toward the Center.* New York: Crossroad Publishing.

Isbell, William H. 1978. The prehistoric ground drawings of Perú. *Scientific American* 239 (October): 140–53.

———. 1980. Solving the mystery of Nazca. *Fate,* October, 36–48.

Kosok, Paul, and Maria Reiche. 1949. Ancient drawings on the desert of Peru. *Archaeology* 2 (Winter): 206–15.

McIntyre, Loren. 1975. Mystery of the ancient Nazca lines. *National Geographic,* May, 716–28.

Nickell, Joe. 1983. The Nazca drawings revisited: Creation of a full-size duplicate. *Skeptical Inquirer* 7, no. 3 (Spring): 36–44.

Reiche, Maria. 1976. *Mystery on the Desert* [1968], rev. ed. Stuttgart: Privately printed.

Setzler, Frank M. 1952. Seeking the secrets of the giants. *National Geographic* 102, 393–404.

Von Däniken, Erich. 1970. *Chariots of the Gods?* New York: G. P. Putnam.

———. 1972. *Gods from Outer Space.* New York: Bantam Books.

Welfare, Simon, and John Fairley. 1980. *Arthur C. Clarke's Mysterious World.* New York: A&W Publishers.

DEATH BY EXTRATERRESTRIALS

THE MYSTERY MONGERS, PARANORMAL HUSTLERS, conspiracy theorists, and UFO hoaxers showed just how far they were willing to go in their quest for publicity when they rushed to promote a man-killed-by-aliens tale. The story unfolded in Northumberland County, Pennsylvania. At about 5:00 A.M. on Sunday, August 4, 2002, thirty-nine-year-old Todd Sees—father of two and a Little League coach—went deer hunting. He rode off on his all-terrain vehicle to scout an area of his eighty-acre tract. When he failed to return, family members searched for him and then alerted authorities. Tracking dogs were soon deployed, followed within hours by an army of volunteers on foot and searchers in helicopters. Sees's four-wheeler was located about two miles away atop Montour Ridge, but when he had not been found by 10:00 that night, the search was temporarily halted (Moore 2002b). The following day, much closer to his home but in a densely wooded area, Sees's body was discovered. An autopsy did not immediately reveal the cause of death, but while toxicology tests were pending, the local Point Township police chief, Gary Steffen, stated: "It's just a waiting game. Something certainly caused his death. The answer has to be in the blood" (Moore 2002a).

Enter "Anonymous." Unnamed sources reportedly provided information to something called the National UFO Reporting Center (NUFORC). Allegedly, a farmer saw a flying disc hover over Montour Ridge, emit a blue-and-white beam, and draw a man into it. "Two days later a naked body except for his underware [sic] was found," stated the source, who "elects to remain totally anonymous." NUFORC's director, Peter B. Davenport (2002), would later apologize for any pain his Internet postings might have caused Sees's family, though he continued to address "unresolved issues." Among these issues were "unconfirmed reports" that the FBI was involved and that the deceased had been badly "disfigured," his face possibly "frozen into a grimace of terror." Why

159

else would family members not be allowed to view the remains? (Davenport 2002; Pilkington 2003). In fact, the investigating officer, Sergeant Seth Cotner, told a reporter that no federal agency was involved, and the coroner had merely advised the family that viewing the remains could be traumatic (Kendron 2002a). There are several possible reasons for the "disfigurement"—all of them more plausible than alien horror. For example, if the deceased lay on his face, various postmortem effects such as lividity—discoloration due to the settling of blood—could be responsible (Geberth 1993). Attack by scavenging animals would be another possibility.

While the stories that Sergeant Cotner termed "ridiculous and far-fetched" continued, I was interviewed by a reporter from a local newspaper. I stated that, according to my analysis, several prima facie elements strongly suggested hoaxing, including the sensational nature of the case, the anonymity of the alleged eyewitnesses, and atypical "abduction" features. For instance, most reputed ET-nabbings are not witnessed, and the few that allegedly are appear to be hoaxes (see Baker and Nickell 1992). I added that I was unaware of any medical examiner ever having declared death by UFO or death by aliens (Kendron 2002b). Nor did the pathologist in the Todd Sees case do so. Instead, Northumberland County coroner James Kelley determined that the hunter's death was due to "cocaine toxicity," and police reported that the manner of death was accidental (Cocaine 2002).

Fortean Times magazine—having prepared an article headed "Killer UFO?" complete with an illustration of a flying saucer beaming up an abductee—responded: "At time of going to press, a Northumberland coroner's report has identified 'cocaine toxicity' as the cause of Sees's death, though for some reason they could not confirm it as an overdose" (Pilkington 2003). (Apparently, the amount of cocaine detected was simply insufficient to warrant the label "overdose.") The article was riddled with errors, including calling Northumberland "Northampton" in one case and giving the wrong dates for Sees's disappearance and recovery. However, the article concluded, probably correctly: "We expect advocates of the UFO hypothesis to claim a whitewash."

References

Baker, Robert A., and Joe Nickell. 1992. *Missing Pieces: How to Investigate Ghosts, UFOs, Psychics, and Other Mysteries*, 199–207. Buffalo, N.Y.: Prometheus Books.

Cocaine blamed in Norry death. 2002. *Press Enterprise* (Bloomsburg, Pa.) staff report, October 10.

Davenport, Peter B. 2002. Internet postings, www.nuforc.org, September 8–30.

Geberth, Vernon J. 1993. *Practical Homicide Investigation,* 2nd ed. Boca Raton, Fla.: CRC Press.

Kendron, Peter, 2002a. Mystery death spawns odd tales. *Press Enterprise Online Newspaper,* www.pressenterpriseonline.com, October 4.

———. 2002b. Skeptic debunks reports. *Press Enterprise* (Bloomsburg, Pa.), October 29.

Moore, Marcia. 2000a. Investigation into man's death. *Daily Item* (Northumberland, Pa.), n.d. (September), reprinted in Davenport 2002.

———. 2002b. Montour Ridge volunteers look for man. *Daily Item* (Northumberland, Pa.), August 5.

Pilkington, Mark. 2003. UFO update: Saucer victim found? *Fortean Times* 165 (January): 16.

FRANKENSTEIN CASTLE

LOCATED IN THE HEART OF EUROPE, Germany has had a more profound impact on the history of the continent than any other country. According to one source: "From Charlemagne and the Holy Roman Empire to Otto von Bismarck's German Reich, Nazism and the rise and fall of the Berlin Wall, no other nation has molded Europe the way Germany has—for better or for worse" (Schulte-Peevers et al. 2002, 17). Today, freed of its own post–World War II division, Germany leads the effort to unite Europe.

In October 2002 I made my second visit to Germany, this time to speak at the biannual symposium of the European Council of Skeptical Organizations and to conduct an investigation workshop for German skeptics at the Center for Inquiry–Europe in Rossdorf. Thanks to the untiring assistance of the center's executive director, Dr. Martin Mahner, I was able to spend the remainder of the sixteen-day trip investigating a number of myths and legends (see also "Haunted Gas Chamber," "Satan's Step," and "The White Lady of Bavaria").

Shelley's Monster Tale

The great monster story and pioneering work of science fiction, Mary Shelley's 1818 novel *Frankenstein,* may have taken its name from a ruined fortress that is otherwise linked to tales of monsters and body snatching (figure 39). Most accounts of the fictional creation of Frankenstein's monster rely on Shelley's own version of events. It was a dark and stormy night in 1816. She (then Mary Godwin) and her future husband, poet Percy Bysshe Shelley, were at the Swiss villa of another famous English poet, Lord Byron, together with two others. They had been reading French translations of German ghost tales when Byron suddenly proclaimed, "We will each write a ghost story" (Hindle 1992).

Mary Shelley would subsequently write in her introduction that the two poets had discussed rumors of animation experiments and speculation that

Figure 39. Ruins of Frankenstein Castle atop Magnet Mountain. (Photo by Joe Nickell)

"galvanism" (electricity) might reanimate a corpse. With such thoughts in mind, she retired after the "witching hour" but did not sleep. Instead, her imagination led her to see—"with shut eyes, but acute mental vision"—"the pale student of unhallowed arts kneeling beside the thing he had put together." She continued: "I saw the hideous phantasm of a man stretched out, and then, on the working of some powerful engine, show signs of life, and stir with an uneasy, half-vital motion. Frightful must it be; for supremely frightful would be the effect of any human endeavor to mock the stupendous mechanism of the Creator of the world" (Shelley 1831).

Shelley does not state why she adopted the name Victor Frankenstein for the monster's creator. However, Radu Florescu, in his *In Search of Frankenstein* (1975, 45–62), makes a convincing case that it was inspired by Burg Frankenstein (i.e., "castle of the Franks' rock"). Located about seven kilometers from Darmstadt, the ruins are those of a castle originally built on a smaller scale in about 1250. Florescu points out that Mary and her lover Shelley had visited the region earlier, traveling by boat down the Rhine in 1814. They surely must have known that they were in "Frankenstein country" and probably spied the castle's distinctive double towers silhouetted atop the mountain. It is even possible that they visited the castle itself or learned of its legends from their German traveling companions. These include the tale of Knight Georg von Frankenstein and a dragonlike monster that was terrorizing the area. Sir Georg was a real person whose tomb in the nearby village of Nieder-Beerbach notes the date of his death in 1531. Although he slew the creature—probably only a snake (the exaggeration being attributable to his popular identification with St. George the dragon slayer)—it succeeded in piercing his armor below the knee, poisoning him (Florescu 1975, 53–69).

A Real-Life Dr. Frankenstein?

Other legends relating to Burg Frankenstein concern an alchemist, Johann Konrad Dippel (1673–1734). Although not a descendant of the Frankensteins, Dippel had been born in the castle and registered at the university as a resident of "Franckensteina." However, after two years marked by "scandalous behavior," he was forced to flee one night due to a "serious incident" rumored to involve body snatching from a local cemetery. Subsequently, Dippel turned to alchemy and claimed to have discovered a secret formula by which he could transmute silver and mercury into pure gold. He also sought to produce an elixir of life and, toward that end, conducted experiments in distilling blood and the boiled residue of bones. Dippel eventually wrote a medical thesis at the University of Leiden (1711), focusing on his previous chemical experiments and animal studies. He practiced vivisection on animals and came to believe that the body was an inert mass animated by a spirit that could be transferred into another corpse to reanimate it (Florescu 1975, 63–86).

The parallels between Victor Frankenstein the fictional character and Johann Konrad Dippel the alchemist are striking, as Florescu (1975, 86) observes. Not everyone accepts the evidence, however. One source cautions that the lack of substantiated information about Dippel's life "leaves much room for doubt, and many of the traits attributed to him may postdate Mary Shelley's novel" (Johann 2002). Also, some of Shelley's admirers resent the implications of the evidence—that her use of a real-life model calls into question her originality (Clerici 2002). However, great writers frequently rely on such sources, adapting them to their creative purposes.

If it is true that Dippel and Frankenstein Castle were sources for Mary Shelley's novel, it seems fittingly ironic that "monsters" have returned to the castle in recent years. Although Martin Mahner and I saw no strange creatures when we prowled the ruins and the surrounding forest, we did encounter posters and ads for spooky goings-on emblazoned "Halloween/Burg Frankenstein." (Though Halloween is not a German tradition, it was imported by Americans stationed at the U.S. Army facilities in nearby Darmstadt.)

References

Clerici, Paul. 2002. Florescu book looks at history behind Frankenstein. www.bc.edu/bc_org/rvp/pubaf/chronicle/v5/O31/florescu.html.

Florescu, Radu. 1975. *In Search of Frankenstein.* Boston: New York Graphic Society.

Hindle, Maurice, ed. 1992. Introduction to Shelley 1831.

Johann Konrad Dippel. 2002. www.english.upenn.edu/~jlynch/Frank/People/dippel.html.

Schulte-Peevers, Andrea, et al. 2002. *Germany.* London: Lonely Planet Publications.

Shelley, Mary. 1831 [1818]. *Frankenstein; or, the Modern Prometheus,* 3rd ed. Reprint, London: Penguin Books, 1992.

INTUITION: THE CASE OF
THE UNKNOWN DAUGHTER

IN THE FALL OF 2003, MY LIFE WAS TRANSFORMED by the news that I was the father of a beautiful, thirty-six-year-old daughter. Based on "intuition," she had confronted her mother with the notion that the man who had helped raise her was not her actual father. As was soon proved by DNA testing, we discovered that she was *my* child. As one who had long been skeptical of much that is labeled intuition, I had to admit that *something* had just happened—something both wonderful and mysterious. With the approval and assistance of my daughter, Cherette, I decided to investigate. As I learned, understanding intuition depends in part on how it is defined.

Sixth Sense?

To New Age writers such as Patricia Einstein, author of *Intuition: The Path of Inner Wisdom,* intuition is an "inner awareness" that functions as a "sixth sense"—that is, a form of extrasensory perception that includes psychometry (gleaning information about people, places, or events by touching objects associated with them). Like other New Agers, she maintains that people have auras (or energy fields) that stem from a larger "universal energy flow," which the ancient Chinese termed *chi.* "Connecting with your intuition," she declares, "is the act of tuning in to the never-ending flow of universal energy." Intuition has frequencies, she explains, and so, "in a sense, tuning in to intuition is like tuning in to a radio station" (Einstein 2002, 1–2, 40–41, 105).

Actually, Patricia Einstein is no Einstein. Although she insists that "instances of psychic healing and psychokinesis (telepathic movement of objects) have been well documented" (Einstein 2002, 37), she provides no documentation herself. In fact, such claims have been repeatedly discredited. For instance, many ballyhooed psychokinetic marvels have been exposed as mere magic tricks (Randi 1982; Korem 1988).

Much effort has been expended in the search for extrasensory phenomena, including the pioneering work of Britain's Society for Psychical Research, founded in 1882, and the scientific research of Dr. J. B. Rhine at Duke University in the 1930s. Rhine was a sincere and dedicated, but credulous, parapsychologist. His first published report on the subject, coauthored with his wife, Louisa, was "An Investigation of a 'Mind-Reading' Horse" in 1929. They believed that the mare, Lady Wonder, was telepathic. However, magician and paranormal investigator Milbourne Christopher (1970, 39–54) visited Lady undercover and determined that she simply responded to subtle cues used by her owner to relay information that had been gleaned from the subjects. Rhine's later card tests—involving a subject's guessing the sequence of symbols on a special deck of cards—engendered considerable controversy, but proof of ESP did not materialize (Christopher 1970, 19–37). Despite the work of others following in Rhine's footsteps, ESP remains unproved, and its existence has not been accepted by mainstream science (see, for example, Kurtz 1985; Hansel 1989; Stenger 1990).

Nevertheless, the belief that intuition is a psychic process persists. It ranges from the relatively harmless, such as New Age shops touting the gemstones hematite and tigereye as having the power to enhance intuition, to the dangerous, such as "medical intuitives" who claim to diagnose illness by reading a person's aura (Nickell 2004).

Dual Processing

But if intuition is not a sixth sense, what is it? Does it exist at all? Do people merely make guesses, then count the hits and disregard the misses? Certainly, our hunches are not always accurate. Elizabeth Loftus, past president of the American Psychological Society, cautions: "Intuition is hot. But often it is perilously wrong." She recommends the book *Intuition: Its Powers and Perils* by David Myers, who, she states, "marshals classic and contemporary science and masterfully shows us why." Skeptic Michael Shermer wrote for the *Los Angeles Times Book Review,* "Myers' book brilliantly establishes intuition as a legitimate subject of scientific inquiry."[1]

As Myers relates, many studies show that quick, impressionistic judgments—though often mistaken—can nevertheless predict some behaviors more successfully than rationally analyzed ones. He observes that we have two very different ways of knowing things (2004, 4):

> Recent cognitive science reveals a fascinating unconscious mind—another mind backstage—that Freud never told us about. More than we realized over a decade ago, thinking occurs not on stage, but off stage, out of sight. . . . Studies of "automatic priming," "implicit memory," "heuristics," "spontaneous trait inference," right-brain processing, instant emotions, nonverbal communication, and creativity unveil our intuitive capacities. Thinking, memory, and attitudes all operate on two levels (conscious and deliberate, and unconscious and automatic)—dual processing, today's researchers call it. We know more than we know we know.

As noted psychologist Robert A. Baker told me—with specific reference to my daughter's intuitive revelation—we humans are constantly responding to subtle cues. Unconsciously, we collect and assemble bits of data—much like pieces of a jigsaw puzzle—often arriving at the realization of some larger concept. No single piece of information is significant, but taken together, the clues may produce something greater than the sum of its parts.

Because we are not *consciously* (i.e., deliberately and analytically) processing data, the results of intuition can be quite startling—bordering on revelation—and can seem quite mysterious. When my daughter's mother, Diana, asked her why she thought the man who raised her was not her real father, she replied, "I don't know. It just came into my mind."

Identifying the Clues

In the case of my daughter's intuition, I sought to identify the clues that might have led to her sense of "knowing" that she had another father. In describing Cherette as a child, Diana notes that she did not have much of a "whimsical mode" but was typically serious and inquisitive. Among the things she wondered about were her eyes, which matched neither her father's nor her mother's (see figure 40; they resemble my ancestors' even more than mine). Although many people remarked that she and her sister did not look like sis-

Figure 40. The author poses with his daughter, who sensed her father through intuition. (Photo by Diana Harris)

ters, she knew that she resembled her mother and did not become suspicious of her parentage—at least not consciously. Nevertheless, her younger brother was adopted, so at some point, the idea that she too could have been adopted would have presented itself. (In fact, her sister once thought that all three of them were adopted.)

There were other clues. At Cherette's wedding, when she was twenty-six, a friend of her mother's inadvertently revealed a family secret: her parents had not been married when she was conceived. Again, that bit of information was not very revealing in itself, but it can now be seen as potentially suggestive— another piece of the puzzle.

Following some medical tests in March 2001, Cherette announced to her mother that she had learned her blood type. Although she did not ask at the time about her parents' blood types—so she did not know that hers was different from theirs and incompatible with her father's—the announcement may have put a thoughtful expression on her mother's face that Cherette read, unconsciously. At the very least, it subtly presented, however obliquely, the issue of genetics.

In June 2003, while she was talking on the phone with her mother, the fact that she had been conceived before her parents' marriage came up again. Cherette said that she did not care about that, as long as her father was indeed her father. Her mother assured her that that was so, but in a way that would be appreciated by fortune-tellers using "cold reading" (an artful method of fishing for information), Cherette thought she detected some equivocation and challenged: "What else haven't you told me? Mom, who is my daddy?"

Soon, Diana conceded that there was a chance that someone else was Cherette's father, but there were only "two possibilities." If her father was not her actual father, she said, then it was a young poet she had been with for a short time before resuming her relationship with her old boyfriend, Cherette's supposed father. Upon learning this, Cherette says, she felt that she probably did have another father, and by the time her mother had tracked me down, both were convinced that I was indeed Cherette's "Daddy" (as she now calls me)—a fact we confirmed by DNA testing.[2] (Not entirely lost on me during our first meeting at Thanksgiving 2003 was the irony that, as a paranormal investigator, I myself was being investigated—the result of intuition, no less!)

Assessment

Although not arrived at consciously, my daughter's sense that she might have had another father could *logically* be inferred from the data. That her brother was adopted raised the question of her own parentage. Since she resembled her mother but not her father, and especially since her eyes were similar to neither parent's, she might conclude that she had a different father. That possibility was enhanced by her parents not having been married when she was conceived. I believe that there were other, more subtle clues as well.

If my assessment is correct, it demonstrates that clues can indeed be rationally assembled unconsciously to uncover a mystery. Myers (2004, 128) observes "that, more than we've realized, our lives are guided by subterranean intuitive thinking." Providing "evidence of intuition's powers," he says, are "*right-brain thinking*—split-brain persons displaying knowledge they cannot verbalize; *thin slices*—detecting traits from mere seconds of behavior; *intuitive expertise*—phenomena of nonconscious learning, expert learning, genius"; and, among many others, "*creativity*—the sometimes spontaneous appearance of novel and valuable ideas" (Myers 2004, 127).

However, he cautions against the perils of intuitive thinking, such as "powerfully flawed intuitions about gambling" (Myers 2004, 225). He also warns of the following: "*memory construction*—influenced by our present moods and by misinformation, we may form false memories and other dubious testimonials; *misreading our own minds*—often we don't know why we do what we do; *hindsight bias*—looking back on events, we falsely surmise that we knew it all along; *overconfidence*—our intuitive assessments of our own knowledge are routinely more confident than correct"; and "*illusory correlation*—intuitively perceiving relationships where none exist" (Myers 2004, 128).

Cautions notwithstanding, I must admit to a new appreciation of intuition, without which I would not have known about my wonderful daughter—and two grandsons! It is enough to warm an old skeptic's heart.

Notes

1. For the Loftus and Shermer quotations, see http://www.yale.edu/yup/books/095317.htm (accessed April 12, 2004).

2. For a follow-up, see my poem "The Discovered Daughter" (with a brief commentary) in *Family Matters: The Newsletter of the Secular Family Network* 7, no. 3 (Fall 2004): 7. On April 1, 2006, I married Cherette's mother, Diana.

References

Christopher, Milbourne. 1970. *ESP Seers and Psychics.* New York: Thomas Y. Crowell.

Einstein, Patricia. 2002. *Intuition: The Path of Inner Wisdom.* London: Vega.

Hansel, C. E. M. 1989. *The Search for Psychic Power: ESP and Parapsychology Revisited.* Buffalo, N.Y.: Prometheus Books.

Korem, Dan. 1988. *Powers: Testing the Psychic and Supernatural.* Downers Grove, Ill.: InterVarsity Press.

Kurtz, Paul. 1985. *A Skeptic's Handbook of Parapsychology.* Buffalo, N.Y.: Prometheus Books.

Myers, David G. 2004. *Intuition: Its Powers and Perils.* New Haven, Conn.: Yale University Press.

Nickell, Joe. 2004. *The Mystery Chronicles,* 207–17. Lexington: University Press of Kentucky.

Randi, James. 1982. *Flim-Flam!* Buffalo, N.Y.: Prometheus Books.

Stenger, Victor J. 1990. *Physics and Psychics.* Buffalo, N.Y.: Prometheus Books.

MYSTERY PAINTING:
THE SHADOW OF THE CROSS

AN ENIGMATIC PAINTING IS EXHIBITED at the Church of San Francisco de Asis (St. Francis of Assisi) at Ranchos de Taos, New Mexico (figure 41). It depicts a barefoot Jesus standing by the Sea of Galilee; however, when the lights are extinguished, the background luminesces as if the sky and sea were shining in moonlight, the figure becomes silhouetted, a cross appears at the left shoulder, and a halo is visible over the head (figure 42) (Michell 1979, 94; Colombo 1999, 70–72). Other mysterious effects are sometimes reported as well.

Background

Known as *The Shadow of the Cross,* the life-size painting was created in 1896 by an obscure French-Canadian artist named Henri Ault who had a studio in the Cobalt, Ontario, region (Rawson 1914, 615–16). Ault apparently denied being responsible for the effect, which he claimed to have discovered (quite fortuitously) upon entering his studio one night. "He believed he was going mad, and he was never able to explain the reason for the transformation," states John Michell (1979, 94).

Reportedly, British scientist and gullible spiritualist William Crookes (1832–1919) was the first to attempt—unsuccessfully—to explain the painting (Michell 1979, 94), which toured Europe and was supposedly an attraction at the 1904 World's Fair in St. Louis. A church brochure claims: "It is not known what causes the background to be luminous. It was painted before radium was discovered and when tested with Geiger counters the results have been negative" (*Shadow* n.d.). Sources even allege that more extensive scientific examinations have been conducted utilizing "light tests and scrapings"—all to no avail (Michell 1979, 94). However, as reported by *New Mexico Magazine,* although a church archivist claimed that the painting had once been analyzed "for all known luminescent substances," she conceded that "she had no docu-

(Left) Figure 41. Historic mission church of San Francisco de Asis in Ranchos de Taos, New Mexico, is home to a "mystery painting." (Photo by Joe Nickell)

(Below) Figure 42. Before-and-after photos of the transformational painting *The Shadow of the Cross* illustrate a mystery that supposedly baffles science. (Photos reproduced courtesy of Sarbo Photography, Albuquerque, N.M.)

mentation of the testing and was not sure who did the test or when" (Gaussoin 1998). Such alleged analyses appear to be apocryphal, representing attempts to convince the credulous that science is trumped by supernatural mystery.

In 1948 the picture was donated to the church, and in the early 1980s it was relocated to a room of the adjacent parish hall, furnished with folding chairs. A videotape provides an introduction to the local parish. But when the lights are turned out and the background begins to glow, subjective impressions can prevail. Observes one source (Crystal 2003): "Soon the silhouette of Jesus grows three-dimensional and appears more like a dark statue than flat image. His robes seem to billow in the breeze."

The church takes a cautious view of the phenomenon, and there are no reported healing cures associated with the painting. Pilgrims' reactions vary. Some exclaim "It's a miracle!" says archivist Corina Santistevan. "There are those who are very touched and very moved and very reverent," she says, "and those who continue to be skeptical. And those who are curious and want a scientific explanation" (Chavez 2002).

Investigation

Being among the latter group, I visited the historic church on October 27, 2003, accompanied by colleague Vaughn Rees. Although photographs are not permitted—and certainly not actual examinations of the painting—we managed to get a close look by staying for two showings and the interval between them.

Some of the picture's touted mysteries are easily explained, such as our docent's claim that Jesus's eyes follow the viewer wherever he or she stands. That is merely the result of a three-dimensional view being "fixed" in a two-dimensional representation, and any portrait in which the subject's eyes gaze directly at the viewer produces the same effect (as discussed earlier in "Haunted Plantation") (Nickell 2003).

The picture is also said to appear more intense the longer one looks at it, but that is to be expected as the viewer's eyes become accustomed to the dark. In the mottled background of the painting, some see a boat, angels, or other images, but these are simply simulacra: pictures perceived in random patterns, as in Rorschach inkblots. Some people report seeing the image of Jesus "vibrate," the docent told us; however, this is attributable to the well-known autokinetic effect, in which a stationary light in the dark appears to be moving due to slight, involuntary eye movements (Schick and Vaughn 1999, 45). All such effects can be augmented by the power of suggestion.

Regarding the appearance of the halo and cross, it must be noted that—contrary to some sources (e.g., Michell 1979, 94; Crystal 2003)—the halo is *always visible,* consisting of a simple outlined ellipse (see figure 42). It merely becomes silhouetted when the background luminesces. Such an effect—as my own experiments demonstrated—can easily be created by painting the halo outline with ordinary opaque paint over a background rendered with a phosphorescent (glow-in-the-dark) one. The same principle can explain the appearing-cross effect, except that the phosphorescent paint would need to visibly match that of the nonglowing background areas—something easily accomplished by an artist. This was my preferred hypothesis to explain the mystery when I first learned of it from Canadian writer John Robert Colombo (1996).

Supporting this hypothesis is the observation that the painting's background—in contrast to the other areas—is badly cracked and flaking, consistent with its having a different composition. Underneath, where the upper layer has flaked off, the background is a very bright blue, suggesting that the picture was repainted—as with a phosphorescent paint.[1] Further corroborative evidence is the fact that the glowing of the paint begins to diminish after a few minutes—just like phosphorescent paint; the painting must be reexposed to light for the effect to continue (Casper 2004).

Proponents' insistence that the picture was created before radium was discovered (by Pierre and Marie Curie in 1898) is largely irrelevant, since nonradium luminous paints had long been available commercially. The first, Balmain's paint (a calcium sulfide phosphor to which a small amount of bismuth compound was added as an "activator"), appeared in 1870 (*Encyclopaedia Britannica* 1911, s.v. "Phosphorescence"; 1960, s.v. "Luminescence"). In 1879 an English patent was awarded "for the use of phosphorescent salts, such as sulphid [sulfide] of lime, of strontium, barium, etc., for the purpose of illumination by mixing them with paint or varnish" (Phosphorescent 1879).[2]

Although in 1896 Ault's *The Shadow of the Cross* was a novelty, some modern artists now produce luminous paintings as a special genre (Duffy 1995). In addition, there are commercial transformational pictures, such as a "daylight" seascape that, in the dark, becomes a "sunset" scene using four glow-in-the-dark colors (Spilsbury 1997).

Conclusions

Evidence suggests that despite his reported protestations to the contrary, artist Henri Ault deliberately and cleverly created the effects in *The Shadow of the Cross*. This type of metamorphosing picture could have been accomplished using glow-in-the-dark pigments or paints that were well known and commercially available at the time the painting was produced. It is no longer much of a mystery, and certainly no miracle, notwithstanding the disingenuous claims of the painting's custodians that science is baffled, while avoiding the testing that could lay the matter to rest.

Notes

In addition to Vaughn Rees and John Robert Colombo, I received research assistance from Timothy Binga and Benjamin Radford. Philip Befumo Jr., product manager of United Mineral & Chemical Corporation (Lyndhurst, N.J.), generously provided a phosphorescent pigment for my experiments. I am also grateful to Paul Loynes for word processing and Lisa Hutter for photographic assistance.

1. Vaughn Rees used a handheld ultraviolet lamp (both short-wave and long-wave) to examine the area around the cross but uncovered nothing remarkable.

2. One source claims that any known luminous paint should have ceased to be phosphorescent by now, due to oxidation (*Shadow* n.d.). Be that as it may, paintings are often given a protective coat of varnish (Laurie 1967, 169–71), which can improve the longevity and brightness of luminous paints (Phosphorescent 2003).

References

Casper, Robert F. 2004. Telephone interview by Joe Nickell, August 25.

Chavez, Lorenzo. 2002. Taos mystery painting puzzles scientists, tourists. August 14. www.archden.org/dcr/archive/20020814/2002081415wn.htm (accessed August 10, 2004).

Colombo, John Robert. 1996. Letter (with enclosures) to Joe Nickell, July 2.

———. 1999. *Mysteries of Ontario*. Toronto: Hounslow Press.

Crystal, Ellie. 2003. Apparitions and miracles. February 14. www.crystalinks.com/apparitions.html (accessed August 10, 2004).

Duffy, Michael. 1995. Anders Knutsson: The experience of light. www.andersknutsson.com/Duffy.htm (accessed October 15, 2003).

Encyclopaedia Britannica. 1911. New York: Encyclopaedia Britannica.

———. 1960. Chicago: Encyclopaedia Britannica.

Gaussoin, Helen. 1998. Ranchos de Taos painting shrouded in mystery. *New Mexico Magazine,* December 21.

Laurie, A. P. 1967. *The Painter's Methods and Materials.* New York: Dover Publications.

Michell, John. 1979. *Simulacra: Faces and Figures in Nature.* London: Thames & Hudson.

Nickell, Joe. 2003. Haunted plantation. *Skeptical Inquirer* 27, no. 5 (September–October): 12–15.

Phosphorescent paint patented. 1879. *Manufacturer and Builder* 11, no. 9 (September): 199.

Phosphorescent pigments. 2003. www.gtamart.com/mart/products/phspgmnt/paints.html (accessed October 20).

Rawson, F. L. 1914. *Life Understood from a Scientific and Religious Point of View.* London: Crystal Press.

Schick, Theodore Jr., and Lewis Vaughn. 1999. *How to Think about Weird Things.* Mountain View, Calif.: Mayfield Publishing Company.

The Shadow of the Cross. N.d. [1996]. Brochure, San Francisco de Asis, Ranchos de Taos, N.M.

Spilsbury Puzzle Company. 1997. Catalog item A3101, "Sunset by the Sea," 80.

SHIPS OF THE DEAD

GHOSTS AND SHIPS SEEM TO GO TOGETHER in the popular imagination, combining the romance of the sea with the spine-tingling lure of hauntings. (See, for example, Horace Beck's *Folklore and the Sea* [1999] and Richard Winer's mystery-mongering *Ghost Ships* [2000].)

Phantom Ships

There are numerous beguiling reports of phantom vessels, most of them linked to shipwrecks and other disasters. In folklore, such ghostly craft are widespread, often as a motif called the Ship of the Dead—a vessel that transports spirits to the afterworld (Guiley 2000, 283–84, 343).

The most famous of the spectral ships is the *Flying Dutchman*. In a version of the legend that appeared in an English magazine in 1821, the ship's captain, having refused to put into harbor during a fierce storm—indeed, even challenging God to sink the vessel—is visited by a glowing form. He attempts to shoot it with his pistol, but the gun blows up in his hand, and the entity dooms the captain to sail the seas forever. One source for the tale—which exists in several variants, indicating the process of folklore—suggests that its origin may lie in the exploits of seventeenth-century Dutch mariner Bernard Fokke. So daring were some of Captain Fokke's voyages that there were whispers about supernatural aid—the rumors intensifying when his ship vanished during one voyage (Cohen 1984, 273–76; Beck 1999, 390–95).

I investigated one historic phantom ship case—that of a fiery spectral vessel reported in Nova Scotia's Mahone Bay. It supposedly originated when a privateer's ship, the *Young Teazer,* was set ablaze in 1813, with all hands perishing. The phenomenon—known as the Teazer Light—was almost always observed on foggy nights about the time of a full moon. I conducted a vigil for the specter in 1999, but it was a no-show. I later came upon the revealing account of someone who had witnessed the fiery ship, only to discover that what he had actually seen was the moon rising behind a bank of fog. The illusion convinced him that this was the explanation for previous sightings of the spectral *Teazer* (Nickell 2001b, 188–89).

Other explanations for wraith ships include actual vessels being seen through fog, rain, or snow. According to Beck (1999, 390), "a ship or even part of her could well be sighted by a lookout and neither seen nor heard by anyone else, or her horn could be heard by only one person—suggesting that it was a spirit ship they had encountered." He adds: "There can be little doubt that anxious hours spent peering into fog and snow will cause seamen to see and hear almost anything they wish. Moreover, thick weather has a tendency to distort objects into outlandish shapes." Mirage effects, outright pranks, and many other factors may contribute to reports of phantom ships, including the occasional encounter of abandoned vessels and derelicts (Beck 1999, 390).

Haunted *Queen Mary*

In addition to spirit ships, there are numerous otherwise ordinary vessels that are reputedly haunted. Prominent among them is the *Queen Mary,* the former ocean liner that, since 1971, has been permanently docked at Long Beach, California. This historic liner is now essentially a floating inn, and I have been among its many overnight guests. Nocturnal encounters with spirits are among the reported phenomena on board.

One woman recalled: "I awoke from a deep sleep around midnight. I saw a figure walking near my daughter's sleeping bag toward the door. I called out. There was no answer. It was then that I noticed my sister was lying next to me. I sat up in bed and watched the person in white walk through the door!" (Wlodarski et al. 1995, 33). This is an obvious example of a "waking dream," actually a type of hallucination that occurs in the twilight between sleep and wakefulness. Such experiences typically include bizarre imagery such as ghosts, angels, aliens, and the like. The encounters can seem quite real, and the person typically insists that he or she was not dreaming (Baker and Nickell 1992, 226–27).

Of course, not all ghost sightings can be explained by waking dreams. Many, in fact, occur during normal everyday activities. Consider the report of

"J. M.," who was at the *Queen Mary's* purser's desk when, he stated, "I caught a brief glimpse out of the corner of my eye, of someone or something moving," or that of "P. T.," who said, "I saw something move out of the corner of my eye . . . a brief glimpse of someone or something" (Wlodarski 1995, 32, 36). Actually, the illusion that something is moving in the peripheral vision is quite common, and either that perception or a different stimulus—perhaps a noise or a subjective feeling—might trigger a mental image. In certain especially imaginative individuals, this might be superimposed on the visual scene— somewhat like a mental version of a photographic double exposure—thus creating a seemingly apparitional event (Nickell 2001b, 290–91).

Data that I have acquired over the years indicate a correlation between haunting experiences and a person's propensity to fantasize. This might explain why such experiences "happened with greater frequency" to one particular female employee on the *Queen Mary*. Reportedly, another frequent percipient "actually *likes* the idea of spending time with the spirits" (Wlodarski 1995, 49, 50).

Aircraft Carrier *Hornet*

Anchored at Alameda, California, the USS *Hornet* was commissioned in 1943 and saw impressive action during World War II in the Pacific. It steamed 150,000 miles, survived 59 attacks, shot down 668 enemy aircraft, and destroyed another 742 on the ground. It later served in the Vietnam War and was the major recovery ship for the *Apollo 11* and *12* lunar landing missions. Decommissioned in 1970, the *Hornet* was mothballed, then sold for scrap in 1993. However, it was saved four years later by a foundation that converted it into a museum (figure 43) (Merideth 2001, 85–99, 232).

Crewmen had dubbed the warship the "Gray Ghost"—apparently because earlier carriers bearing the same name had been sunk, and because its gray color caused it to blend into hazy backgrounds (Merideth 2001, x). The moniker may have helped inspire notions that the ship is haunted. "Paranormal activity" has been reported since mid-1995 (Haunting 2004), when members of the public began to be invited on board. In 2001 a press release seeking funds to help with restoration efforts promoted the carrier as a "Ship of Spirits." Halloween 2001 offered a special opportunity to capitalize on the

Figure 43. The "haunted" aircraft carrier USS *Hornet* is a floating museum at Alameda, California. (Photo by Joe Nickell)

popularity of ghosts, with a flyer advertising a "Monster Bash aboard the Gray Ghost" drawing costumed visitors at $25 each. Another flyer titled "Don't Miss the Boat" advertised overnight stays for young people and promised, among other things, "real ghost stories"—all for a bargain rate of $50 per child.

Such promotional efforts have been aided by ghost hunter Loyd Auerbach and local spirit medium Aann Golemac. Auerbach, who uses a magnetometer in pseudoscientific fashion as a ghost detector (*Best* 2001), claims that spirits aboard the warship have patted him on the back (Knight 2001), although this could be merely imagined self-congratulation. Golemac has visited the *Hornet* several times and insists that it is filled with spirits. She asserts, "When we leave our bodies, we can go back and visit the places that were important to us" (Knight 2001). Actually, there is no scientific proof of that assertion, but Golemac is undaunted: "If a person is skeptical, then they are just in denial" (Reports 2004).

I may be one of those skeptics she has in mind. While investigating the aircraft carrier with colleague Vaughn Rees, I found no evidence of any odd entities on board—other than, well, haunted people. Many reputedly para-normal occurrences on the ship are merely unidentified noises, and there are countless sources of these on such an old, rambling metal ship (Hull 2000). A man sleeping aboard one night who felt something tugging at him was prob-ably experiencing a waking dream; he admitted being unsure whether he was awake or not (*America's* 2003). As I explained on a television documentary on the *Hornet,* many seemingly real experiences may actually be illusory. And once the idea of a ghost attaches itself to a place, anything unusual that hap-pens there is considered evidence of haunting (*Best* 2001).

A climate of ghost promotion not only intensifies the effects of suggestion but also can invite pranks, as I have learned firsthand at many sites over the years. I suspect that pranks have occurred on the USS *Hornet.* For example, the reported fall of a wrench during one overnight session may have been merely ghostly theatrics intended to spook a youth group (Nickell 2001a). I find it ironic when a volunteer tour guide states, "The spirits are real pranksters" (Hull 2000).

In contrast to those who report ghostly shenanigans are others who have had no paranormal experiences, including one man who had served as a docent on the *Hornet* for two years. He suggested that people who experience ghosts do so because they are believers (Nickell 2001a).

Star of India

Moored in San Diego's harbor is the three-masted, black-hulled ship the *Star of India* (figure 44). Christened *Euterpe* and launched in 1863 from the Isle of Man, the ship sailed for thirty-five years under the British flag. It brought Indian jute to England, transported European emigrants to New Zealand and Australia, and carried sugar from Hawaii to San Francisco. Before becoming an Alaskan salmon-fishing vessel in 1898—by then, rechristened *Star of India*—the ship experienced many troubling incidents, including collisions, a nonviolent mutiny, and several deaths of crew members and passengers (Lamb 1999).

Towed to San Diego in 1927 to become a floating museum, the *Star of India* suffered neglect through the Great Depression, World War II, and beyond. Restoration was finally completed in 1976, and it is now "the oldest active sailing ship in the world." Sometime along the way—apparently in the

Figure 44. The three-masted *Star of India* is "the oldest active sailing ship in the world" and reportedly has stowaway spirits. (Photo by Joe Nickell)

1920s, after the ship was retired—the *Star of India* allegedly acquired some ghostly residents (Lamb 1999).

In October 2001—accompanied by a group of local skeptics (including Keith Taylor), a newspaper reporter, and a television crew—I boarded the *Star* for a private nighttime pre-Halloween investigative tour. On board were unmistakable "ghosts," each dressed in a period costume for the occasion. Three scenes—each supposedly reflecting a real, recorded tragedy aboard the *Star of India*—were dramatized. These "scary yarns," as the local newspaper dubbed them (LaFee 2001), told about a lad who fell from atop the main mast, a Chinese sailor who was crushed by the ship's heavy anchor chain, and a drunken immigrant who committed suicide by slashing his throat (figure 45).

But do the ghosts of these tragic figures indeed haunt the *Star*? The answer depends on whom one asks. Some crew members were dismissive of any ghosts, while others had experiences to relate—the same dichotomy reported by John J. Lamb (1999) in *San Diego Specters*. Lamb quotes Joseph Ditler,

Figure 45. A "ghost," sporting a bloody bandage, is all dressed up for Halloween aboard the *Star of India.* (Photo by Joe Nickell)

director of development for the San Diego Maritime Museum, as stating: "All ships are haunted, but some more than others. *Star of India* has a very special atmosphere. I'm not prone to flights of imagination, but if you stand on the decks you can't help but sense the spirits of the seamen and passengers who sailed on her." As a poet, I understand these feelings, although I would replace the verb *sense* with *imagine.*

To study different people's experiences on the *Star of India,* I handed out copies of my "Ghost Encounters Questionnaire," seven of which I received back. The experiences related were similar to others that had been reported aboard the ship (Lamb 1999) and at other "haunted" places as well. These included eerie chills, feelings of ghostly presences, and the like—all of which are easily attributable to subjective impressions. As I told a reporter (LaFee 2001), some places—particularly those imbued with history and especially those with a reputation of being haunted—possess an "ambiance" that can inspire such feelings.

A few experiencers reported hearing unexplained sounds. For instance, one man "heard chains down in the orlop [deck]" (the lowest deck of a ship). Another, on a calm morning, heard a "sloshing" in a freshwater tank; it stopped when he fetched a shipmate to verify the sound but resumed after the latter had left, shaking his head. ("I found something to do elsewhere," the man confessed.) Perhaps these incidents had some real but unnoticed cause, such as wind rattling something in the first instance or a sea creature splashing in the latter. If not, the sounds may have been merely mental impressions—familiar ship sounds surfacing from memory.

My limited number of respondents exhibited a good range of experiences (extending from one person with no ghostly encounters to others having low, medium, and high levels). Similar to my previous studies (Nickell 2001b, 84–85, 299), there was a correlation between an individual's level of ghost experiences and the number of personality traits associated with a propensity to fantasize (Wilson and Barber 1983). With the *Star of India,* as with other supposedly haunted sites, it appears that it is not the *places* that are haunted but the *people.*

USS *The Sullivans*

The destroyer USS *The Sullivans* was named for five brothers from Waterloo, Iowa—George, Francis, Joseph, Madison, and Albert Sullivan—who enlisted in the navy and served together aboard a light cruiser, the USS *Juneau.* In late 1942 the cruiser was sunk by a torpedo from a Japanese submarine, killing most of the sailors on board. Of the brothers, only George Sullivan survived, but he succumbed soon afterward (*Sullivans* n.d.).

President Franklin D. Roosevelt directed that one of the new destroyers under construction be named for the five brothers—the only navy destroyer ever to bear the name of more than a single person. USS *The Sullivans* was launched at San Francisco on April 4, 1943, sporting an Irish shamrock on the forward stack. The ship fought in the Philippines and elsewhere during World War II and later served during the Korean War and the Cuban blockade, as well as assisting with rescue efforts for the nuclear submarine USS *Thresher*. Decommissioned in 1965, *The Sullivans* arrived for display in Buffalo, New York, in 1977, and in 1986 it was designated a national historic landmark. Its famous name has been passed on to another destroyer (USS n.d.).

Following a familiar pattern, ghost claims became attached to *The Sullivans* only after it was mothballed. Workers, guards, and guides—often unnamed and cited secondhand—began to report strange incidents that were supposedly "unexplained" and therefore attributed to a ghostly cause. But incidents that are unexplained are not necessarily *unexplainable.* For example, apparitions could be tricks of the mind, and other incidents might be explained as misperceptions or outright pranks.

Pranks seem especially worthy of consideration when we are told that the spirit antics occur "especially on Friday the thirteenth" (Hauck 1996). This source (which erroneously refers to the destroyer as "the USS *Sullivan*") fails to explain why that date would be significant. In fact, the Sullivan brothers' ship was torpedoed on November 13, 1942—a Friday. However, friggatriskaidekaphobes—superstitious folk who fear Friday the thirteenth (Christopher 2004)—should recall that it was the *Juneau,* not *The Sullivans,* that was the brothers' death ship. They were never aboard the destroyer. Moreover, there is no credible evidence that Fridays falling on the thirteenth of the month are particularly jinxed for the U.S. Navy. Therefore, if there are more "ghost" incidents aboard *The Sullivans* on those days, pranking is a possible explanation. Other spooky dates, like Halloween, can also invite certain people to engage in "Boo!" type behavior.

In any case, the Friday-the-thirteenth link apparently no longer exists. In fact, the "haunting" of the ship appears to be declining on the whole. Ghosts were not mentioned in the brochures and flyers I obtained on a visit, accompanied by Center for Inquiry intern Dawn Peterson. A docent on the ship told us that he had had no ghostly experiences on board, although he had worked there for six years (Bart 2003).

Figure 46. Mysterious blurring of one of the five Sullivan brothers' pictures—aboard their namesake ship—is duplicated in this experimental photo. (Photo by Joe Nickell)

To me, the most interesting phenomenon reported aboard *The Sullivans* concerns a room (Area 43) designated the "Sullivan Bros. Memorial," with framed photographs of each of the five brothers. According to a television documentary, *Haunted History: New York* (2000), whenever one takes a photograph of the row of pictures, four of them appear normal, while that of George is indistinct—rendered as "a big blur of light." Dawn Peterson and I conducted several experiments and were able to duplicate the effect shown in the documentary (figure 46). Since George's picture is in the center, one tends to stand squarely in front of it when photographing the gallery; thus, its glass reflects the camera's flash, producing the blurring. The fact that the glass is the nonglare type helps soften the reflection, producing a diffuse, more mysterious effect.

Among other historic ships, *The Sullivans* appears to be no more haunted than any other—that is, not at all.

References

America's Most Haunted. 2003. Travel Channel, January 5.

Baker, Robert A., and Joe Nickell. 1992. *Missing Pieces: How to Investigate Ghosts, UFOs, Psychics and Other Mysteries.* Buffalo, N.Y.: Prometheus Books.

Bart, John. 2003. Interview by Joe Nickell, June 24.

Beck, Horace. 1999. *Folklore and the Sea.* Edison, N.J.: Castle Books.

Best Kept Secrets of the Paranormal. 2001. Learning Channel, September 23.

Christopher, Kevin. 2004. Horrified by Friday the 13th? CSI press release, February 10.

Cohen, Daniel. 1984. *The Encyclopedia of Ghosts.* New York: Dorset Press.

Guiley, Rosemary Ellen. 2000. *The Encyclopedia of Ghosts and Spirits.* New York: Checkmark Books.

Hauck, William Dennis. 1996. *Haunted Places: The National Directory,* 290–91. New York: Penguin Books.

Haunted History: New York. 2000. History Channel documentary, September 22.

The Haunting of the USS *Hornet.* 2004. www.dr-assoc.com/hornet-9–30–02.htm (accessed April 20).

Hull, Dana. 2000. USS *Hornet*—staff and visitors report seeing and hearing strange things. *San Jose Mercury News,* August 11.

Knight, Heather. 2001. Backyard haunts. *San Francisco Chronicle* (Contra Costa and Tri-Valley ed.), October 26.

LaFee, Scott. 2001. Haunting pro goes on ghostly iron ship, October 31. www .signonsandiego.com/news/uniontrib/wed/currents/news_1c31paranormal.html.

Lamb, John J. 1999. *San Diego Specters: Ghosts, Poltergeists, and Phantasmic Tales,* 153–58. San Diego: Sunbelt Publications.

Merideth, Lee William. 2001. *Gray Ghost.* Sunnyvale, Calif.: Historical Indexes.

Nickell, Joe. 2001a. Interviews with staff of USS *Hornet,* October 25.

———. 2001b. *Real-Life X-Files: Investigating the Paranormal.* Lexington: University Press of Kentucky.

Reports of zombie-like figures. 2004. www.100megsfree.

Ship of spirits. 2001. Media release, March 28. www.uss-hornet.org/news_events/ press_releases/press_releases_2001.html (accessed April 20, 2004).

The Sullivans. N.d. Display sign aboard USS *The Sullivans,* Buffalo and Erie County Naval and Military Park, Buffalo, N.Y. (visited June 24, 2003).

USS *The Sullivans* history. N.d. In informational brochure, Welcome to the Buffalo and Erie County Naval and Military Park, Buffalo, N.Y. (obtained June 24, 2003).

Wilson, Sheryl C., and Theodore X. Barber. 1983. The fantasy-prone personality. In *Imagery: Current Theory, Research, and Application,* ed. Anees A. Sheikh. New York: John Wiley & Sons.

Winer, Richard. 2000. *Ghost Ships: True Stories of Nautical Nightmares, Hauntings, and Disasters.* New York: Berkley Books.

Wlodarski, Robert, et al. 1995. *A Guide to the Haunted* Queen Mary. Calabasas, Calif.: G-Host.

FORTUNE-TELLING, MEXICAN STYLE

In Ciudad Juárez in 2003, I was able to have my fortune told by a canary! The bird's partner was a sidewalk vendor who wore a shirt emblazoned with tarot cards. To prognosticate, he picked up a pinch of birdseed and let his charge out of its cage, whereupon it plucked two folded paper slips from a rack. The little bird waited to receive its reward and then dutifully hopped back into its cage. Then I paid up: five pesos for each fortune slip, and $5 for the privilege of taking a photograph.

From another prescient canary in Tijuana I obtained two more fortune slips, offering a welter of predictions and advice. One of the four slips was in English: "You shall soon receive good news in the mail about the matter that so concerns you. But before this, some one shall rather mysteriously get in touch with you. I can tell you no more as I cannot read your mind." I was intrigued by the latter admission. As for the fortunes, I tried to assess them fairly. Unfortunately, the events that best matched the vague predictions had already occurred by the time I received the slips. What birdbrain prognostications!

Also in Tijuana, on the Day of the Dead, colleague Vaughn Rees and I visited a professional fortune-teller whose sign offered *Lectura de las cartas y Palma de la Mano* (card readings and palmistry). His place of business was one flight up. "Sir Omar" gave me his business card, which stated that he was a *Maestro en Ciencias Occultas* (master of occult sciences) who offered *Soluciona tus Problemas* (solutions to your problems). An outgoing man, he told us that he had worked in the same place for twenty-eight years. His tarot cards looked nearly that old. (I was later able to purchase a similar set, approximately the size of a regular deck but with tarot-like suits of swords, cups, wands, and coins.) He agreed to do my reading in his struggling English for 100 pesos (about $10).

I falsely told the cartomancer that my reason for coming was that I had

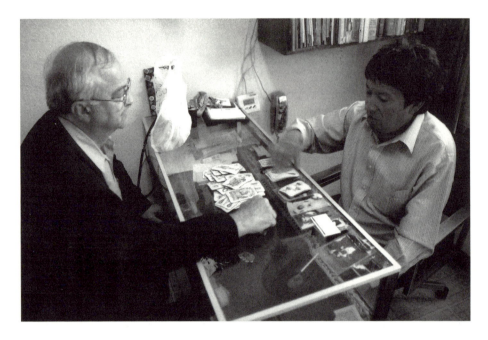

Figure 47. Tijuana cartomancer *(right)* reads the fortune of investigator Joe Nickell. (Photo by Vaughn Rees)

recently been diagnosed with terminal cancer. My persona was that of a frightened man who could think of little else. Sir Omar had me cut the cards into three stacks, after which he began the reading (figure 47). He told me that a black-magic curse had been placed on me in 1978 by a "dark woman," but it had now been lifted. (I regarded this as utter nonsense.) He stated that my health was in the hands of the medical profession but that he foresaw my having a long future. (He was simply telling me what he thought I wanted to hear.) Money and even the love of a much younger woman (twenty-one years younger, he specified) would be mine in abundance. (He was obviously just dispensing happy possibilities, which, after all, cost him nothing.) Then he asserted that someone would try to borrow a sum of $7,000 from me and that I should decline the request. (Years later, that still has not occurred.) Sir Omar ended by allowing me three questions, but I insisted that nothing mattered except my health. He repeated what he had said earlier, indicating that I would pull through and live a long time. He wrote his phone number on the back of his business card and suggested that I call him in several months.

The alleged clairvoyant, in my opinion, merely sold optimism, with any success depending on what skeptics call the "Barnum effect." Named for showman P. T. Barnum, who strove to provide something for everyone, this refers to people's tendency to take a vague, generalized statement and try to fit it to their own situation (French et al. 1991). The soothsayer may have hoped that his optimistic statements and cautionary foretellings would function as self-fulfilling prophecies, prompting me to help bring about what I expected to occur. The bottom line is that he failed to divine anything that was truly enlightening, completely missed important things that were actually occurring in my life, and was apparently oblivious to the actual state of my health or the true nature of my visit. He did succeed in collecting 100 pesos, however.

Reference

French, Christopher C., et al. 1991. Belief in astrology: A test of the Barnum effect. *Skeptical Inquirer* 15, no. 2 (Winter): 166–72.

HEALING SPAS

IN VARIOUS CULTURES, WATER HAS BEEN touted for its curative power—attributed to its mineral properties, thermal effects, and even supposed supernatural qualities. Here I look at ancient baths and more recent spas; in the next chapter I discuss legendary "fountains of youth" and reputed miraculous healing shrines such as that at Lourdes, France.

Ancient Baths

Hydrotherapy—the internal or external use of water to treat disease—is among the earliest "healing" practices. Indeed, drinking or bathing in springs, streams, or pools for therapeutic purposes predates recorded history.

There is archaeological evidence of mineral springs in Asia during the Bronze Age (circa 3000 BC), and biblical references allude to the practice. For example, Joshua (19:35) refers to the city of Hammath (from the Hebrew word for "hot springs") located at Tiberius in Israel, one of the world's oldest spas. And 2 Kings 5:10 tells of Elisha instructing a Syrian to wash seven times in the Jordan River to cure his "leprosy."

In ancient Greece, springs were believed to have supernatural powers because they were supposedly the dwelling places of gods. Therapeutic centers called *Asclepieia*—after Asclepius, the mythological god of health—were built at mineral springs throughout the Greek realm. The Romans followed the practice, translating the deity's name to Aesculapius and establishing baths across their empire (Swanner 1988, 16–20). One was at Bath, England, so named for its hot springs attended by a great temple.

In the Americas, the native peoples also believed in the miraculous curative powers of mineral waters. Aztec emperor Montezuma was carried on a litter from Tenochtitlan (today's Mexico City) across a mountain to a spa called Agua Hedionda. There he bathed in the invigorating spring and sipped the waters to recuperate from his strenuous life. In 1605 the conquering Catholic Spaniards established a health-cure community at the site, transforming it into a spa that later became fashionable among both Europeans and Americans (Swanner 1988, 20).

The Mohawks of the Iroquois Nation, in what is now Saratoga County, New York, held the mineral springs of that area to be sacred, a gift of their great deity Manitou. According to spa physician Grace Maguire Swanner (1988, 20, 95), they attempted to keep the existence of the springs a secret from the white invaders.

Later Spas

In 1326 an ironmaster in southeastern Belgium learned of a secluded spring that was reputed to have healing properties. When he received relief from his own ailments, he founded a health resort there named Spa, from an old Walloon (French dialect) word meaning "fountain" (Swanner 1988, 14). It gained fame in the sixteenth century for both its water and its climate, and the term *spa* began to be applied to similar resorts. By the eighteenth century, Spa had become "the most fashionable resort in Europe for the medicinal use of such waters" (*Encyclopaedia Britannica* 1960, s.v. "Spa"; see also *Collier's Encyclopedia* 1993, s.v. "Spa").

In my travels I have visited several famous spas both in Europe and in the United States. In Italy, for example, during the October 8–10, 2004, World Skeptics Congress in Abano Terme (near Padua), I stayed at one of the numerous spa-hotels in the city, which calls itself "the world's spa capital." The naturally heated springs there were important in Roman times, according to reports by Pliny the Elder (*Colli* 2004, 7; Abano n.d.). Today, thermal- and mud-bath health and beauty treatments promise that "you can regain your vigor, relax and achieve that lost sense of well-being" (*Colli* 2004, 6; Abano n.d.). Although I did not partake of the treatments, I felt reinvigorated simply being in Abano.

Along with Italian paranormal investigator Luigi Garlaschelli, I visited the historic spa site at Pozzuoli, only a few miles from Naples and Mount Vesuvius, the volcano that destroyed Pompeii. In fact, the ancient healing waters at Pozzuoli are actually in a volcano. Known as the Vulcano Solfatara, it formed

4,000 years ago and last erupted in 1198. Today it spouts sulfurous steam, small "volcanoes" of hot mud, and jets of bubbling sand (*Benvenuto* 2004, 15). A well in the crater became famous in the late Middle Ages for its mineral waters, which supposedly cured sterility and ulcers. "Natural saunas" elsewhere in the crater yielded sulfurous vapors that were considered beneficial for respiratory ailments, and hot mud was used to treat rheumatism. The crater is in the region known as the Phlegraean Fields, which contains thermomineral waters said in ancient times to be capable of "healing wounds both old and new, relieving the whole body, ridding the heart of evil and arthritis, slimming heavy limbs, making the sad rejoice" (*Benvenuto* 2004, 7).

Germany is rife with spas. In 2002 I traveled with skeptic Martin Mahner to southern Bavaria to visit the spa at Bad Tölz, a colorful, baroque town at the foothills of the Alps (figure 48). A farmhand found a spring there in 1845, and the realization that local residents never developed goiters eventually led to the discovery that the water contained iodine, an element needed by the thyroid gland (Bad Tölz n.d.). (Elsewhere in Europe and the United States, waters containing other elements—such as lithium, used to treat manic depression,[1] and radon, a radioactive gas supposedly effective in treating rheumatism—were promoted to increase the patronage at those spas.) Such cause-and-effect evidence represents the "nucleus of truth" that may be behind some spa therapies, according to Peter Kröling (2002), a physician and professor of spa treatments. Germany, he observed, has approximately 300 spas, all licensed by the federal government, and each has a medical staff that includes a *Badearzt* ("spa doctor").

American spas followed the popularity of the European resorts, and I have been able to visit many of them. In fact, the former Cole Hotel in my hometown of West Liberty, in the hills of eastern Kentucky, was a sort of poor-man's spa, although its heyday was before my time. A 1911 advertisement for its "Health-giving Mineral Waters" typifies claims of the era: "The water contains 25 grains of solid matter to the gallon, composed mainly of Carbonates of Calcium, Magnesium and Sodium, and traces of Chlorides and Sulphates of Sodium and Potassium, and a trace of Carbonate of Strontium." The analysis, signed by "Alfred M. Peters, Chemist," concluded, "This water is very wholesome and has great medicinal value" (Nickell 1988, 98). Actually, all water except distilled water contains dissolved salts, and it became customary to set

Figure 48. Spa at Bad Tölz, Germany, as shown on a 1939 postcard. (Author's collection)

the level at fifty grains per gallon (twice that of the Cole Hotel water) to justify the designation *mineral water* (Swanner 1988, 32).

America's "Queen of the Spas" was the celebrated Saratoga Springs of New York. By 1783, George Washington had sipped water from one of several springs in the area, High Rock Spring, and later recommended it to one of his former Revolutionary War officers as a remedy for rheumatism. By 1790, taverns there were housing guests seeking the health-giving waters. In the 1820s, spas (as well as summer vacations) were becoming fashionable among the wealthy, and none would become more popular than Saratoga (White 1985, 86–87; Swanner 1988, 105–6). The crude early taverns were followed by larger and larger hotels, medical offices, and, by the 1880s, Dr. Strong's Sanatorium, advertised as "a popular resort for health, change, rest or recreation of the year." Amenities included "elevator, electric bells, steam, open fireplaces, sun parlor and promenade on the roof, croquet, lawn tennis." Family prayers were offered daily "at no additional charge" (Swanner 1988, 128). An article in the December 9, 1887, edition of the *London Times* portrayed the spa in its grandeur:

Everybody who is anybody comes to Saratoga, because here can be found an aggregation of people of a character to be met nowhere else.

The throng is essentially cosmopolitan, and comes from all parts of the country, besides many who cross the Atlantic. . . . Saratoga is the place in America to see diamonds. Their glitter dazzles the eye at every turn, as they sparkle under the brilliant electric lights illuminating the evening scene.

"Fine equipages" drove people around the area, and certain eateries provided "elaborate fish and game dinners at high prices" (American 1887).

The springs still flow at Saratoga, and I toured the area on one of my trips to search for the Lake Champlain monster (Nickell 2003). I drank some of the salty, naturally carbonated water and sought out the famous Island Spouter—spewing from a tiny island in Geyser Creek in the nearby state park (figure 49). I also stopped at historic Ballston Spa, which had been flourishing as a resort while Saratoga was still a wilderness. Some of its numerous springs—including one supposedly discovered during a séance with Benjamin Franklin, and two with a high lithium content—provided water that was bottled and sold for its allegedly healthful properties (Swanner 1988, 89–94). Some unscrupulous companies sold ordinary tap water in bottles bearing counterfeit labels (figure 50) (Saratoga n.d.).

Among the other historic spas I have visited are Sharon Springs and Clifton Springs in New York, Cambridge Springs in Pennsylvania, and Lithia Springs in Georgia—each worthy of a chapter by itself.

The Verdict

Seemingly supportive of the grandiose claims made for mineral springs are testimonials from visitors. However, according to psychologist Terence Hines (1988, 236–37), "One can find testimonials attesting to the effectiveness of almost anything," such as those given for "snake oils" that allegedly cured even "consumption" (tuberculosis). Hines adds: "It is safe to say that if testimonials play a major part in the 'come on' for a cure or therapy it is almost certainly worthless. If the promoters of the therapy had actual evidence for its effectiveness, they would cite it and not have to rely on testimonials."

Figure 49. "Island Spouter," depicted on a 1941 postcard, is a natural geyser in the state park at Saratoga Springs, New York. (Author's collection)

Figure 50. Various mineral-water bottles include one *(front)* from Saratoga Springs, New York. Others *(back, from left)* are from Olympian Springs, Kentucky; Buffalo Lythia Water from Buffalo Lythia Springs, Virginia; and a drink from Cloverdale Spring, Newville, Pennsylvania (containing mineral water, Lithia, and lime flavor). Also shown is an antique drinking cup purchased near Sharon Springs, New York. (Photo by Joe Nickell, from his collection)

Even some spa advocates concede that the beneficial effects are not solely due to the various elements in the water. Benefits are also obtained from the water's mechanical and thermal effects on the body; hot- and cold-water applications are commonly prescribed for various therapeutic purposes—not to mention the psychosomatic benefits, or the so-called placebo effect (Swanner 1988, 32–37; Kröling 2002).

Potential negative effects are rarely considered. For example, at Saratoga, laws on radioactivity required the posting of signs warning that the water's radium content might be harmful, but spa advocate Swanner (1988, 37) found that "ridiculous," saying, "If the mineral waters have deleterious physiologic effects, they have yet to be demonstrated." This seems to be an attempt to shift the burden of proof and to suggest, counterintuitively, that a wide variety of positive effects can be obtained from ingesting certain substances, but never any negative effects.

Nonetheless, it is quite obvious that the spas—offering a change of scenery, rest, distraction from one's ills (provided by almost any physical treatment), and the power of positive thinking—represent a successful, if temporary, prescription for many ailments.

Note

1. According to Andrew Skolnick: "Levels of lithium that cause dangerous toxicity are rather close to therapeutic levels. This is especially so for people with severe cardiovascular or kidney disease. Therefore, it's likely that any natural waters with high enough lithium levels to have any beneficial psychological effect would also cause substantial illness and death."

References

Abano in History. N.d. Typescript supplied by Abano Terme tourism office, October 2004.

The American spa. 1887. *London Times,* December 9. Quoted in Swanner 1988, 136–37.

Bad Tölz. N.d. [2002]. Tourist information brochure, English version.

Benvenuto nei Campl Flegrel (Welcome to the Phlegraean Fields). 2004. Pozzuoli, Italy, Tourist Office, October.

Colli. 2004. Tourism brochure. Padova, Italy: Turismo Padova Terme Euganee, June.

Collier's Encyclopedia. 1993. New York: P. F. Collier.

Encyclopaedia Britannica. 1960. Chicago: Encyclopaedia Britannica.

Hines, Terence. 1988. *Pseudoscience and the Paranormal.* Amherst, N.Y.: Prometheus Books.

Kröling, Peter. 2002. Interview by Joe Nickell with Martin Mahner, Munich, Germany, October 16.

Nickell, Joe. 2003. Legend of the Lake Champlain monster. *Skeptical Inquirer* 27, no. 4 (July–August): 18–23.

Nickell, W. Lynn. 1988. *The Changing Faces of West Liberty.* Berea, Ky.: Kentucky Imprints.

Saratoga Springs visitor center. N.d. Display text (viewed August 2, 2002).

Swanner, Grace Maguire. 1988. *Saratoga: Queen of the Spas.* Utica, N.Y.: North Country Books.

White, William Chapman. 1985. *Adirondack Country.* Syracuse, N.Y.: Syracuse University Press.

MIRACULOUS SPRINGS

As discussed in the previous chapter, spas offer supposed physiological benefits—along with obvious psychological gains—to those who suffer from a wide variety of ailments. However, as one advocate of spa therapy notes (Swanner 1988, 21), whereas the touted effects are now explained "on a scientific basis," in early times, mysticism prevailed. Here I investigate so-called fountains of youth and "miraculous" healing springs like that at Lourdes, France.

Fountain of Youth

The legend of a fountain of youth may have originated in northern India. By the seventh century, the tale had arrived in Europe, where it was widely discussed during the Middle Ages. In 1546 the German Renaissance artist Lucas Cranach produced a celebrated painting of the miraculous spring that depicted frail, wrinkled women entering the pool and youthful beauties exiting at the other side (Who 2000). But Cranach's *The Fountain of Youth* is allegorical: "The fountain spouting water from the spring into the pool bears the statues of Venus and Cupid—evidence that this is actually a fountain of love rather than youth, and that the power of love is the true source of immortality" (Fountain 2005a).

Earlier, the Spanish explorer Juan Ponce de León (1460–1521) had reportedly searched for the fabled spring. Having accompanied Columbus on his second voyage to America (1493), he conquered Puerto Rico in 1509 and then—as a reward for that service—received permission from Spain to search for a land called "Bimini." According to Native American legend, the region had a fountain with marvelously curative water. Supposedly, those who drank from it would never age.

Ponce de León organized an expedition and set off with three ships in March 1513, allegedly to locate the Bimini spring. On March 27 he landed

Figure 51. Postcard from the 1940s illustrates a spring in St. Augustine, Florida, promoted to tourists as the Fountain of Youth sought by Ponce de León. (Author's collection)

near present-day St. Augustine, believing that he had arrived on an island and unaware that he was the first European to explore Florida. He claimed the land for Spain and then continued his search for Bimini, sailing through the Florida Keys and on to Cuba, but finding nothing. Discouraged, he and his crew abandoned their quest and sailed for Spain.

In 1521 Ponce de León returned with two shiploads of soldiers in an attempt to conquer the Native Americans and colonize Florida. He landed on the west coast of the "island" but met a large force of resisting natives. During the fierce engagement, Ponce de León was mortally wounded by an arrow. He was carried to the ship and taken to Cuba, where he died in July 1521 (Ponce de León 2005).

Although Ponce de León failed to locate the fountain of youth, today, a popular tourist destination at St. Augustine is billed as that very site. As stated on a mid-1940s postcard (figure 51):

The Fountain of Youth attracts visitors to St. Augustine. According to tradition, it is the exact spot where Juan Ponce de León, the Spanish explorer, in search of the Fountain of Youth, landed April 2, 1513, and planted a cross (as shown in the foreground of picture) and took possession of the "New World" in the name of the King of Spain.

Note that the caption merely cites "tradition"—meaning a handed-down tale.

Indeed, there is no real evidence that Ponce de León found the spring at St. Augustine during his search for the fountain of youth. The spring—actually a *former* spring that quit flowing and is now tapped by a well shaft—was commercialized by a man named Walter B. Fraser. Fraser arrived in the city in 1927 and sought to promote St. Augustine as a tourist site; he later became mayor and state senator (Fountain 2005c). Moreover, according to one source, "Historians do not unanimously honor at full value the beautifully romantic story that Ponce [de León] was seeking to find the fountain of youth" (Fountain 2005b).

Miracle Healing Springs

Around the world are various alleged "miracle" springs, many promoted by Roman Catholics. The most famous of these is Lourdes in southern France. There, in 1858, fourteen-year-old Bernadette Soubirous (1844–1879) claimed to see apparitions of the Virgin Mary that directed her to the spring at the back of a grotto (figure 52). Soon, rumors of miraculous healings surfaced, along with tales of miracles that occurred in Bernadette's youth. In 1933 the late visionary was canonized and became St. Bernadette (Jones 1994).

Meanwhile, in 1884 the Lourdes Medical Bureau was founded and has since recognized 67 miracle cures at the site. An additional 6,800 cases that were said to be "medically inexplicable" did not meet the church's criteria to be declared miraculous. The existence of a disease must be proved, and the cure must be "instantaneous" as well as "complete and permanent" (Nickell 1998; Morris 2004)

However, *miracle* is not a scientific term or concept. Since the Lourdes miracle claims are derived from those cases that are held to be "medically inexplicable," claimants are engaging in a logical fallacy called arguing from ignorance—that is, drawing a conclusion based on a lack of knowledge. Moreover, some cases appear to be nothing more than the result of poor

Figure 52. An old print from the "miracle" spring at Lourdes, France, features a statue depicting the Virgin Mary as she supposedly appeared to a visionary in 1858. (Author's collection)

investigation. For instance, doctors who examined one 1976 certification pronounced it "vague" and "obtuse," labeling the documents "a lot of mumbo jumbo" and "unscientific and totally unconvincing" (Nickell 1998, 150–51).

There are additional indicators that Lourdes lacks any true healing properties. One is that many cases have alternative explanations. For example, some concern illnesses—such as multiple sclerosis—that are known to exhibit spontaneous remission. Other "cures" may be attributable to misdiagnosis, psychosomatic conditions, prior medical treatment, the body's own healing

203

power, and other effects. Also, some types of miracle healings never occur at Lourdes, as indicated by the comment of French writer Anatole France. On visiting the shrine and seeing the discarded crutches and canes, he exclaimed, "What, what, no wooden legs???" (Nickell 1998, 150–51).

Still another reason for skepticism is that those who seem eminently deserving of healing may receive no benefits at all. For example, Bernadette herself failed to be aided by the spring's touted curative powers. Having been sickly as a child, she was bedridden for the last years of her life and died at the young age of thirty-five (Nickell 1998, 149; Jones 1994).

Then there is the case of ailing Pope John Paul II, who visited Lourdes in August 2004. The eighty-four-year-old pontiff—who had Parkinson's disease and knee and hip debilities—struggled through Mass, gasping and trembling. In a rare reference to his own condition, he assured other ill pilgrims that he shared their suffering. Poignant as that statement was, it underscored the fact that the claimed healing powers of Lourdes were ineffective even for the head of the church that promotes its miracle cures. He died the following year.

As the evidence indicates, Lourdes offers pilgrims only the illusion of miracles. The overwhelming millions of visitors to the shrine receive no benefits, unless false hope can be considered one. They are instead drained of money that enriches the town of Lourdes by some $400 million annually—money that could be better spent on medical science.

Attributable in part to the success of Lourdes, other "curative" waters are (so to speak) springing up elsewhere. One is at Tlacote, Mexico, where a ranch owner claimed that his well water could cure any disease, including AIDS. Scientists determined that the well yielded only ordinary water but noted that it was safe to drink.

A different verdict was rendered in the case of water on the Rockdale County, Georgia, property of Nancy Fowler, a woman who claimed to see scheduled apparitions of the Virgin Mary. Mrs. Fowler stated that her well water had been blessed when Jesus Christ himself appeared to her. However, a sample of the water was found to be contaminated with coliform bacteria and therefore unsuitable for drinking. The Rockdale County Health Department asked the visionary to post a sign at the well to warn people of the possible danger (Nickell 1998, 153). (I later drank the water after it had been treated and suffered no ill effects.)

Then there is the "Lourdes of the Bronx"—as the *New York Times* dubbed it—where curative water flows from a rocky replica of the French grotto. The fake spring is only piped city water, but the parish priest blesses the water annually in a special rite. The parish business manager says of some people's claims of miracles at the local shrine: "I can't prove anything but the faith they had in the Lord and themselves. I do know there is something here you can't touch, see or feel. But there is something here" (Gonzalez 1992).

That "something" is the aura of the miraculous attending ordinary water set in a religious context and offered to the credulous—especially those who are desperate for help.

References

The Fountain of Youth. 2005a. Web gallery of art. www.wga.hu/html/c/cranach/lucas_ e/8/0fountain.html (accessed July 1).

———. 2005b. www.fountainofyouth.com (accessed July 7).

———. 2005c. http://tfn.net/Springs/FountainofYouth.html/c/cranach/ (accessed July 1).

Gonzalez, David. 1992. At Lourdes of Bronx, where cooling hope flows. *New York Times,* May 27.

Jones, Alison. 1994. *The Wordsworth Dictionary of Saints.* Ware, England: Wordsworth Editions.

Morris, Linda. 2004. Priest offers $5,000 to disprove miracles of Lourdes. *Sydney Morning Herald,* August 30.

Nickell, Joe. 1998. *Looking for a Miracle: Weeping Icons, Relics, Stigmata, Visions and Healing Cures.* Amherst, N.Y.: Prometheus Books.

Ponce de León, Juan. 2005. http://library.thinkingquest.org/J0002678F/ponce_de_ leon.htm (accessed July 1).

Swanner, Grace Maguire. 1988. *Saratoga: Queen of Spas.* Utica: N.Y.: North Country Books.

Who wants to live forever? 2000. *Economist,* December 23, 23–24.

UFOS OVER BUFFALO!

FLYING SAUCERS BUZZING BUFFALO? The "rock jocks" from Buffalo radio station WEDG's popular morning show "Shredd & Ragan" challenged us in July 2003 to explain several UFOs that a listener had caught on video. We accepted.

The Evidence

I confess that I was not eager to accept this pig-in-a-poke deal, being hopelessly overextended already and always leery of frivolous claims. (One can spend a huge amount of time trying to explain some anomaly that is of interest to one puzzled person—or even an attention-seeking hoaxer.) However, Center for Inquiry communications director Kevin Christopher twisted my overworked arm, noting that the case was destined to garner attention and that, being local, it was more accessible to investigation; he also assured me that other staffers—including three summer interns—would be glad to provide yeoman's service. Kevin prevailed, and I would later tell him (quoting a famous letter from President Abraham Lincoln to General Ulysses S. Grant), "You were right, and I was wrong."

I insisted on one thing, however: receipt of an affidavit from the eyewitness detailing the conditions under which his video had been made and attesting that it was unaltered. This was immediately forthcoming (Szeglowski 2003), and, with greetings from his partner Ted Shredd, Tom Ragan personally delivered a copy of the videotape to us.[1] Viewing the video, besides Kevin and me, were experienced videographer and editor Tom Flynn, *Skeptical Inquirer* managing editor Benjamin Radford, assistant communications director John Gaeddert (who chronicled our project's activities), and interns Dawn Peterson, Benjamin Hyink, and Chris Lauer.

The video—which was made near downtown Buffalo at about 6:50 P.M.

206

Figure 53. UFOs near downtown Buffalo, New York, were caught on amateur video. Local radio hosts challenged CSICOP to investigate. (Courtesy of *Skeptical Inquirer* magazine)

on Sunday, July 13, 2003—depicted several "bright lights in the eastern sky," as the amateur videographer himself termed the UFOs (figure 53). "After observing these lights with my girlfriend and child for several moments," he stated, "I then grabbed my video camera"—a handheld Canon 8mm model—"and began to film these lights." He then quickly obtained a tripod to steady the camera (Szeglowski 2003).

The Investigation

Two unusual effects on the video—the lights blinking simultaneously and the whole picture going dark at one point—were readily explained by our video expert Tom Flynn: the blinking was an effect of the "searching" function of the camera's autofocus when image details are especially poor, and the image darkening was almost certainly caused by the inadvertent pushing of the fade-out button. These effects were not actually observed in the sky but rather viewed through the camera—both by the eyewitness and by his girlfriend, using the camcorder's flip-out LCD screen. Flynn called our attention to the moment when the screen was unfolded from the camcorder body.

But what were the lights—the UFOs—themselves? We could see that, in relation to the power lines, they were moving slowly and so were not stars or planets. Given the position of the sun, behind the camera, we thought it likely that the objects were not transmitting light but simply *reflecting* sunlight. After eliminating such possibilities as birds, gliders, helicopters, satellites, and other aerial phenomena, we settled on two basic hypotheses. Some thought that the shining objects could be distant airplanes, while I brought up the possibility of balloons.

After viewing the video, Ben Radford circulated a memo citing evidence that the UFOs were apparently drifting rather than flying. He dubbed them "Unidentified Floating Objects," consistent with balloons (Radford 2003). Chris Lauer, pursuing a double major in meteorology and computer science at North Carolina State University, ruled out weather balloons, which he had experience observing. However, he agreed that small helium-filled party balloons were a good possibility. Even those subscribing to the airplanes hypothesis agreed that conducting some simple experiments with balloons was a good idea. We performed them at approximately the same time of day and under similar conditions as the UFO sighting.

Our first set of experiments (July 25) was a failure. Our initial balloon releases were too far from the video and still cameras, but when we corrected that problem, we discovered that flat, shiny, Mylar balloons tilted in the wind, flashing like signal mirrors. So, for the second set of experiments (July 28), we used round, sixteen-inch white balloons (figure 54), and their similarity to the UFOs was immediately apparent. On video, the results were striking (figure 55), even replicating the "blinking" effect. Everyone agreed with Flynn's assessment of "98 percent confidence that we have identified the mechanism" responsible for the UFOs.

Seemingly corroborative evidence was provided by our team's student meteorologist. Lauer (2003) determined from posted airport records that on the day in question, the winds were from the southwest at nine miles per hour. This was consistent with the left-drifting, receding UFOs in the video, which (since the camera faced east) indicated that the objects were drifting

Figure 54. Dawn Peterson prepares to release balloons as part of an experiment to replicate the UFO video. (Also shown are Paul Kurtz, Joe Nickell, John Gaeddert, and Ben Radford.) (Courtesy of *Skeptical Inquirer* magazine)

Figure 55. Balloons replicated the appearance of the UFOs in the video. (Courtesy of *Skeptical Inquirer* magazine)

northeastwardly, as expected. Also, someone noted that white, helium-filled balloons might have been released in keeping with a local wedding custom.

The Presentation

To see how convincing our results would be to others, we decided to play a little trick on our radio friends. Keeping the details of our solution a secret, Kevin Christopher invited Tom Ragan to a video presentation at the Center for Inquiry. At the showing, while I made introductory remarks about the original UFO video, Flynn played a clip from *our* video. Ragan acknowledged that the segment looked like the original video he had seen. I then confessed the trick, and we played both videos for him to judge. He agreed that ours was a convincing replication.

Before our appearance on "Shredd & Ragan," the radio duo's producer put our video clip on the station's Internet site (wedg.com 2003), along with the original video that had already been airing. The unscientific poll showed that a greater percentage of respondents actually thought that ours was more con-vincing than the original (52.39 percent versus 49.4 percent).[2] Subsequently, on August 25, Tom Flynn and I appeared as guests on "Shredd & Ragan." With quips and banter, we explained the approach we had taken, and both Shredd and Ragan concluded on air that we had convincingly solved the mystery. Our group had transformed the UFOs into IFOs: identified floating objects.

Notes

1. The original 8-mm tape had been transferred to a VHS tape.
2. After we revealed on "Shredd & Ragan" how our video had been produced, the positive poll results naturally declined.

References

Gaeddert, John D. 2003. Project chronology and notes, July 30.
Lauer, Chris. 2003. Memo to Kevin Christopher, August 8.
Radford, Benjamin. 2003. Memo to project members, July 22.
Szeglowski, Jack. 2003. Notarized affidavit accompanying UFO video, July 17.
wedg.com/snr/ufosighting.html. 2003. Accessed July 28 and August 20.

SECOND SIGHT:
THE PHENOMENON OF
EYELESS VISION

Natasha Demkina claims a special ability: she can supposedly peer inside people's bodies, observe their organs, and diagnose malfunctions and diseases (Girl 2004; Baty 2004). For a Discovery Channel documentary, *The Girl with X-ray Eyes,* CSICOP (now CSI) was asked to test the seventeen-year-old Russian girl's alleged visionary abilities.

Natasha's alleged ability falls under the heading of clairvoyance ("clear seeing"), also known as second sight. This is the purported perception of objects, people, or events other than by the normal senses—that is, a form of extrasensory perception (ESP). Mystics claim that there are various states of clairvoyance, including two that are relevant to Natasha's claims: X-ray clairvoyance, "the ability to see through opaque objects such as envelopes, containers, and walls to perceive what lies within or beyond," and medical clairvoyance, "the ability to see disease and illness in the human body, either by reading the aura or seeing the body as transparent" (Guiley 1991, 111–13). Needless to say, like other forms of ESP, neither of these alleged abilities has been scientifically verified.

X-ray Clairvoyance

Demonstrations of X-ray clairvoyance date back many centuries, as do revelations that they can be accomplished by deception. For example, in the sixteenth century, Reginald Scot explained how a trickster could use an accomplice to receive secret information. "By this means," he wrote in his classic treatise *The Discoverie of Witchcraft* (1564), "If you have aine invention [any inventiveness] you may seem to doo a hundreth miracles, and to discover the secrets of a mans thoughts or words spoken a far off."

Just such feats were being performed in 1831 by the "Double-sighted Phenomenon," an eight-year-old Scottish lad named Louis Gordon M'Kean.

Blindfolded and facing away from the audience, the kilted youth readily identified watches, coins, snuffboxes, and the like. He could also repeat what others had spoken, even though they whispered the words at a distance of 100 yards (Nickell 1992, 70).

Similar performances were put on by an English woman known only as the "Mysterious Lady." She appeared at the Egyptian Hall in Piccadilly in 1845 and also toured New England, where she apparently came to the attention of Nathaniel Hawthorne. He portrayed a strikingly similar clairvoyant, named the "Veiled Lady," in his 1852 novel *The Blithedale Romance* (Dawes 1979, 147; Nickell 1991, 126–37).

A contemporary of the Mysterious Lady was Scotland's John Henry Anderson, styled the "Wizard of the North." His magic act featured his blindfolded daughter, billed as the "Second-Sighted Sybil." Anderson would leave the stage for this routine, going into the audience to select the objects for remote viewing (Dawes 1979, 110–11).

To thwart skeptics who might have guessed that a prearranged code was being used, some performers utilized a method in which not a single word was uttered. This technique was employed in 1848 by the great French conjurer Robert-Houdin (from whom young Ehrich Weiss would derive the name Houdini). He performed *La Second Vue* (Second Sight) with his young son Emile. The boy's eyes were bandaged, and his father rang a bell to indicate when an object was being held up for identification. There are many clever ways of accomplishing such a feat (Nickell 1992, 73–74).

The ability to see while apparently securely blindfolded is a magician's secret used by many who lay claim to mysterious powers. One such alleged power is known variously as dermo-optical perception, paroptic vision, skin vision, or simply eyeless sight. Supposedly, this involves reading printed matter by means of the fingertips, divining colors by holding objects to the cheek, and similar demonstrations. The phenomenon has appeared in various guises over the centuries, being associated, for example, with mesmerism in the 1840s.

Experimental work in both the United States and the Soviet Union in the 1960s sparked new interest in eyeless sight. For example, in 1962 a Soviet newspaper reported that twenty-two-year-old Rosa Kuleshova could read with her middle finger and accurately describe magazine pictures. Before long, other Soviet women discovered that they too possessed this amazing gift. Ninel Kulagina, a housewife in Leningrad, not only could read while blindfolded but also could propel small objects across a table, apparently by mere concentration (Christopher 1975, 77–86).

In the United States, *Life* magazine's June 12, 1964, issue carried accounts of these Russian marvels. Years earlier (April 19, 1937), *Life* had featured the phenomenon of dermo-optical perception. At that time, it was being demonstrated by a thirteen-year-old California lad named Pat Marquis, "the boy with the X-ray eyes."

Alas, each of the various X-ray wonders was soon discredited. Pat Marquis was tested by ESP pioneer J. B. Rhine and was caught peeking down his nose. When the Soviet marvels were tested in ways that did not allow them to peek, the remarkable phenomenon ceased.

As magicians know, it is difficult to prevent a determined trickster from peeking, since there are numerous ways to do it. For example, one ten-year-old Soviet girl took advantage of her turned-up nose, which helped her circumvent a pair of opaque goggles. Many circus entertainers, such as high-wire walkers, jugglers, knife throwers, and archers, have long employed trick blindfolds (Christopher 1975, 81–86; Gardner 1987, 63–73).

Among the most famous of the eyeless-sight feats is the celebrated "blindfold drive," which has a long and colorful history. The "thought reader" Washington Irving Bishop (1856–1889) performed it with a horse-drawn carriage in the late 1880s, and many others followed suit. In modern times, automobiles have been used. I have even performed the feat myself, wearing an examined blindfold followed by a black cloth sack placed over the head and tied at the neck (figures 56 and 57).

Laypeople observing such feats often come up with imaginative theories to explain them. A British performer—only one of many who claimed the title the "Man with the X-ray Eyes"—prompted several unique guesses when he drove a car around a farmyard while blindfolded. One observer opined that the alleged visionary had "fiber optics up his nose," and another thought that he possessed "supersensitive hearing which detected the sound of squeaking mice hidden in straw bales." The actual secrets are far simpler (Nickell 1992, 69–80).

Figures 56 and 57. The author dons an opaque blindfold, followed by a black cloth hood. He then performs the celebrated "blindfold drive" feat—a supposed demonstration of "second sight." (Photos for author by Robert H. van Outer)

But what about a performer whose ability to perceive is apparently limited neither by blindfolding nor by solid metal shielding? Such a "phenomenal mystifier"—as the Great Houdini called him—was Joaquin Maria Argamasilla, the "Spaniard with X-ray Eyes." He could tell time from a watch whose case was snapped shut or read a calling card or message locked in a box. Houdini investigated the Spanish marvel in 1924 and determined that Argamasilla used a simple blindfold and was obviously peeking. Houdini maneuvered into position behind the mystifier, allowing him to peer over Argamasilla's shoulder. Houdini discovered that the Spaniard opened the watch case a trifle under cover of a sweeping motion, and the lid of the padlocked box could be raised slightly at the corner, permitting a brief glimpse of the contents. Houdini offered a test by supplying two boxes, neither of which could be opened even slightly. He later wrote, "Argamasilla failed by refusal to make a test in both instances" (Gibson and Young 1953, 248–57).

Another X-ray clairvoyant appeared on the *Jerry Springer Show* in 1992, where he seemingly divined the contents of a locked and guarded refrigerator. I was on the show as well and was suspicious of the whole performance. I challenged the marvel to a test of his ability using sealed envelopes, which he failed. Later, I analyzed a videotape of the fridge stunt. The descriptions of the various items were not *visually* accurate (for instance, the psychic described a *carton* rather than a *jug* of milk) but only *cognitively* so—consistent with the hypothesis that the alleged clairvoyant had been tipped off as to the refrigerator's contents (Nickell 2001, 54–59).

To date, no one has demonstrated convincingly, under suitably controlled conditions, the existence of X-ray sight or any other form of clairvoyance or ESP.

Medical Clairvoyance

The other type of alleged clairvoyance is medical intuition, a resurgent pseudoscientific fad based on so-called energy medicine. It involves psychically divining people's illnesses and, often, recommending treatment.

The approach is as ancient as it is primitive, being akin to the magical, divinatory efforts of shamans, medicine men, or witch doctors or to the practice of astrological medicine in the Middle Ages (Porter 1997, 14, 25). A forerunner of modern spiritualists, Andrew Jackson Davis (1826–1910) was known as the "Poughkeepsie Seer" for his ability to diagnose illnesses while in a supposed mesmeric trance. Another was Antoinette (Mrs. J. H. R.) Matteson (1847–1913), a "clairvoyant doctress" and spiritualist who, suitably self-entranced, divined formulas for her custom-bottled "Clairvoyant Remedies" (Nickell 2004).

The most famous medical clairvoyant was "Sleeping Prophet" Edgar Cayce (1877–1945), who gave diagnostic and prescriptive readings while supposedly hypnotized. His early studies of osteopathy, homeopathy, and other quaint theories of healing influenced his approach, and in addition to osteopathic manipulations he prescribed electrical treatments, special diets, and various strange remedies. According to Martin Gardner (1957, 218), these included such medicines as "oil of smoke" (to treat a leg sore), "peach-tree poultice" (for a baby's convulsions), and "bedbug juice" (to treat dropsy).

Cayce's touted successes at diagnosis and treatment are not surprising. His diagnoses were obviously aided by letters he had received containing specific details about the illnesses for which readings were sought. Moreover, Cayce's responses were laced with such expressions as "perhaps" and "I feel that," thus avoiding positive declarations. Even so, he sometimes gave these supposedly psychic diagnoses for persons who had already died (Randi 1982, 189–92). As for Cayce's supposedly successful treatments, they might have been due to the body's natural healing ability, the spontaneous remission of some conditions, the placebo effect, delayed results of prior medical intervention, and other factors, including misdiagnosis and selective reporting of positive outcomes (the dead do not give testimonials). (See Nickell 1998, 131–66.)

In recent years, the practice of medical clairvoyance has gained new impetus from some popular books. These include *Second Sight,* written by Judith Orloff (1996), a psychiatrist who fancies that she has psychic abilities, and the best-selling *Why People Don't Heal and How They Can,* by Caroline Myss (1997), "who has a background in theology" (Koontz 2000, 102). As is typical of self-styled medical intuitives, Orloff and Myss have many of the traits associated with a fantasy-prone personality (Nickell 2004, 214–16).

Girl with X-ray Eyes

Natasha Demkina's claimed ability combines features of both X-ray clairvoyance and medical clairvoyance. Yet she declined my suggestion that she attempt to identify simple, easily recognizable objects—such as a pair of scissors—merely placed inside my sport coat. This seemed to me a far easier and potentially less ambiguous test than looking through both clothing and flesh and identifying subtle alterations in organs. However, she told me (through a translator) that—inexplicably—she could only "see" through living tissue, leaving me to wonder whether some of her touted successes were dependent on the ambiguity that necessarily results from such a descriptive process.

Although a few medical intuitives purport to see the body as transparent, most do not; instead, they claim to get their knowledge by reading the subject's "aura" or by some other—even more remote—means. Some nineteenth-century practitioners had curious techniques: one offered "Medical Diagnosis by Lock of Hair," while another worked via his "Spirit-Physicians" (*Medium* 1875).

Natasha's claimed power, then, is rather distinctive, but it also seems to be nonexistent. In Britain she appeared on ITV's *This Morning,* and at first she seemed to impress the program's resident physician, Chris Steele. She said that he might have problems with his stomach, liver, pancreas, and kidneys; however, subsequent medical tests revealed Natasha's claims to be erroneous. As for the CSICOP test conducted in New York City on May 1, 2004, she failed to demonstrate the power of X-ray vision (see Hyman 2005; Skolnick 2005).

References

Baty, Phil. 2004. Scientists fail to see eye to eye over girl's "x-ray vision." *Times Higher Education Supplement,* December 10.

Christopher, Milbourne. 1975. *Mediums, Mystics and the Occult.* New York: Thomas Y. Crowell.

Dawes, Edwin A. 1979. *The Great Illusionists.* Secaucus, N.J.: Chartwell Books.

Gardner, Martin. 1957. *Fads and Fallacies in the Name of Science.* New York: Dover.

———. 1987. *Science: Good, Bad and Bogus.* Buffalo, N.Y.: Prometheus Books.

Gibson, Walter B., and Morriss N. Young, eds. 1953. *Houdini on Magic.* New York: Dover.

The Girl with the X-ray eyes. 2004. *Fortean Times* 182 (May): 4–5.

Guiley, Rosemary Ellen. 1991. *Harper's Encyclopedia of Mystical and Paranormal Experience.* New York: HarperCollins.

Hyman, Ray. 2005. Testing Natasha. *Skeptical Inquirer* 29, no. 3 (May–June): 27–33.

Koontz, Katy. 2000. The new health detectives. *New Age* (January–February): 64–66, 102–10.

The Medium and Daybreak. 1875. London, August 13, 527.

Myss, Caroline. 1997. *Why People Don't Heal and How They Can.* New York: Harmony Books.

Nickell, Joe. 1991. *Ambrose Bierce Is Missing and Other Historical Mysteries.* Lexington: University Press of Kentucky.

———. 1992. *Mysterious Realms.* Buffalo, N.Y.: Prometheus Books.

———. 1998. *Looking for a Miracle: Weeping Icons, Relics, Stigmata, Visions and Healing Cures.* Amherst, N.Y.: Prometheus Books.

———. 2001. *Real-Life X-Files.* Lexington: University Press of Kentucky.

———. 2004. *The Mystery Chronicles: More Real-Life X-Files.* Lexington: University Press of Kentucky.

Orloff, Judith. 1996. *Second Sight.* New York: Warner Books.

Porter, Roy. 1997. *Medicine: A History of Healing.* New York: Barnes & Noble.

Randi, James. 1982. *Flim-Flam!* Buffalo, N.Y.: Prometheus Books.

Scot, Reginald. 1564. *The Discoverie of Witchcraft.* Reprint (from a 1930 English edition), New York: Dover, 1972.

Skolnick, Andrew A. 2005. Natasha Demkina: The girl with normal eyes. *Skeptical Inquirer* 29, no. 3 (May–June): 34–37.

MONSTERS IN THE LAKES

THE PHENOMENON OF LAKE MONSTERS deserves book-length treatment, which my colleague Benjamin Radford and I provided in *Lake Monster Mysteries: Investigating the World's Most Elusive Creatures* (2006). Although the famous alleged monster habitats, such as Scotland's Loch Ness and North America's Lake Champlain, tend to get the most attention, there are numerous less well-known domains.

One of these is Canada's Lake Simcoe, some forty miles north of Toronto. It supposedly holds a monster known as Igopogo (after its more famous relative Ogopogo in Lake Okanagan, British Columbia), among other appellations. Residents of Beaverton, on the eastern shore, call it Beaverton Bessie, while others refer to it as Kempenfelt Kelly, after Kempenfelt Bay, which has the lake's deepest water and claims the most monster sightings. Sources refer vaguely to early "Indian legends" of the monster and sporadic reports of a "sea serpent" in the lake during the nineteenth century. Important sightings occurred in 1952 and 1963 (Costello 1974, 229), and a "sonar sounding of a large animal" in 1983 was followed by a videotape in 1991 of "a large, seal-like animal" (Eberhart 2002, 242–45).

Significantly, according to John Robert Colombo in his *Mysterious Canada* (1988, 153), "No two descriptions of Kempenfelt Kelly coincide." Nevertheless, cryptozoologist George M. Eberhart (2002, 244) attempted a portrait:

Physical Description: Seal-like animal. Length, 12–70 feet. Charcoal-gray color. Dog- or horse-like face. Prominent eyes. Gaping mouth. Neck is like a stovepipe. Several dorsal fins. Fishlike tail.
Behavior. Basks in the sun.

In August 2005, supported by Discovery Canada's science program *Daily*

Planet and by the tourism department of the city of Barrie, Radford and I went in search of the elusive creature. We conducted interviews and searched Kempenfelt Bay using a boat equipped with sonar and an underwater camera.

First, however, we visited the home of retired businessman Arch Brown, who claimed to have coined the name "Kempenfelt Kelly" and to have personally witnessed four sightings of the legendary monster. He acknowledged that he was predisposed to believe. His Scottish father had told him of the Loch Ness monster, and since he had formerly resided in British Columbia, he was well aware of Ogopogo. When he moved to Barrie many years ago, he said, he was prompted by local reports to be "on the lookout" for the monster, spending many hours at the task (Brown 2005).

Over the years, Brown had had no fewer than four sightings—all from a distance, unfortunately. Once he saw the creature from an estimated quarter of a mile away but nevertheless described it as being ten feet long and having a dark gray, serpentlike body and a dog-shaped head. It swam, he told us, with an undulating, up-and-down motion. Less seriously, he added that it had "an impish look" and a kind disposition that kept it from frightening children (Brown 2005). Like many of the other sightings, his could reasonably be explained by otters swimming in a line, diving and resurfacing. Our boat captain, Jerry Clayton (2005), specifically mentioned otters as a likelihood for some sightings. Brown (2005) himself acknowledged that there are otters—as well as beavers, minks, and other animals—in the vicinity, although he did not believe that any of these were responsible for his sightings.

As for the 1983 sonar report, Clayton showed us on his sonar screen what were clearly individual fish, as well as occasional larger forms that he attributed to schools of small fish being "read" by the sonar as a single unit. The underwater camera showed only nonmonstrous fish. Clayton (2005) told us that he had been on Lake Simcoe for eighteen years. "I've dragged a lot of lines for a lot of miles here on this lake, and—nothing," he said.

Although widely reported, lake monsters are of doubtful reality—for a variety of reasons. For example, for some hitherto unknown species to continue to reproduce over time, there would have to be a sizable breeding herd—in which case a floating or beached carcass should eventually be encountered. It also seems unlikely that there would be some multimillion-year-old creature (such as the often suggested plesiosaur) in a lake that (like Lake Champlain) is only roughly 10,000 years old (see Nickell 2003).

At least two lakes from my native Kentucky are even less likely to hold the monsters they are alleged to contain. Cryptozoologist Roy P. Mackal's *Searching for Hidden Animals* (1980, 220) mentions Herrington Lake and Kentucky Lake as the subjects of monster reports that may be worthy of investigation. And George Eberhart's *Mysterious Creatures: A Guide to Cryptozoology* (2002, 682) specifically cites a fifteen-foot "prehistoric creature" that was reportedly seen several times in Herrington Lake in 1972. Neither author provides further information about the Kentucky Lake sightings. The problem with both sets of reports is that the two lakes are *man-made!* According to *The Kentucky Encyclopedia* (Kleber 1992, 532), Herrington Lake was formed in 1925, and Kentucky Lake in 1944. How (monster promoters should be asked) can lakes of such construction and recent vintage be populated by prehistoric or exotic animals?

The answer, of course, is that such sightings are fostered at least in part by wishful thinking. I suspect that if an alleged monster-bearing lake could be drained, and thus the absence of any monster conclusively demonstrated, the sightings would continue when the lake was refilled.

References

Brown, Arch. 2005. Interview by Joe Nickell.

Clayton, Jerry. 2005. Interview by Benjamin Radford.

Colombo, John Robert. 1988. *Mysterious Canada.* Toronto: Doubleday Canada.

Costello, Peter. 1974. *In Search of Lake Monsters.* New York: Coward, McCann & Geoghegan.

Eberhart, George M. 2002. *Mysterious Creatures: A Guide to Cryptozoology.* Santa Barbara, Calif.: ABC-CLIO.

Kleber, John, ed. 1992. *The Kentucky Encyclopedia.* Lexington: University Press of Kentucky.

Mackal, Roy P. 1980. *Searching for Hidden Animals.* New York: Doubleday.

Nickell, Joe. 2003. Legend of the Lake Champlain monster. *Skeptical Inquirer* 27, no. 4 (July–August): 18–23.

Radford, Benjamin, and Joe Nickell. 2006. *Lake Monster Mysteries: Investigating the World's Most Elusive Creatures.* Lexington: University Press of Kentucky.

THE "NEW" IDOLATRY

FOR A LIVE, PRIME-TIME TELEVISION PROGRAM, I was asked to evaluate claims that a statue in Sacramento streamed tears of blood. The case prompted me to take a retrospective look at a wide variety of related phenomena, ranging from weeping icons to perambulating statues, many of which I personally investigated over the years.

Idolatry

Belief that an effigy is in some way animated (from *anima,* "breath") not only challenges science's natural-world view but also crosses a theological line. It moves from veneration (reverence toward an image) to idolatry (image worship), in which the image is regarded as the "tenement or vehicle of the god and fraught with divine influence" (*Encyclopaedia Britannica* 1960, s.v. "Idolatry"). Religious prohibitions against idolatry are ancient. In the Old Testament, the second commandment is an injunction against "graven images," but only those that were adored or served (Exodus 20:4–5); others were explicitly allowed (Exodus 25:18). Influenced by Islam and Judaism, a movement of iconoclasts (Greek for "image breakers") lasting from about 723 to 842 sought to carry out the injunction, destroying countless religious works and persecuting those who made and venerated them. In the ninth century, iconoclasm was declared a heresy.

Images proliferated, being widely used for ornamental, instructional, and devotional purposes. In the Orthodox Church, image veneration largely focused on icons (wood panels painted in the Byzantine tradition) and was generally more elaborate than the veneration in Roman Catholicism, which tended to favor statues (*Collier's Encyclopedia* 1993, s.v. "Images").

A new iconoclasm arose during the Protestant Reformation in sixteenth-century Europe. Reformers such as Martin Luther and John Calvin listed image worship among the church's excesses. Ironically, Catholic Bibles (unlike Protestant ones) contain an extra, fourteenth chapter of Daniel that condemns idolatry with a story. The tale involves the Babylonian idol of Bel (or Baal), which consumed vast quantities of food and wine—or so it seemed. The apparent miracle convinced King Cyrus to worship the idol. However, Daniel sifted ashes on the floor of the sealed temple and so recorded the footprints of the priests and their families who used "secret doors" to enter and devour the offerings. As Daniel reasoned to the king, the idol consisted only of brass-covered clay and "never ate or drank anything." Nor, he might have added by way of extrapolation, do statues move, weep, bleed, or otherwise become animated. Or was Daniel wrong?

Animated Statues

In September 1995, reminiscent of the idol of Bel, statues of Lord Ganesh and other Indian deities throughout the Hindu world began to sip spoonfuls of milk offered to them. Some observers noticed milk pooling at the bottoms of the statues, but they could not explain how it was getting there. The secret was discovered by government scientists, who offered a statue milk mixed with red dye and noted that although the liquid disappeared from the spoon, it coated the statue due to surface tension. (This is the same principle that causes two drops of liquid that are brought together to form a single drop.) The spoon was naturally tilted a bit, and the milk was imperceptibly drawn over the wet (ritually washed) idol. I was able to study the phenomenon when Indian skeptic Vikas Gora visited my paranormal investigation lab in May 2001. He had witnessed the original "miracle" and taught me how to make statues and figurines seem to drink (Nickell 2001, 312–15).

In contrast to this singular Hindu case, Roman Catholicism has yielded several modern instances of allegedly animated statues. In 1981, for example, in a church at Thornton, California, a sculpted Virgin Mary not only altered the angle of her eyes and the tilt of her chin, churchgoers reported, but also wept and even strolled about the church at night. Although no one actually witnessed the latter, the statue was frequently found several feet from its usual location, standing at the altar. A bishop's investigation, however, failed to support the miracle claims. Investigating clerics determined that the purported movement of the statue's eyes and chin were merely due to variations in photographic angles. Worse, they branded the weeping and perambulations a probable hoax. For their efforts, the investigators were denounced by some believers, even being called "a bunch of devils" (Nickell 1998, 67).

In 1985 came reports that a figure of the Virgin in a grotto at Ballinspittle, Ireland, had begun to sway gently. Thousands of pilgrims, eager to witness the phenomenon, flocked to the village to view the statue, which was adorned with a halo of blue lights. It remained for a group of scientists from University College, Cork, to discover the truth. They too saw the figure sway, yet a motion-picture camera revealed that no such movement had occurred, and they soon determined that the effect was an illusion. According to the science magazine *Discover* (Those 1985, 19):

> It is induced when people rock gently back and forth while looking at the statue. At dusk, when the sky is grey and landmarks are obscured, the eye has no point of reference except the halo of blue lights. Therefore, say the scientists, the eye is unable to detect the fact that one's head and body are unconsciously moving. The viewer who sways is likely to get the impression that not he but the statue is moving.

Other phenomena were reported in Pennsylvania in 1989. The case began on Good Friday at the Holy Trinity Church in Ambridge, a quiet Ohio River mill town fifteen miles northwest of Pittsburgh. During the service, a luminous, life-size crucifixion figure of Christ reportedly closed its eyes. At first, no one claimed to have seen the eyelids actually moving; it was only noted that when the statue had been relocated in January, the eyes had been about one-third open, but during the special three-hour prayer meeting, the eyes were observed to be shut. However, the pastor of the church was soon reporting additional claims: "At times the eyes seem to be opening and a little later seem to close again." An investigation was launched by the diocese, with a commission appointed to examine the evidence and report on the astonishing phenomenon. After careful study of the before-and-after videotapes, the commission found "no convincing evidence" that the statue had closed its eyes during the Good Friday service. When close-up views of the face from each videotape showed the eyes in a similar, partially open position, the commission rejected claims that a miracle had occurred. Commission members stated that they believed the witnesses were sincere but could have been deceived by the church's lighting and by the angles of viewing. In the wake of the commission's report, the pastor was barred from celebrating Mass, and he responded by resigning (Nickell 1998, 65–66).

But if that statue's eyes did not close, what about another's that allegedly opened? They belonged to a "sleeping" figure of Jesus that a Hoboken, New Jersey, street "preacher" had rescued from a garbage bin. He claimed in July 2005 that while he was cleaning the figurine it opened its right eye. Stories soon spread of the statue "blinking" its right eye, turning its head, and performing other unverifiable feats. Actually, the statue's eyes were never closed. I studied high-resolution photos of the figure and determined that it had glass eyes and that portions of its upper and lower right eyelids had been broken off, explaining the opening-eye effect (Nickell 2005).

Other statue animations have been reported, including chameleonesque effects. For example, the previously mentioned eye-closing statue at Ambridge, Pennsylvania, also reportedly changed color—from vivid tones on Good Friday to dull ones afterward. However, these were attributed to the lighting and to pious imagination.

Similar explanations applied to a thirty-inch figure of Mary in a church at Paterson, New Jersey, that reportedly changed color in 1992. One witness saw the base of the statue turn a "dark, dark pink," while another said the figure "turned the brightest blue." The statue was actually white with pink and blue tones, and the effect appeared to correlate with the emotive force of the believers. Not surprisingly, many people were unable to witness the color change and went away disappointed (Nickell 1998, 66–67).

Still other statues, at a Marian apparition site in Conyers, Georgia, supposedly had even more remarkable signs of life: they were said to have heartbeats! I was asked by an Atlanta television station to investigate these claims (and others), but I found no heartbeats detectable by stethoscope (figure 58). In fact, as people reached up to feel the throbbings, they were feeling either the pulse in their own thumbs or the effects of pious imagination (Nickell 1996).

Figure 58. At a Marian apparition site at Conyers, Georgia, the author examines a statue of the Virgin Mary that some pilgrims claim has a heartbeat. (Photo for author by William Evans)

Exuding Effigies

Not only statues but also icons and other images may seemingly become animated (icons are common in Orthodox churches). According to D. Scott Rogo, in his *Miracles: A Parascientific Inquiry into Wondrous Phenomena* (1982, 161):

226

Cases of religious statues, paintings, icons, and other effigies that suddenly begin to bleed or weep have been documented throughout history. Before Rome was sacked in 1527, for instance, a statue of Christ housed in a local monastery wept for several days. When the city of Syracuse in Sicily lay under Spanish siege in 1719, a marble statue of St. Lucy in the city cried continually.

Similar manifestations have been reported in modern times. Interestingly, Syracuse was the site of another "weeping" statue in 1953. It was reported that the liquid was consistent with real tears, although doubts were raised about the scientific competency and impartiality of the investigators. The woman who owned the original statue had received it as a wedding gift in March, and it began to weep in her presence in late August, the culmination of several weeks of upheaval in her household. She was pregnant, and for several weeks she had been suffering "seizures," fainting spells, and attacks of blindness. Local doctors were unable to diagnose her condition, and she may have been seeking attention. That case was followed by an epidemic of similar manifestations across Roman Catholic Italy. Rogo (1982, 178) remarked that they were "no doubt spawned by wide press coverage of the Syracuse miracle."

Two other Italian cases are especially instructive. In one that took place in Pavia in 1980, no one witnessed the initial weeping, and the woman who owned the plaster bas-relief was caught surreptitiously applying "tears" with a water pistol. In 1995 an epidemic of crying effigies followed one that began weeping bloody tears in Sardinia. However, DNA tests on the blood revealed that it belonged to the statue's owner. Her attorney explained, "Well, the Virgin Mary had to get that blood from somewhere" (Nickell 1997b).

Another instructive case transpired in 1985 when a statue of the Virgin began first weeping and then bleeding in the home of a Quebec railroad worker. Soon the phenomenon spread to other nearby icons, statues, and crucifixes. Thousands of pilgrims waited in the brutal winter cold to view the "miracle"—as many as 12,000 in a single week. The local bishop went largely ignored when he implied that the affair was a false miracle. Then, suddenly, the Associated Press reported that it was "all a hoax—not even a very clever hoax." Newsmen from the Canadian Broadcasting Corporation had been permitted to borrow an icon and had it examined. They found that blood had been mixed with animal fat so that when the room warmed from the body heat of the pilgrims, the substance would liquefy and flow realistically. The owner confessed that he had used his own blood to produce the effects (Nickell 1998, 58).

The results are not always so definitive. An icon I investigated in Astoria, New York, on May 11, 1991, was no longer weeping, and my stereomicroscopic examination showed little. However, a videotape of the earlier weeping revealed that the "tear" rivulets flowed from *outside the eyes* and were greatly disproportionate to the diminutive size of the saint's face, observations that suggested a rather crude hoax (Nickell 1998, 54).

Later, the priest who had presided over the Astoria church during the weeping phenomenon relocated to a Toronto church, and one of its icons mysteriously began to weep. I was called in on the case twice: first by the *Toronto Sun* newspaper, and later by attorneys for the parent church. With a fraud squad detective standing by, I took samples of the oily "tears" for analysis by the Ontario Center of Forensic Sciences. The substance proved to be a nondrying oil, as I had surmised on inspection; its use is an effective trick, since one application remains fresh-looking indefinitely. Because no one could prove how the oil got on the icon, the legal case went nowhere, but the church's North American head pronounced it a hoax. And it turned out that the priest had previously been defrocked and excommunicated for working in a brothel in Athens (Nickell 1997a).

An interesting feature of the exuding icons is the variety of substances involved, along with some apparent trends. In Catholicism, the images tended to yield watery tears or blood until relatively recently, when there was an occasional shift to oil—seeming to tap into the Greek Orthodox tradition, which has received media attention of late. And in the Russian Orthodox tradition, the icons tend to exude myrrh (a fragrant resin) or myrrh-scented oil, as in a case I investigated in Moscow. The "myrrhing" involved an icon of the assassinated Czar Nicholas II, and it occurred at a time when there was a campaign to bestow sainthood on him and his family (Nickell 2002).

Investigative Approach

As these examples show, news reports of "weeping" and other animated effigies are occurring more frequently. Not a single one has ever been authenticated by science. However, rather than simply dismiss such claims, I actually investigate them—whenever possible.

It is not unusual for me to be refused access. For example, for a TV documentary about a comatose "miracle" girl named Audrey Santo, near whom icons and figurines dripped oil, producers requested that I be permitted to visit her Worcester, Massachusetts, home. The girl's mother agreed at first but then, on advice from a priest closely associated with the case, withdrew permission for my visit. I could only comment on the very suspicious circumstances of the case, including the fact that one test of the oil had revealed it to be 20 percent chicken fat (Nickell 1999).

One weeping icon was brought to me from Syria by a BBC producer. Suspiciously, it ceased to stream oil as soon as it left its owner, a member of the Chaldean Catholic Church. Alas, nothing—neither pleas nor insults, not even slicing onions before it—seems able to make it cry again, although I keep it as part of my paranormal collection (Nickell 2004).

Sometimes, I am contacted on short notice, such as when CNN asked me to assess the case of the aforementioned Sacramento statue that appeared to be crying blood. Fortunately, I had been able to examine photos and videos of the supposed weeping, allowing me to observe that the streams of "blood" came only from Mary's left eye, and that one of the rivulets actually began above and outside the eye itself. Moreover, the streams were not flowing but remained static, as if the red substance had merely been *applied* to the statue. Thus, when I appeared on *Paula Zahn Now* on December 2, 2005, I told the host that I had good news and bad news: the bad news was that the weeping was fake; the good news was that few of the faithful would believe me.

I also told the *Sacramento Bee* that the weeping was a "clumsy, obvious hoax" (Kollars and Fletcher 2005). When a church spokesperson, the Reverend James Murphy, said that there were no plans to investigate the incident, I responded: "If a statue is a fraud or a hoax, or even just a mistake, it should be determined and that should be that. If it's a fake, then it should be repudiated." However, Murphy expressed an all-too-typical attitude, stating, "If people view this as a miracle and it brings them closer to God, then that's a good thing" (Milbourn 2005). But such an end-justifies-the-means approach is untenable, especially given the seriousness of the matter: an affront to science, religion, ethics, good sense, and truth, all rolled in one.

References

Collier's Encyclopedia. 1993. New York: P. F. Collier.

Encyclopaedia Britannica. 1960. Chicago: Encyclopaedia Britannica.

Kollars, Deb, and Ed Fletcher. 2005. Weeping or not, Mary is a magnet. *Sacramento Bee,* December 7.

Milbourn, Todd. 2005. No probe is planned of "weeping" statue. *Sacramento Bee,* November 29.

Nickell, Joe. 1996. Examining miracle claims. *Deolog,* March 4–5, 14, 23.

———. 1997a. Something to cry about: The case of the weeping icon. *Skeptical Inquirer* 21, no. 2 (March–April): 19–20.

———. 1997b. Those tearful icons. *Free Inquiry* 17, no. 2 (Spring): 5, 7, 61.

———. 1998. *Looking for a Miracle.* Amherst, N.Y.: Prometheus Books.

———. 1999. Miracles or deception? The pathetic case of Audrey Santo. *Skeptical Inquirer* 23, no. 5 (September–October): 16–18.

———. 2001. *Real-Life X-Files.* Lexington: University Press of Kentucky.

———. 2002. Moscow mysteries. *Skeptical Inquirer* 26, no. 4 (July–August): 17–20, 24.

———. 2004. Gewezen wenend icoon [Formerly weeping icon]. *Skepter,* March, 41.

———. 2005. "Winking Jesus" statue: Mystery solved! *Skeptical Inquirer* 29, no. 6 (November–December): 7–8.

Rogo, Scott D. 1982. *Miracles: A Parascientific Inquiry into Wondrous Phenomena.* New York: Dial Press.

Those who sway together pray together. 1985. *Discover,* October, 19.

PSYCHIC SLEUTH
WITHOUT A CLUE

Despite the lack of scientific confirmation of their alleged powers, psychics continue to gain popularity in a credulous society. Some have undergone makeovers, transforming themselves from ordinary psychics to psychic sleuths and beyond—communicants with the great beyond, in fact. One such purveyor is Phil Jordan, whose flagging career has been given new impetus by popular TV mediums who purport to communicate with the dead. Jordan has climbed aboard that spiritualist bandwagon, so I donned a disguise to get close to him and check out his alleged powers.

Lesser Light

Phil Jordan, psychic sleuth–cum–spiritualist, was, he says, "raised on dreams" and experienced clairvoyant visions from about the age of six. Prompted in part by "severe unemployment," he decided to offer "psychic consultations" to the public. Two years later, he launched his reputation as a psychic detective by supposedly locating a missing five-year-old boy. Although Jordan claims to have been helpful in other cases, it is this one that receives the most attention in his autobiography *I Knew This Day Would Come: A Personal Journey to Psychic Self-Awareness* (Jordan 1999, 58–64).

The case—the rescue of Tommy Kennedy in Tioga County, New York— began on August 3, 1975. Young Kennedy had wandered away from his family at Empire Lake, and searchers feared that he might have fallen into the water and drowned. Using psychometry (or object reading, an alleged type of ESP), Jordan supposedly received impressions from the boy's discovered T-shirt. Jordan announced, "He's alive," and produced a sketch, claiming, "that's where they will find him." Subsequently, Jordan led searchers into the woods, where "they found the exhausted five-year-old, under a tree in the exact location sketched by the psychic the night before" (Randles and Hough 2001).

Unfortunately, the story has become "mythologized," according to Kenneth L. Feder and Michael Alan Park, who investigated the Kennedy case for my book *Psychic Sleuths* (Nickell 1994). They demonstrated how facts have been exaggerated and the story subjected to various embellishments. For example, the psychic's own accounts (Jordan 1977, 1999) fail to mention the T-shirt. That detail was provided in Arthur Lyons and Marcello Truzzi's *The Blue Sense: Psychic Detectives and Crime* (1991, 74), citing *Fate* magazine and the tabloid *National Enquirer*. It was repeated by Jenny Randles and Peter Hough in their credulous *Psychic Detectives* (2001, 86–88), which, astonishingly, ascribes the Kennedy case to 1982.

Moreover, Jordan's map was vague and contained erroneous details. It was apparently of little use in the search, during which Jordan supposedly received vibrations telling him "to go here, to go there" (Feder and Park 1994). Jordan had, by his own admission, chosen an area of the woods that "no one had searched" (although Randles and Hough [2001] report otherwise). "Just as I was ready to give up," he says, "I looked down and saw the footprint of a young barefoot human headed up the trail." Even with such good luck, Jordan happened to be elsewhere—in a ravine—when other searchers in the party actually located the lost child. They had heard him "yelling for help" (Jordan 1999, 58–63).

A 1989 television re-creation further exaggerated the story, leading Feder and Park (1994) to conclude, "It is curious indeed that this case, with all of its contradictions and odd coincidences, is considered an example compelling enough to be singled out in a television documentary more than a decade after the fact." And, of course, it has also been featured in mystery-mongering books such as that by Randles and Hough (2001).

Revealingly, the powers of Jordan and his ilk were illuminated by something of a national test case when Washington, D.C., intern Chandra Levy went missing for many months. Thousands of self-proclaimed psychics offered "clues"—Sylvia Browne, for example, visualized "some trees down in a marshy area"—but their offerings were of no use whatsoever. After Levy's remains were accidentally discovered in late May 2002, some of the failed psychics attempted to match their vague speculations with the known facts (Radford 2002). This technique, called "retrofitting," is a mainstay of alleged psychic detectives (Nickell 2001, 125–26).

Makeover

In 2001 Phil Jordan's fame as a psychic seemed to be in decline. However, in that year he purchased the Gould Hotel in Seneca Falls, New York, and began offering "Psychic Dinner Floorshows" twice a week. Also, on Saturdays, he scheduled "The Spirit Connection," which his promotional literature describes as "a show similar to *The John Edwards* [sic] *Show* on TV" (Phil Jordan 2003).

Jordan, who was made an honorary sheriff's deputy for his efforts in the Tommy Kennedy case, is also a licensed funeral director and ordained minister of a nondenominational Christian church. Potentially, he could help police find a missing body, secure the crime scene, supply a coffin, preach at the funeral, and give periodic updates on the person from the spirit realm.

To assess Jordan's spiritualistic ability, I decided to sign up for one of his shows. Since I had featured him in a chapter of one of my books (Nickell 1994), I thought it best to adopt a pseudonym and disguise my appearance. As "Johnny Adams," a somewhat homely old yokel with slicked-back hair and nerdy horn-rims, I attended Jordan's session on August 9, 2003, with some four dozen other hopefuls. Arriving early, I soon found my small table, its nameplate lettered with a red felt marker, "ADAMS 1."

Sitting on a stool, Jordan tried to provide readings for nearly every sitter. Some of his first readings seemed to leave the targeted individual puzzled, prompting a blank look—albeit sometimes a nodding head—that seemed to say, "I'm trying to make a connection." His was a standard "cold-reading" technique, in which the reader artfully fishes for information and tosses out vague statements that he hopes the sitter will interpret and validate. His most accurate reading seemed to occur when he told a woman about "John"—described as having worn a helmet of some kind—who had passed over. The lady was baffled, but another woman several feet behind her claimed the reading as her own and supplied some information that allowed Jordan to offer further statements that she seemed willing to accept.

After a fifteen-minute break, Jordan resumed, answering a few questions and continuing with the readings. Then, looking at me, he said that he really had to go to "this gentleman" next. He stated that he saw a woman, possibly my mother, who had swollen legs before her passing. I regarded that as a miss. He also mentioned a man who had "raised hogs." That could describe my grandfa-

Figure 59. Phil Jordan, alleged clairvoyant and medium, at the bar of his Seneca Falls, New York, hotel where he gives spiritualist readings. (Photo by "Johnny Adams," a.k.a. Joe Nickell)

ther Nickell (who was a farmer as well as a member of the Kentucky state legislature), except that he was anything but the plainspoken, matter-of-fact type the medium described. Jordan also claimed to tune in on a man who worked for a railroad, but that was utterly meaningless to me. I have also been unable to relate to someone named "Charlie" that Jordan foresaw having a positive influence on my life in the near future—how near was not specified.

One might have thought that—if he were really clairvoyant—Jordan would have done better. He could have mentioned my mother's Alzheimer's or at least foreseen the life-transforming news that arrived shortly after my reading: the discovery of a daughter (along with two grandsons) I had not known about. (I really should not pick on Jordan alone, because this profound fact also went unmentioned for thirty-six years by countless palmists, card readers, astrologers, clairvoyants, and mediums. It makes you wonder: where are their powers when you really need them?) And with me so near, shouldn't Jordan at least have gotten the name "Nickell"? Couldn't he have announced, "I see an impostor," or sensed the tremendously negative vibrations coming from my direction?

After the reading, Jordan inscribed a copy of his self-published book to me, addressing me as "Johnny," and happily posed for a photograph (figure 59). He seemed, well, totally clueless.

References

Feder, Kenneth L., and Michael Alan Park. 1994. The mythologized psychic detective: Phil Jordan. In Nickell 1994, 115–29.

Jordan, Phil. 1977. Psychic's search for a missing child. *Fate,* August, 60–65.

———. 1999. *I Knew This Day Would Come: A Personal Journey to Psychic Self-Awareness.* Privately printed.

Lyons, Arthur, and Marcello Truzzi. 1991. *The Blue Sense: Psychic Detectives and Crime.* New York: Mysterious Press.

Nickell, Joe, ed. 1994. *Psychic Sleuths: ESP and Sensational Cases.* Buffalo, N.Y.: Prometheus Books.

———. 2001. *Real-Life X-Files: Investigating the Paranormal,* 125–26. Lexington: University Press of Kentucky.

"Phil Jordan the psychic venue." 2003. *Innsights* (Official Newspaper-Menu of the Gould Hotel) 1, no. 4 (Summer): 1.

Radford, Benjamin. 2002. Psychics wrong about Chandra Levy. *Skeptical Inquirer* 26, no. 6 (November–December): 9.

Randles, Jenny, and Peter Hough. 2001. *Psychic Detectives: The Mysterious Use of Paranormal Phenomena in Solving True Crimes,* 86–88. Pleasantville, N.Y.: Reader's Digest.

SATAN'S STEP

MUNICH'S TWIN-TOWERED FRAUENKIRCHE (Church of Our Lady), erected in 1468–1488, has a curious legend. It stems from an impression in the foyer's pavement that is said to be *Der Teufelstritt,* the "devil's step." Supposedly, the architect, Jörg von Halspach, made a pact with Satan, who agreed to supply money for the church's construction so long as it was built without a single window; otherwise, the builder would forfeit his soul. When the church was completed, the architect led the devil to a place where he could view the well-lit nave but no windows could be seen, due to their being hidden by the great pillars. Furious at the deception, the devil stamped his foot, "leaving his black hoofed footprint in the pavement" (McLachan 2001). Actually, the imprint (figure 60) is not a hoofed one at all but rather "a footprint of a human being," as it is correctly described in a church flyer (Black n.d.).

One could write an entire treatise on footprints in stone, including those of fairies; various holy persons, including the Buddha, Christ, angels, and Christian saints; and others, notably the devil (Thompson 1955, 2:178–79). Of these, some may be attributable to imagination applied to natural markings in rock, while others have been pious frauds.

As to the folktale of the *Teufelstritt,* it exists in a number of variants, providing evidence of the oral tradition behind it. The greatest divergence in the varied tales is whether Satan stamped his foot in anger or out of triumph and glee. The latter versions, including the church's own flyer, tend to omit any interaction between builder and the devil and instead have Satan sneaking a view of the newly built church. Standing on the spot from which no windows can be seen, and finding a windowless building laughable, "in triumphal happiness he stamped into the floor, where he left this footprint in the ground." But when he took another step, he saw that there were many windows: "Out of an anger he changed himself into a great wind and hoped he could blow the

Figure 60. The "devil's footprint" in the foyer of a Munich cathedral. (Photo by Joe Nickell)

building down. But he failed; and since that time there is always a wind blowing around the towers" (Black n.d.).

Despite the variations, all the accounts focus on the concept of a vantage point from which none of the huge windows can be seen. This is a real effect, but only if we ignore the great stained-glass window on the opposite end of the church. Although that is a replacement (the church was largely destroyed by bombs during World War II but later underwent years of restoration), unfortunately for the legend makers, there was a window there at the time of the church's completion in 1488. The legend of the invisible windows therefore must have originated after 1620, when the window was blocked by a baroque high altar and remained so until 1858 (*Die Frauenkirche* 1999, 10), thus completing the illusion of no windows.

Moreover, examining the Frauenkirche's legendary footprint, I concluded that it was incompatible with its accompanying folktale. Whereas the foyer's pavement is a checkerboard pattern of red and gray marble, the imprint is not in one of those paving stones. Instead (as shown in figure 60), it is in a smaller inset square—apparently made of concrete and covered over (except for the footprint) with a hard, mustard-colored material that has suffered some cracking and breaking.

The church warden admitted that the imprint was not genuine, stating that the floor had been restored and that the *Teufelstritt* was merely a reconstruction. He was uncertain whether the "original" footprint had been destroyed or perhaps was in a museum or in storage somewhere. However, the other evidence of a post-1620 creation demonstrates that the *Teufelstritt* and its attendant legend are apocryphal.

One possibly innocent explanation is that the original footprint was put there by a stonemason when the floor was reportedly redone in 1671 (Schmeer-Sturm 1998). It could have been placed to mark the spot where churchgoers could observe what was, after all, an intriguing little illusion. Then, after that purpose was no longer remembered, the legend was born.

References

The black footprint. N.d. Flyer from Frauenkirche, Munich, Germany.

Die Frauenkirche in München. 1999. Regensburg, Germany: Schnell & Steiner.

McLachan, Gordon. 2001. *The Rough Guide to Germany,* 75. London: Rough Guides.

Schmeer-Sturm, Marie-Louise. 1998. *Die Schwarzen Führer: Munchen, Oberbayern.* Freiburg, Germany: Eulen Verlag.

Thompson, Stith. 1955. *Motif-Index of Folk-Literature.* 6 vols. Bloomington: Indiana University Press.

UNDERCOVER IN TIJUANA

ACCORDING TO QUACKWATCH (WILSON 2004)—an online source of information about doubtful medical treatments—the story of Laetrile is one of quackery, crime, and death. The drug is chemically related to amygdalin, a substance that occurs naturally in the pits of apricots and certain other fruits. Laetrile is outlawed in the United States.

The so-called father of Laetrile, "Doctor" Ernst T. Krebs Jr., was the son of a physician who promoted various alleged cures for cancer and other serious illnesses. The younger Krebs had only a bachelor of arts degree and a "doctor of science" degree from a now-defunct Bible college. The Krebses claimed that cancer tissues contain an abundance of an enzyme that causes amygdalin to release cyanide, which in turn destroys cancer cells. (Noncancerous tissues are supposedly protected by another cyanide-neutralizing enzyme.) Later, when enforcement agencies sought to ban the drug, the Krebses claimed that amygdalin is a vitamin—vitamin B_{17}—and asserted that cancer results from a deficiency of that vitamin. These claims have been discredited (Wilson 2004).

Repeated studies—including that of the Cancer Advisory Council in 1962–1963—found that Laetrile has no value as a cancer treatment. At a 1977 U.S. Senate subcommittee hearing chaired by Senator Edward Kennedy (D-Mass.), the senator concluded that Laetrile's promoters were "slick salesmen who would offer a false sense of hope" (Wilson 2004).

Publicity about Laetrile sent many desperate cancer victims to Mexico, including, in 1980, Hollywood actor Steve McQueen. Despite the glowing testimonial he gave at the beginning of his treatment, McQueen soon died. Although the Laetrile movement reached its peak in the 1970s, the drug continues to be sold through toll-free telephone numbers, Internet sites, shell companies, and other means (Wilson 2004). An organization called the Cancer Control Society, which has a post office box in Modesto, California, offers bus tours of cancer treatment clinics in Tijuana, including those offering Laetrile (Cancer 2004).

Colleague Vaughn Rees and I sought to learn the extent of Laetrile availability in Tijuana. On the Day of the Dead, 2003, we scouted out several places—including various herb shops and pharmacies—looking for the drug. However, none of the people we questioned seemed to know anything about it. Inquiry at an information booth yielded the telephone number of one hospital that offered "alternative" treatments, but a call revealed that Laetrile was not among them. A visit to another hospital was likewise negative (although it did offer homeopathic treatments). However, a receptionist was willing to provide us with the names and addresses of clinics that did prescribe Laetrile.

One of these was a large, modern, respectable-looking facility called the Oasis of Hope Hospital. I told a receptionist that I had been diagnosed with prostate cancer and that my doctor had offered no hope. "Frankly," I said, putting a tremor in my voice, "I'm scared." (In fact, a few months earlier I had required a prostate biopsy, which proved negative. Later, I briefly discussed this planned undercover role with an oncologist.) The receptionist nodded, businesslike, and told me to have a seat and wait while she summoned someone to talk with me. Vaughn hovered in the vicinity, playing the part of someone assisting a sick friend. Soon, a young woman from "Customer Service" (as her card read) sat down with me, and I repeated my story in more detail. I made it clear that I was not there to be admitted but had only made a side jaunt to check out my options while visiting my friend in California. I said that I had heard about something called Laetrile, but I deliberately fumbled the pronunciation. I was given a form to fill out so that my name would be on file—"no obligation," I was promised. I listed my occupation as "retired." I then received a packet of materials. One brochure, promoting the Oasis-operated "Contreras Cancer Care Center," admitted that:

> The programs are eclectic and often include:
> - Laetrile, Enzymes, Mega-doses of Vitamins
> - Regenerating Agents
> - Immune Modulating Agents
> - Prayer Therapy

• Shark Cartilage (100% Pure)
• Antioxidants
• Hormone Therapy
• O-Zone [*sic*]

Another brochure, called the "Oasis of Hope Activity Schedule," listed such offerings as "Laetrile use and care / Important to attend" and a video by Dr. Ernesto Contreras titled "What the Bible Says about Disease." Dr. Ernesto Contreras Sr., a former pathologist with the Mexican army, was an early Laetrile promoter who employed translators to accommodate his numerous American patients. Business was so good in 1970 that he constructed the facility since named Oasis Hospital (Wilson 2004). A color brochure pictures Contreras holding hands with apparent patients, their eyes closed and heads bowed in prayer.

After returning home, I received from Oasis Hospital in San Ysidro, California, additional materials, including a video with the message, "It is no wonder why more than 40,000 Americans have sought refuge at the Oasis of Hope Hospital." States the narrator, "Although conventional chemotherapy and radiation treatments are available, the heart of the program is alternative therapy." This features "metabolic therapy" that utilizes "a steady diet of organic foods and mega-doses of vitamins," including Laetrile. Prayer is encouraged. According to Dr. Francisco Contreras (whose voice is accompanied by inspirational music), "In this hospital the medical director is Jesus Christ, and *that* makes a difference."

Non-Christians should be insulted by this appeal, but the attempt to imply Jesus's endorsement of something as dubious as Laetrile should offend Christians as well. Everyone should beware of the snake-oil approach.

References

Cancer Control Society. 2004. www.cancercontrolsociety.com (accessed March 16).
Wilson, Benjamin. 2004. The rise and fall of Laetrile. www.quackwatch.org/01QuackeryRelatedTopics/Cancer/laetrile.html (accessed March 15).

LEGENDS OF CASTLES AND KEEPS

DURING THE MIDDLE AGES, THE CASTLE (from the Latin *castellum,* "small fortification") arose as the private fortress of a monarch or a nobleman. Its central tower (like the Tower of London) is called a *keep,* a term also applied to a fort or other stronghold, or even a jail. Castles offer a romantic, often Gothic allure. If they are not haunted, I like to say, they ought to be. Besides supposedly being inhabited by specters, they are usually the focus of other legends as well.

I have explored and written about many castles and keeps, including Burg Frankenstein and Plassenburg castle in Germany (Nickell 2003a, 2003b), the Kremlin fortress in Moscow (Nickell 2002), and the Old Melbourne Gaol in Australia (Nickell 2001). Here are some others that I have investigated over the years.

Blarney Castle

The well-known term *blarney* refers to the gift of eloquence, attributed especially to the Irish. It is variously defined as cajoling, flattering talk; smooth, deceitful speech; or even nonsense. Legendarily, kissing the Blarney Stone is supposed to endow one with the powers of eloquence and persuasion.

Reportedly, Queen Elizabeth I (1533–1603) coined the term *blarney* during the lengthy, tiresome negotiations concerning control of the fortress. The titular owner, Cormac McCarthy, Earl of Blarney, dutifully followed the protocols of sixteenth-century diplomatic prose and wrote grandiose letters that praised the queen, without, however, relinquishing the land. Her regal feathers ruffled, Elizabeth is said to have huffed, "This is all blarney—he never says what he means!" (O'Dwyer 2000, 222).

The stone is located in the castle at Blarney in County Cork, Ireland. Built in 1446, it is among the largest Irish tower castles (figure 61). A spiral stone stairway leads up to three levels. (Originally, the first tier consisted of the kitchen and armory, the second the dining hall, and the third the chapel.) A smaller stair leads to the battlements and the Blarney Stone. The stone is actually one of the great lintels in the parapet and is reached by dangling upside down in the gap between the parapet and the wall (as shown in a photo in Constable and Farrington 2004, 94). Even though there are parallel iron bars at the bottom of the small shaft to keep one from plummeting to one's death, and a pair of vertical iron rails to hold on to, the experience can be somewhat frightening. This is especially the case for those of us with acrophobia—I don't even like being this tall! I survived the experience in 1971, but instead of getting the "gift of gab," I was left speechless! (Of course, since I am of Irish ancestry, that effect was very brief.)

One legend about the castle is intriguing and may stem from the fact that a limestone cave and dank dungeons are located near the castle (O'Dwyer 2000, 223; Nickell 1971). In 1651, after Oliver Cromwell's forces had conquered castle after castle (Limerick, for example, falling to siege tactics), Blarney claimed a sort of "moral victory" over the rebels. Allegedly—at least "according to Irish folklore"—the castle's entire garrison secretly escaped through a tunnel beneath the massive tower (Constable and Farrington 2004, 118).

The similarity of the word *blarney* to the American *baloney* (or *boloney*), meaning "nonsense," cannot go unnoted—especially since the latter is a popular skeptics' epithet. (For example, Carl Sagan, in his 1995 *The Demon-Haunted World: Science as a Candle in the Dark,* included a chapter titled "The Fine Art of Baloney Detection.") Attempts to explain *baloney* as deriving from *bologna sausage* (e.g., Barnhart 1988, 73) are unconvincing. Some sources note that that connection is conjectural or frankly admit that the etymology is unknown (*Webster's* 1986, 34); others offer different theories—for instance, that it may come from the Spanish *pelone,* meaning "balls" (Hendrickson 1997, 87).

I have long suspected that *baloney* might actually be a corruption of *blarney* itself. Foreign or other unfamiliar expressions are often corrupted to a familiar one. For example, "Pennsylvania Dutch" is a corruption of Pennsylvania *Deutsch* (i.e., German immigrants). I finally discovered one scholarly source that acknowledges that *baloney* was "possibly influenced" by *blarney* (Lighter

Figure 61. Sketch of Blarney Castle from the author's travel journal of 1971.

1994, 82). In any case, a fine distinction between the two words was expressed by Fulton John Sheen in 1938: "Baloney is flattery so thick it cannot be true, and blarney is flattery so thin we like it" (Bartlett 1955, 973).

Rock of Cashel

Another Irish castle represents an impressive sight: in County Tipperary, atop a gigantic limestone outcropping that rises abruptly to a height of 358 feet, stands a stone fortress wall enclosing the ruins of great medieval structures, including the Irish-Romanesque Cormac's Chapel (consecrated 1134), a thirteenth-century Gothic cathedral, and a ninety-foot round tower. The last, built shortly after 1101, is the oldest part of "one of the most interesting assemblages of ruins in Ireland" (*Encyclopaedia Britannica* 1910, s.v. "Cashel"). It is known as the Rock of Cashel but is also called St. Patrick's Rock.

Legends about the castle range from the fanciful to the historical. The former is typified by a tale claiming that the rock was hurled by the devil when he spied a church being built at Cashel. Fortunately, the evil one had bad aim, and the Christians were undaunted (O'Dwyer 2000, 179). A much more likely story is that St. Patrick—the Briton who legendarily endured danger and hardship to convert Ireland to Christianity—baptized King Aenghus of Munster at Cashel in about AD 450, thus establishing Cashel as a bishopric.

Patrick himself is largely a legendary figure. Although pious tales have him single-handedly Christianizing Ireland, the fact is that "this work took many more years than these legends allow" (Jones 1994, 189). The most famous legends of St. Patrick have him using the shamrock to explain the doctrine of the Trinity and expelling snakes from the isle; hence, these became his emblems (Jones 1994, 189). Although snakes are indeed absent from Ireland, that is not due to any saintly magic: there were never any snakes to expel. Because of climatic conditions and Ireland's having become separated by the Irish Sea from the other British Isles before they were separated from Europe, the Emerald Isle lacks snakes and other reptiles as well as such common English mammals as the mole, the weasel, and two varieties of mice (*Encyclopaedia Britannica* 1978, s.v. "Ireland").

Not surprisingly, some say St. Patrick's Rock is haunted. I saw no ghosts when I visited many years ago, but I can understand how folk have fancied "sper'ts av kings an' bishops that rest on Cashel" (McAnally 1888, 49). At the time, I wrote in my journal (Nickell 1971): "the wind added 'atmosphere,' and with the cold grey sky, the cold grey stone, and the old graves, made an eerie place of 'The Rock.'"

Heidelberg Castle

Perched atop a ridge overlooking Heidelberg, the *Schloss* (castle) is the center-piece of the scenic views of the city. Its grandiose ruins of striking red sand-stone are well preserved and represent "one of Germany's finest examples of a Gothic-Renaissance fortress" (Schulte-Peevers et al. 2002, 543). During the Second World Skeptics Congress held in the picturesque city in July 1998 (see Frazier 1998), I found time to visit the castle, accompanied by fellow skeptic and former U.S. Air Force Major James McGaha.

Legends abound. For example, one concerns the castle terrace, where one can see a supposed "footprint" in the stone. This is purported to have been caused by a knight leaping from a third-story window when the prince made an early return to his wife's bedroom (Schulte-Peevers et al. 2002, 543). Of course, such an explanation of the alleged imprint is ridiculous, since it would have taken a superhuman leap to make an impression in the stone. Indeed, the common footprint-in-the-stone motif is typically attributed to the supernatural (see Nickell 2003a).

Still another legend at Schloss Heidelberg is obviously recounted not for its factual value but for its punch line. The tale focuses on the *Grosses Fass* ("great cask"), an enormous wine vat standing two stories tall in the cellar. Once the largest functioning wine vat in the world, it was reputedly made from 130 oak trees and had a capacity of some 50,000 gallons. According to the legend, in the eighteenth century, the vat's guardian was a dwarf named Perkeo, a court jester with a tremendous thirst for wine. Some say that he could consume the contents of the great cask in a single draught (Perkeo 2005); a more reasonable source states that he only attempted to empty the cask by drinking eighteen bottles daily for fifty years. One day, however, Perkeo substituted a glass of water—by accident, say most raconteurs—and died instantly (Inowlocki 1999, 70–71; Knight 2002, 303).

The anecdote may have grown from a proverbial kernel of truth. Apparently, under the rule of Carl Phillip, a Tyrolean dwarf did serve as the court jester—a role that clever dwarfs often filled (Nickell 2005, 107). Perkeo was supposedly a nickname deriving from his response when offered wine: "Perche no?" (Why not?). An antique statue of Perkeo today stands next to the great cask (Knight 2002, 303; Perkeo 2005).

Castillo de San Marcos

The seventeenth-century Spanish-built Castillo de San Marcos in St. Augustine, Florida, is the oldest masonry fort in the continental United States. Constructed of coquina, a soft limestone formed by cemented seashells, the fort was a response to a 1668 raid by English pirates. Construction started in 1672 and was completed after twenty-three years. The Castillo guarded Florida until that territory was ceded to England in 1763, and it imprisoned Americans during the Revolutionary War (Brownstone and Franck 1989, 8). It was returned to Spain in 1783, then purchased by the United States in 1819. Today it is a national monument operated by the National Park Service.

Of the many legends of the Castillo, none is more gruesome, more spine-tingling, or more often repeated—and less substantiated—than that of the ghostly lovers in the fort's dungeon. As it is summarized in *Haunted Places: The National Directory* (Hauck 1996, 125):

> An eerie glow accompanied by the faint odor of a woman's perfume is sometimes detected near a wall in the dungeon of this 1672 Spanish fort. The wall was the ghastly tomb of Señora Dolores Marti and Captain Manuel Abela. Señora Dolores was the wife of Colonel Garcia Marti, assigned to the Spanish garrison in 1784. When Colonel Marti found out his wife was having an affair with Abela, he chained them to a wall in the dungeon and mortared a new wall of coquina stone in front of them.

In the next century, an engineer noticed that a section of wall sounded hollow when tapped. "He chipped away the mortar, and the lantern he held illuminated two skeletons" (Moore 1998, 43). Another raconteur stated more specifically: "There before him hung two skeletons, chained to the wall" (Lapham 1997, 147). That writer—along with his illustrator—seemed to be unaware that bones are not wired together like the articulated skeletons in science class; rather than hanging as a unit, they would have fallen apart, landing in a heap on the floor.

In fact, the legend represents an interesting example of how facts are embellished over time by those intent on fostering mystery. First of all, there is no "dungeon" in the Castillo, despite its having been used as a prison on various occasions (Brownstone and Franck 1989, 8). The area in question was actually a small room that was part of the powder magazine; when it proved too humid for storing gunpowder, it was sealed off. It was rediscovered not in 1833, 1838, or 1938, as variously stated (Hauck 1996, 125–26; Cain 1997, 22), but in 1832, "when a cannon fell through from the gundeck" (National n.d.; Harris 2004).

Although "bones" were reportedly found among the debris in the room, whether they were human is far from certain. Concedes one source: "Many rumors and stories developed about the bones. Tour guides shortly after the turn of the century concocted all kinds of fascinating tales involving the 'dungeon room.'" Indeed, "some stories were quite fantastic" (Cain 1997, 22), including, of course, the fable of the governor sealing his wife and her lover in that chamber. One source acknowledges that "history does not record the event" (Lapham 1997, 146); another, though agreeing, nevertheless offers the hope that "perhaps some visitors may still experience an eerie feeling when visiting the small room in the northeast corner" (Cain 1997, 22).

In 2004 when I visited the Castillo (for the third time), I was impressed with the professionalism of the staff. One told me, "There aren't any ghosts," explaining that he had slept there all night on occasion and experienced nothing. He said that places with genuine history did not need to use ghosts for tourist promotion—unlike those that "don't have anything else" (Cipriani 2004). The Castillo de San Marcos certainly has plenty of real history.

References

Barnhart, Robert K., ed. 1988. *Chambers Dictionary of Etymology.* Edinburgh: Chambers.

Bartlett, John. 1955. *Bartlett's Familiar Quotations,* 13th ed. Boston: Little, Brown.

Brownstone, David M., and Irene M. Franck. 1989. *Historic Places of Early America.* New York: Atheneum.

Cain, Suzy. 1997. *A Ghostly Experience: Tales of St. Augustine.* St. Augustine, Fla.: Tour Saint Augustine.

Cipriani, John. 2004. Interview by Joe Nickell, March 23.

Constable, Nick, and Karen Farrington. 2004. *Ireland.* New York: Barnes & Noble Books.

Encyclopaedia Britannica. 1910. New York: Encyclopaedia Britannica.

———. 1978. Chicago: Encyclopaedia Britannica.

Frazier, Kendrick. 1998. Science and reason, foibles and fallacies, and doomsdays. *Skeptical Inquirer* 22, no. 6 (November–December): 5–8.

Harris, Bruce (Castillo bookstore manager). 2004. Interview by Joe Nickell, March 23.

Hauck, Dennis William. 1996. *Haunted Places: The National Directory.* New York: Penguin Books.

Hendrickson, Robert. 1997. *Encyclopedia of Word and Phrase Origins.* New York: Facts on File.

Inowlocki, Tania, ed. 1999. *Fodor's UpCLOSE Germany.* New York: Fodor's Travel Publications.

Jones, Alison. 1994. *The Wordsworth Dictionary of Saints.* Hertfordshire, England: Wordsworth Editions.

Knight, Christina, ed. 2002. *Fodor's Germany 2002.* New York: Fodor's Travel Publications.

Lapham, Dave. 1997. *Ghosts of St. Augustine.* Sarasota, Fla.: Pineapple Press.

Lighter, J. E., ed. 1994. *Random House Historical Dictionary of American Slang.* New York: Random House.

McAnally, D. R. 1888. *Irish Wonders.* Reprint, New York: Gramercy Books, 1996.

Moore, Joyce Elson. 1998. *Haunt Hunter's Guide to Florida.* Sarasota, Fla.: Pineapple Press.

National Park Service. N.d. Self-guided map, Castillo de San Marcos National Monument (copy obtained March 23, 2004).

Nickell, Joe. 1971. Personal travel journal, January 6–8.

———. 2001. Mysterious Australia. *Skeptical Inquirer* 25, no. 2 (March–April): 15–18.

———. 2002. Moscow mysteries. *Skeptical Inquirer* 26, no. 4 (July–August): 17–20, 24.

———. 2003a. Germany: Monsters, myths and mysteries. *Skeptical Inquirer* 27, no. 2 (July–August): 24–28.

———. 2003b. Legend of the white lady. *Skeptical Briefs,* March, 10–11.

———. 2005. *Secrets of the Sideshows.* Lexington: University Press of Kentucky.

O'Dwyer, Deirdre, ed. 2000. *Let's Go Ireland.* New York: St. Martin's Press.

Perkeo. 2005. www.zum.de/Faecher/G/BW/LandesKunde/rhein/hd/schloss/mona/perkeo 1.htm (accessed July 28).

Sagan, Carl. 1995. *The Demon-Haunted World: Science as a Candle in the Dark.* New York: Random House.

Schulte-Peevers, Andrea, et al. 2002. *Germany,* 3rd ed. Melbourne, Australia: Lonely Planet Publications.

Webster's New Encyclopedia of Dictionaries. 1986. Baltimore: Ottenheimer Publishers.

ALIEN ENCOUNTERS

Since Robert A. Baker's pioneering article appeared in *Skeptical Inquirer* (Baker 1987–1988), a controversy has raged over his suggestion that self-proclaimed alien abductees exhibit an array of unusual traits that indicate a fantasy-prone personality. Baker cited the "important but much neglected" work of Wilson and Barber (1983), who listed certain identifying characteristics of people who fantasize profoundly. Baker applied Wilson and Barber's findings to the alien-abduction phenomenon and found a strong correlation. Baker explained that whereas a cursory examination by a psychologist or psychiatrist might find an "abductee" to be perfectly normal, more detailed knowledge about the person's background and habits would reveal, to such a trained observer, a pattern of fantasy proneness.

For example, Baker found Whitley Strieber—author of *Communion,* which tells the "true story" of Strieber's own alleged abduction—to be "a classic example of the [fantasy-prone personality] genre." Baker noted that, in addition to being a writer of occult and highly imaginative novels, Strieber exhibited such symptoms as being easily hypnotized, having vivid memories, and experiencing hypnopompic hallucinations (i.e., waking dreams), as well as exhibiting other characteristics of fantasy proneness. A subsequent but apparently independent study by Bartholomew and Basterfield (1988) drew similar conclusions.

Wilson and Barber's study did not deal with the abduction phenomenon (which at the time consisted of only a handful of reported cases), and some of their criteria seem less applicable to abduction cases than to other types of reported phenomena, such as psychic experiences. Nevertheless, although the criteria for fantasy proneness have not been codified, they generally include such features as having a rich fantasy life, showing high hypnotic susceptibility, claiming psychic abilities and healing powers, reporting out-of-body experiences and vivid or waking dreams, having apparitional experiences and religious visions, and exhibiting automatic writing. In one study, Bartholomew, Basterfield, and Howard (1991) found that of 152 otherwise normal, functional individuals who reported that they had been abducted by aliens or had persistent contact with extraterrestrials, 132 had one or more major characteristics of a fantasy-prone personality.

Somewhat equivocal results were obtained by Spanos and colleagues (1993, 631), although their "findings suggest that intense UFO experiences are more likely to occur in individuals who are predisposed toward esoteric beliefs in general and alien beliefs in particular and who interpret unusual sensory and imagined experiences in terms of the alien hypothesis. Among UFO believers, those with stronger propensities toward fantasy production were particularly likely to generate such experiences."

A totally dismissive view of these attempts to find conventional psychological explanations for the abduction experience is found in the introduction to psychiatrist John Mack's *Abduction: Human Encounters with Aliens* (1994). Mack states unequivocally: "The effort to discover a personality type associated with abductions has also not been successful." According to Mack, because some alleged abductions reportedly take place in infancy or early childhood, "Cause and effect in the relationship of abduction experiences to building of personality are thus virtually impossible to sort out" (Mack 1994, 5) But surely it is Mack's burden to prove his own thesis that the alien hypothesis has a basis in fact beyond mere allegation. Otherwise, the evidence may well be explained by the simpler hypothesis of abductees being fantasy-prone personality types. (Because such people have traits that cut across many different personality dimensions, conventional personality tests are useless. Some "abductees" who are not fantasy prone may be hoaxers, for example, or exhibit other distinctive personality traits or psychological problems.) Mack's approach to the diagnosis and treatment of his "abductee" patients has been criticized by many of his colleagues (e.g., Cone 1994).

Methodology

To test the fantasy-proneness hypothesis, I carefully reviewed the thirteen chapter-length cases in Mack's *Abduction,* selected from the forty-nine patients he most carefully studied out of seventy-six "abductees." Since his presentation was not intended to include fantasy proneness, certain potential indicators of that personality type—such as a subject's having an imaginary playmate—would not be expected to be present. Nevertheless, Mack's rendering of each personality in light of the person's alleged abduction experiences was sufficiently detailed to allow the extraction of data pertaining to several indicators of fantasy proneness. They are the following.

1. *Susceptibility to hypnosis.* Wilson and Barber rated "hypnotizability" as one of the main indicators of fantasy proneness. In all cases, Mack repeatedly hypnotized the subjects without reporting any difficulty in doing so. Also, under hypnosis, the subjects did not merely recall their alleged abduction experiences: all of them *reexperienced* and *relived* them in a manner typical of fantasy proneness (Wilson and Barber 1983, 373–79). For example, Mack's patient "Scott" (No. 3) was so alarmed at "remembering" his first abduction (in a pre-Mack hypnosis session with another psychiatrist) that, he said, "I jumped clear off the couch" (Mack 1994, 81); "Jerry" (No. 4) "expressed shock over how vividly he had relived the abduction" (112); similarly, "Catherine" (No. 5) "began to relive" a feeling of numbness and started "to sob and pant" (140).

2. *Paraidentity.* I use this term to refer to a subject's having had imaginary companions as a child (Wilson and Barber 1983, 346–47) or, by extension, claiming to have lived past lives or having a dual identity of some type. Of their fantasy-prone subjects, Wilson and Barber stated: "In fantasy they can do anything—experience a previous lifetime, experience their own birth, go off into the future, go into space, and so on." In addition, "While they are pretending, they become totally absorbed in the character and tend to lose awareness of their true identity" (Wilson and Barber 1983, 353, 354).

Thus, as a child, "Ed" (No. 1) stated: "Things talked to me. The animals, the spirits . . . I can sense the earth" (Mack 1994, 47); "Jerry" (No. 4) said that he had had a relationship with a tall extraterrestrial being since age five (113). At least four of Mack's subjects (Nos. 5, 7, 9, and 10) claimed to have had past-life experiences (160–62, 200, 248, 259), and seven (Nos. 3, 6, 7, 8, 9, 11, and 12) said that they had some sort of dual identity (92–93, 173, 200, 209, 243, 297, 355–56). For example "Dave" (No. 10) considered himself "a modern-day

Indian," while "Peter" (No. 11) under hypnosis said that he *becomes* an alien and speaks in robotic tones (275, 277, 297). In all, eleven of Mack's thirteen featured subjects exhibited paraidentity.

3. *Psychic experiences.* Another strong characteristic of fantasy proneness, according to Wilson and Barber (1983, 359–60), is having telepathic, precognitive, or other types of psychic experiences. All of Mack's thirteen subjects claimed to have experienced one or more types of alleged psychical phenomena, with most of them reporting telepathic contact with extraterrestrials. "Catherine" (No. 5) also claimed that she could "feel people's auras," "Eva" (No. 9) said that she could perceive beyond the range of the five senses, and "Carlos" (No. 12) claimed to have "a history of what he calls 'visionary' experiences" (Mack 1994, 157, 245, 332).

4. *"Floating" or out-of-body experiences.* Wilson and Barber (1983, 360) state: "The overwhelming majority of subjects (88 percent) in the fantasy-prone group, as contrasted to few (8 percent) in the comparison group, report realistic out-of-the-body experiences" (which one subject described as "a weightless, floating sensation" and another called "astral travel"). Only one of Mack's thirteen subjects (No. 2) failed to report this; of the other twelve, most described, under hypnosis, being "floated" from their beds to an awaiting spaceship. Some said that they were even able to drift through a solid door or wall, a further indication of the fantasy nature of the experience (more on this later). Also, "Eva" (No. 9) stated that she had once put her head down on her desk to nap and saw herself "floating from the ceiling. . . . My consciousness was up there. My physical body was down there" (Mack 1994, 237). In the case of "Carlos" (No. 12), "flying is a recurring motif in some of his more vivid dreams" (338).

5. *Vivid or "waking" dreams, visions, or hallucinations.* A majority of Wilson and Barber's subjects (64 percent) reported that they frequently experienced a type of dream that is particularly vivid and realistic (Wilson and Barber 1983, 364). Technically termed *hypnagogic* or *hypnopompic* hallucinations (depending on whether they occur while the person is going to sleep or waking, respectively), they are more popularly known as waking dreams or,

in earlier times, as night terrors (Nickell 1995, 41). Wilson and Barber (1983, 364) reported that several of their subjects "were especially grateful to learn that the 'monsters' they saw nightly when they were children could be discussed in terms of 'what the mind does when it is nearly, but not quite asleep.'" Some of Wilson and Barber's subjects (six of twenty-seven in the fantasy-prone group, compared with none in the comparison group of twenty-five) also had religious visions, and some had outright hallucinations (Wilson and Barber 1983, 362–63, 364–65, 367–71).

Of Mack's thirteen selected cases, all but one (No. 13) reported some type of especially vivid dream, vision, or hallucination. For example, "Scott" (No. 3) said that he had been having "visual hallucinations" since age twelve; "Jerry" (No. 4) recorded in his journal "vivid dreams of UFOs" as well as "visions"; and "Carlos" (No. 12) had the previously mentioned "visionary" experiences and dreams of flying (Mack 1994, 82, 112). Almost all of Mack's subjects (Nos. 1–11) had vivid dreams with strong indications of hypnagogic or hypnopompic hallucination (38, 56, 80, 106, 132, 168–69, 196, 213, 235, 265–67, 289).

6. *Hypnotically generated apparitions.* Encountering apparitions (which Wilson and Barber define rather narrowly as "ghosts" or "spirits") is another characteristic of a fantasy-prone personality (found in only 16 percent of their comparison group). A large number of the fantasizers also reported seeing classic hypnagogic imagery, including such apparition-like entities as "demon-type beings, goblins, gargoyles, monsters that seemed to be from outer space" (Wilson and Barber 1983, 364).

Mack's subjects had a variety of such encounters, both in their apparent waking dreams and under hypnosis. All thirteen subjects reported seeing one or more types of outer-space creatures during hypnosis.

7. *Receipt of special messages.* Fifty percent of Wilson and Barber's fantasizers (contrasted with only 8 percent of their comparison subjects) reported the feeling that some spirit or higher intelligence was using them "to write a poem, song, or message" (Wilson and Barber 1983, 361).

Of Mack's thirteen abductees, all but one clearly exhibited this characteristic, usually in the form of receiving a telepathic message from the extraterrestrials. The message was usually similar to the one given to "Arthur" (No. 13) "about the danger facing the earth's ecology" (Mack 1994, 381). Interestingly, many of these messages just happen to echo Mack's own apocalyptic notions (3, 412), indicating that Mack may be leading his witnesses. In the case of "Eva" (No. 9), the aliens, who represented a "higher communication" (243, 247), purportedly spoke through her and described her "global mission." "Jerry" (No. 4) produced a "flood of poetry" yet stated, "I don't know where it's coming from"; "Sara" (No. 7) had been "spontaneously making drawings with a pen in each hand," although she had never used her left hand before; and "Peter" (No. 11), who has "always known that I could commune with God," stated that the aliens "want to see if I'm a worthy leader" (99, 192, 288, 297).

Results

One of Mack's subjects ("Sheila," No. 2) exhibited four of the seven fantasy-prone indicators, and another ("Arthur," No. 13) exhibited five; the rest showed all seven characteristics. These results are displayed in figure 62.

Although not included here, healing—that is, the subjects' feeling that they have the ability to heal—is another characteristic of the fantasy-prone personality noted by Wilson and Barber (1983, 363). At least six of Mack's thirteen subjects exhibited this trait. Other traits not discussed by Wilson and Barber but of possible interest are as follows (with the number of Mack's thirteen subjects that exhibit it): having seen UFOs (9), New Age or mystical involvement (11), Roman Catholic upbringing (6 of 9 whose religion was known or could be inferred), previously being in a religio-philosophical limbo or quest for the meaning of life (10), and involvement in the arts as a vocation or avocation (5). For example, though apparently not an artist, a healer, or a UFO sighter, "Ed" (No. 1) had "a traditional Roman Catholic upbringing" and, as a bit of a loner, feels "lost in the desert"; in addition to "talk[ing] to plants," he has "practiced meditation and studied Eastern philosophy in his struggle to find his authentic path" (Mack 1994, 39, 41–42). "Carlos" (No. 12) is an artist, writer, and "fine arts professor" involved in theatrical productions; he has seen UFOs, has a "capacity as a healer," was raised a Roman Catholic, is interested in numerology and mythology, and calls himself "a shaman/artist teacher" (Mack 1994, 330, 332, 340–41, 357).

Also of interest, I think, is the evidence that many of Mack's subjects fan-

Case Number from Mack's *Abduction*

Fantasy Proneness Markers	1	2	3	4	5	6	7	8	9	10	11	12	13
1. Susceptibility to Hypnosis	•	•	•	•	•	•	•	•	•	•	•	•	•
2. Paraidentity (Imaginary Companions, Past Lives, Dual Identies)	•		•	•	•	•	•	•	•	•	•	•	•
3. Psychic Experiences	•	•	•	•	•	•	•	•	•	•	•	•	•
4. 'Floating' or Out-of-Body Experiences	•		•	•	•	•	•	•	•	•	•	•	•
5. Vivid or 'Waking' Dreams/Visions/ Hallucinations	•	•	•	•	•	•	•	•	•	•	•	•	
6. Hypnotically Generated Apparitions	•	•	•	•	•	•		•	•	•	•	•	•
7. Receipt of Special Messages	•		•	•	•	•	•	•	•	•	•	•	•

Figure 62. Alien encounter cases from John Mack's *Abduction* were studied for fantasy proneness. (Courtesy of *Skeptical Inquirer* magazine)

tasized while under hypnosis. For example, in addition to aliens, "Ed" (No. 1) said he saw earth spirits that he described as "mirthful little playful creatures" (Mack 1994, 48). "Joe" (No. 6) saw "mythic gods, and winged horses" and also "remembered" being born (170, 184). "Catherine" (No. 5), "Sara" (No. 7), "Paul" (No. 8), and "Eva" (No. 9) said they had past-life experiences or engaged in time travel while under hypnosis. Several said they were able to drift through solid doors or walls, including "Ed" (No. 1), "Jerry" (No. 4), "Catherine" (No. 5), "Paul" (No. 8), "Dave (No. 10), and "Arthur" (No. 13). "Carlos" (No. 12) claimed his body was transmuted into light. In all, eleven of Mack's thirteen subjects (all but Nos. 2 and 3) fantasized under hypnosis. Of course, it may be argued that there really are "earth spirits" and "winged horses" or that extraterrestrials truly have the ability to time travel or dematerialize bodies or that any of the other examples I have given as evidence of fantasizing are actually true. However, once again, the burden of proof is on the claimant, and until that burden is met, the examples can be taken as evidence of the subjects' ability to fantasize.

Conclusions

Despite John Mack's denial, my study of his best thirteen cases shows high fantasy proneness among his subjects. Whether the same results would be obtained with his other subjects remains to be seen. Nevertheless, my study supports the earlier opinions of Baker and of Bartholomew and Basterfield that alleged alien abductees tend to have fantasy-prone personalities. Certainly, that is the case for the very best subjects selected by a major advocate.

References

Baker, Robert A. 1987–1988. The aliens among us: Hypnotic regression revisited. *Skeptical Inquirer* 12, no. 2 (Winter): 147–62.

Bartholomew, Robert E., and Keith Basterfield. 1988. Abduction states of consciousness. *International UFO Reporter,* March–April.

Bartholomew, Robert E., Keith Basterfield, and George S. Howard. 1991. UFO abductees and contactees: Psychopathology or fantasy-proneness? *Professional Psychology: Research and Practice* 22, no. 3, 215–22.

Cone, William. 1994. Research therapy methods questioned. *UFO* 9, no. 5, 32–34.

Mack, John. 1994. *Abduction: Human Encounters with Aliens.* New York: Simon & Schuster.

Nickell, Joe. 1995. *Entities: Angels, Spirits, Demons and Other Alien Beings.* Amherst, N.Y.: Prometheus Books.

Spanos, Nicholas P., Patricia A. Cross, Kirby Dickson, and Susan C. DuBreuil. 1993. Close encounters: An examination of UFO experiences. *Journal of Abnormal Psychology* 102, no. 4, 624–32.

Wilson, Sheryl C., and Theodore X. Barber. 1983. The fantasy-prone personality: Implications for understanding imagery, hypnosis, and parapsychological phenomena. In *Imagery, Current Theory, Research and Application,* ed. Anees A. Sheikh, 340–90. New York: Wiley.

RETURN FROM THE DEAD

FIGURE 63 DEPICTS AN ANTIQUE lithographed poster advertising a story slated to appear in the *Boston American* newspaper. Finding a "10-6-06" in the corner, I was able to track down a microfilm copy of the October 14, 1906, issue of that paper, which actually related four stories of people who had "come back from the dead." I wondered how century-old narratives would compare with present-day ones describing what we now term near-death experiences.

The main story, the one dramatized by the poster artist, told how Mrs. James A. Haskins of 82 Oak Street, Middleboro, Massachusetts,[1] had "apparently died during a recent attack of pleuro-pneumonia." It was alleged that "for twenty-three minutes her heart ceased beating, no breath could be detected, and she made no sign of life when her eyes were closed by the nurse." (Obviously, this was only apparent; otherwise, she would have suffered irreversible brain damage.)

The twenty-three-year-old Mrs. Haskins told a moving account, dictating it after her recovery. She stated that she had suffered a fever of 104.5 degrees, had a fitful pulse, and experienced shortness of breath, whereupon she declared, "Mother, I'm going to die." Soon she obtained relief: "I felt as if I had been lifted from my bed and was floating up and away on light fleecy clouds. At the same time I heard the nurse say: 'Well, she's gone.'" She felt the nurse close her eyes and heard her mother sobbing. "Then," Mrs. Haskins said, "my little dead baby, Doris, came to me. I held out my arms to her and held her close to my breast. Oh, I was so happy. Baby and I were together again. That was all I thought of or cared for." Little Doris, the first of her three children, had died a few years earlier at eight months old. Now, Mrs. Haskins noted, "she looked happy and healthy," although "she wore the short skirts and white stockings and shoes that she was buried in." She added: "Her coming back to me was not a shock. It seemed perfectly natural that she should come in that way. So I gathered her

Figure 63. Poster from 1906 illustrates what would now be termed a near-death experience. (Author's collection)

up in my arms and together we floated away in perfect happiness." In time, though, Mrs. Haskins felt herself gasping for breath, the pain of her illness returned, and she was caught up in her own mother's arms. "Returning to life was the hard part," she insisted. "Dying was peace and happiness."

Mrs. Haskins's encounter has much in common with today's typical near-death experience (NDE)—a term coined by physician Raymond Moody in the 1970s to describe the mystical experiences of some who return from death's door. Although each individual's experience is unique, *Harper's Encyclopedia of Mystical and Paranormal Experience* (Guiley 1991, 399) states:

> In an NDE people generally experience one or more of the following phenomena in this sequence: a sense of being dead, or an out-of-body-experience in which they feel themselves floating above their bodies, looking down; cessation of pain and a feeling of bliss or peace-

fulness; traveling down a dark tunnel toward a light at the end; meeting nonphysical beings who glow, many of whom are dead friends and relatives; coming in contact with a guide or Supreme Being who takes them on a life review, during which their entire lives are put into perspective without rendering any negative judgments about past acts; and finally, a reluctant return to life.

This sequence generally describes Mrs. Haskins's reported experience, except for a few elements. She did not mention the dark tunnel but did refer to "brightness." There was no life review by a guide or deity, but, perhaps significantly, Mrs. Haskins described herself as "not very religious," adding, "I am not a spiritualist, either, and had never before seen the apparition of my dead baby, though I have thought and dreamed of her often." Spiritualism, the supposed communication with the dead, was still a popular belief in 1906. (Interestingly, a one-paragraph account of the incident in the May 18, 1906, weekly *Middleboro Gazette* referred to Mrs. Haskins's experience as an example of "suspended animation" and made no mention of the encounter with her deceased infant daughter.)

Viewed scientifically, out-of-body experiences are actually hallucinations that can occur under anesthesia when one is nowhere near death, when one is falling asleep or even just relaxing or meditating, or during attacks of migraine or epilepsy. The tunnel-travel experience is also a hallucination, attributable to the particular structure of the visual cortex—the portion of the brain that processes visual information (Blackmore 1991) — or to pupil widening due to oxygen deprivation (Woerlee 2004). And the life review results from the dying, oxygen-starved brain stimulating cells in the temporal lobe and thus arousing memories.

It is not surprising that people's longing for dead loved ones should manifest in dreamlike imagery. During more than three decades of investigating the paranormal, I have encountered many such claims of direct contact with the dead, typically reported through dreams, waking dreams (hallucinations that occur in the twilight between wakefulness and sleep), apparitions (which tend to be perceived during daydreams or other altered states of consciousness), and deathbed visions (which are similar to NDEs). Having one of these experiences is probably physiological, but the content of the experience is probably psychological and cultural (Nickell 2002). Yet the NDE has aspects, says Blackmore (1991), "that are ineffable—they cannot be put into words." The event can seem so real, so powerful in its import, that even though it is "essentially physiological," it can profoundly change the lives of those who experience it.

Of the other three cases related in "Came Back from the Dead," only one follows the essential NDE pattern. Richard Howland of Brooklyn was on his deathbed when he apparently died, and his sorrowful wife, Mollie, sent for the undertaker. When he arrived, they found Howland sitting upright and calling, "Where's Mollie?" He told them that his body had grown cold, and he felt his spirit being transported into strange surroundings; at the end of the road he was traveling was "a great and glorious white light." Then "some invisible intelligence" spoke, assuring him of "eternal happiness" and concluding, "You may return." Howland found himself in his body again and spent many hours talking with his wife until "his spirit passed away finally."

The next case involved a man named Edward McElroon of Yonkers who had suffered a skull fracture and underwent surgery. During the operation his heart stopped beating, and he could not be revived. His body was taken to the morgue but was later seen to exhibit "a slight tremor of the chest muscles," whereupon the doctors were recalled and they resuscitated him. After two days he recovered consciousness, but the narrative ends without mentioning any NDE.

The fourth and final case is suspect in the extreme. Henry Hutchinson of Croydon, England, supposedly gave a first-person account of dying and his spirit being lifted up "in a vortex of light." He heard the physician pronounce him dead, was dressed on the following day for his funeral, and "for three days I was exposed upon a bier" to friends and family. The undertakers roughly forced him into a too-narrow coffin, one placing his knee in Hutchinson's chest to accomplish it. The lid was nailed shut, and Hutchinson recalled hearing a sermon preached over his grave before the sod struck the coffin. He lay buried alive "for many hours," after which he became aware of his coffin being exhumed and transported a great distance. "Soon after," he said, "I heard the sound of many voices; hands touched me, and . . . some one raised the lid of my eyes," so that "I saw myself in the amphitheater of a dissecting room in the midst of a great body of students!" Fortunately, he continues, they first decided to "galvanize" him, and the electrical jolt was applied: "At the second discharge every one of my nerves trembled like the strings of a harp, and my body rose to a sitting posture, with stiff muscles, open and staring eyes. They extended me again; the professor approached and made a light cut through the ligaments of my breast. At this moment an enormous change took place in my whole body, I succeeded in crying out; the bonds of death were separated, and I returned to life." Believe it or not!

Hutchinson's narrative reads like fiction. It is unlikely that an unembalmed body would be left unburied for four days, but if it were, the fact that it showed no obvious signs of decomposition should have provoked astonishment. If he had family and friends, why not find a coffin that fit him? The knee-in-the-chest detail seems particularly literary. Then there are the fortuitous elements of grave robbers digging him up, someone raising one of his eyelids (enabling him to glimpse his presence in a medical amphitheater), and the application of a reanimating electrical current—as was done to Frankenstein's monster.

As these stories demonstrate, examples of people recovering from "death"—sometimes with near-death experiences to tell—extend back a century; indeed, they are probably as old as humankind.

Note

1. The Resident and Business Directory of Middleboro, Massachusetts, for the years 1906–1907 lists not "James" but John A. Haskins at 82 Oak Street; he was a shoemaker. Mrs. Haskins's doctor, mentioned in the article (with an erroneous middle initial "H"), was also listed in the directory: Thomas S. Hodgson at 47 South Main Street.

References

Blackmore, Susan. 1991. Near-death experiences: In or out of the body? *Skeptical Inquirer* 16, no. 1 (Fall): 34–35.

Came back from the dead! 1906. *Boston American,* October 14, 14.

Guiley, Rosemary Ellen. 1991. *Harper's Encyclopedia of Mystical and Paranormal Experience.* New York: HarperCollins.

Nickell, Joe. 2002. Visitations: After-death contacts. *Skeptical Briefs* 12, no. 3 (September): 7–10.

Woerlee, G. M. 2004. Darkness, tunnels, and light. *Skeptical Inquirer* 28, no. 3 (May–June): 28–32.

RIDDLE OF
THE GLOWING STATUES

Two women noticed it first, on about August 4, 2003: the eyes of the Virgin Mary statue on the church's bell tower had begun to glow; so had the statue's halo and sacred heart. Subsequently, the same features of a Jesus statue on the tower's opposite side were also observed to shine mysteriously. Soon, thousands of pilgrims and curiosity seekers had flocked to the site: St. Joseph the Provider Catholic Church in Campbell, Ohio, just south of Youngstown (Horton 2003; Kubik 2003).

On Site

I decided to take in the spectacle and conduct an investigation. Donning a suitable disguise as a pilgrim, including an ostentatious cross hanging around my neck—I drove to Campbell on Saturday, August 16, 2003. As I neared the site I occasionally stopped to ask for directions and thus get feedback from local residents.

At my first stop at a fast-food restaurant in nearby Hubbard, Ohio, I asked a workman about the "miracle statues." Climbing down from his stepladder, he said he had not heard about them but cautioned, "I wouldn't put much faith in statues." Closer to the church, a convenience-store clerk was familiar with the stories about the supposedly miraculous phenomenon but offered a condescendingly skeptical smile while giving directions.

Arriving at the church in the afternoon, I decided to change into the persona of an investigative journalist—complete with photographer's vest, camera, and notebook. In this way, I could freely go about my business of taking numerous photographs, making experiments (more on this presently), and conducting interviews.

As luck would have it, I was able to catch St. Joseph's busy young priest, Michael Swierz, as he was hurrying into the church. I identified myself as a writer with "*Skeptical Inquirer,* the science magazine." He flashed a smile and repeated what he had recently told the Associated Press: that there was a ready explanation for the phenomenon. He stated that during the 1970s the statues' halos, eyes, and hearts had been covered with gold leaf. He thought that rain might have washed away the grime or that some chemical reaction might have taken place, causing the gold to shine more brightly (Priest 2003; Swierz 2003). Swierz told me that the real miracle was that the phenomenon had brought together so many diverse people from such far-flung places.

Examination

It seemed easy to confirm the priest's basic explanation. During the afternoon I was able to observe that the gilded areas, especially the sacred heart of the Mary statue (which faces west), were shining brightly while the sun was out, but they dimmed whenever clouds obtruded. Several other statues on the grounds—all lacking gilding—failed to shine. (Local photographer John Yavorsky shared my observation and, equipped with a telephoto lens, kindly shot an extra roll of film for me. See figure 64.)

A few people insisted that the phenomenon occurred even at night, supposedly disproving the shining hypothesis and indicating that the statues were indeed glowing. I resolved to return in the evening, when a crowd was expected to gather.

After securing lodging and eating supper, I returned for the evening gathering—or "show," as the *Cleveland Plain Dealer* termed it (Horton 2003). I brought along a pair of binoculars and a flashlight and joined the latest crowd of pilgrims trampling the grass of the church's east and west courtyards. After dark, the two statues continued to shine much as before (albeit without the fluctuations caused by waxing and waning sunlight). However, there were obviously streetlights and church security lights as sources of illumination, as well as significant ambient light. I observed that the shining changed with the angle of viewing. Also, when I played the beam of my flashlight across each statue's gilded areas, there were distinct flashes of light. These practical experiments clearly demonstrated that the light was being reflected, not transmitted. In other words, there was no glowing, only the shining to be expected from the areas covered with gold leaf.

Figure 64. One of two supposedly miraculous statues at an Ohio Catholic church whose eyes, halo, and sacred heart reportedly began to "glow." (Photo for author by John Yavorsky)

The following day, I made my third visit to the church grounds. I talked with a volunteer who was loading a vehicle with supplies for a church picnic. He said that the gilding on the statues dated from about 1973 or 1974. Plans to have it redone sometime around 1991 had been judged too costly and had not been carried out. The man stated that he had noticed the effect for years but had thought nothing of it until recently, when it began to receive attention. He thus confirmed the suggestion of Monsignor Robert Siffrin, vicar-general of the Youngstown, Ohio, Catholic Diocese. Monsignor Siffrin said that the statues had likely always reflected light and that people had previously noticed it without drawing attention to it. He agreed with Father Swierz "that light is reflected off the gold leaf" (Kubik 2003).

Further Observations

I spent much time studying the two statues with binoculars, which gave me a good look at the shining areas. Having been a professional sign painter in my youth (Nickell 2001), with hands-on experience in applying gold leaf, I recognized its distinctive appearance on the church statues. It was surely genuine gilding and not the "gold leaf paint" mentioned in some news accounts (Kubik 2003). ("Gold" paint is typically made with bronze powder as a pigment, and it soon tarnishes [Owen 1958]. Only genuine leaf has the look and brilliance of gold, like that on the church's statues. It is widely used for such outdoor applications, including the famous gold dome of the Denver, Colorado, capitol [Green 2003].)

A brief discussion of the process of surface gilding (distinct from glass—or window—gilding) might be instructive. The process involves the use of either a "quick" (varnish-based) or "slow" (linseed oil) size, the latter permitting "a more brilliant burnish" and enhancing durability. The size is brushed over a suitably primed surface and allowed to dry to "a hard, dry-feeling tack," whereupon incredibly thin squares of beaten gold are then laid on (Owen 1958, 57). The leaves may be purchased "loose" (interleaved between the pages of a book) or in "patent" form (lightly adhered to a paper backing); patent gold is preferred for gilding in the wind (Owen 1958, 57–59; Duvall 1952, 52, 65–66; Sutherland 1889, 6–7). Finally, after the leaves have been applied in overlapping fashion, they are burnished and then covered with a protective coat of varnish. "This will cut down on the brilliance of the leaf somewhat," notes one authoritative text (Owen 1958, 59), "but durability will be insured."

My observations of the supposedly glowing statues in Campbell revealed that, not unexpectedly, the gold was missing in places, and where it was present, some areas were brighter than others. I suspect that some of the protective overcoating is still on the duller areas but has largely worn off the rest, causing them to shine even more brightly.

I found nothing that seemed even remotely supernatural at the site, although much miracle mongering was going on. Some people claimed, for example, that reddish streaks below the Jesus statue were evidence of miraculous "blood," even though these came not from the body (e.g., the heart or areas of Jesus's crucifixion wounds) but from the bottom of the boxlike base. I thought it much more likely that they were rust stains from the hardware that secured the statue to the bell tower.

Emotional belief is not easy to counter with dispassionate reason and evidence, however. One woman who saw me taking photographs and scribbling notes asked my opinion of the "glowing" phenomenon. When I explained my findings and concluded that the gold was merely shining, she managed a smile and said, "I prefer not to believe that," showing that some minds are inoculated against disproof.

References

Duvall, Edward J. 1952. *Modern Sign Painting.* Wilmette, Ill.: Frederick J. Drake.

Green, Mike. 2003. Colorado Capitol Walk, June 22. www.angelfire.com/co3/avaconvention2003/taw/denvercapitolarticle01.html (accessed October 13).

Horton, John. 2003. Skeptics, believers flock to statues. *Cleveland Plain Dealer,* August 14.

Kubik, Maraline. 2003. Campbell statue: It's no miracle, but it's nice, officials say. *Vindicator* (Youngstown, Ohio), August 9. www.vindi.com/print/278677665434201.shtml (accessed August 18).

Nickell, Joe. 2001. Adventures of a paranormal investigator. In *Skeptical Odysseys,* ed. Paul Kurtz, 219–32. Amherst, N.Y.: Prometheus Books.

Owen, Robert E. 1958. *New Practical Sign Painting.* Milwaukee, Wis.: Bruce Publishing Company.

Priest offers explanation for glowing statue. 2003. www.onnnews.com/story
.php?record=26055 (accessed August 15).

Sutherland, William. 1889. *The Art and Craft of Sign-writing.* Reprint, New York:
Crescent Books, 1989.

Swierz, Michael. 2003. Interview by Joe Nickell, August 16.

THE WHITE LADY OF BAVARIA

IT IS SAID THAT EVERY TOWN IN FRANCONIA (the northern region of the state of Bavaria in Germany) has a legend of *Die Weisse Frau*—the White Lady—a ghostly figure that walks about at night terrifying people. Perhaps it is she who is referred to in the local jokelore: As I was told by a guide during a midnight ghost tour of old Bamberg, a visitor approached a woman and asked if there were ghosts in the city. She replied, "I've lived here 500 years and never seen one."

The White Lady's saga is most firmly attached to the old fortress known as the Plassenburg, high above the town of Kulmbach. Originally built in the twelfth and thirteenth centuries, it was a residence for the Franconian princes. It was torched by marauding Bavarians in 1554 but rebuilt and enlarged, beginning in about 1560 (Plassenburg n.d.). Remarkable especially for its uniquely ornamented courtyard (figure 65), it has been termed "the most important Renaissance castle in the country" (Knight 2002, 208).

According to tradition, the White Lady was a woman named Kunigunde von Orlamünde (figures 66 and 67), whose husband's ancestors had built the castle. After his death, she wished to marry a certain Albrecht von Hohenzollern, who said that he would marry her if not for the "four eyes between us." Supposedly, his cryptic reference was to his parents, but Kunigunde thought he meant her two children, so she determined to kill them. To make it appear that they died naturally, she used a needle—a "golden needle," in one of the many variants— to pierce their skulls. Racked by a guilty conscience, she went to Rome, where the pope promised her forgiveness if she devoted her life to monastic work. Thereafter, she walked on her knees from Plassenburg to the valley of Berneck to establish a monastery. In some versions, she fell dead in the attempt; in others, she founded a monastery called Heaven's Crown but died in her early thirties. Ever since, she haunts all the castles of the dynasty of the Hohenzollern—even

Figure 65. Courtyard of the Renaissance castle known as the Plassenburg, located in Franconia. (Photo by Joe Nickell)

appearing at various family castles simultaneously—and brings bad luck or foreshadows misfortune (Wachler 1931; Die sage 2002).

As noted, there are many variant tales (one gives the protagonist's name as *Katharina* von Orlamünde [Die sage 2002]), which is evidence of oral tradition at work. One such version was told to me (with my colleague Martin Mahner translating) by our castle guide, who acknowledged the existence of the variants but noted that they contain many similarities, invariably including the motif of the potential marriage.

The castle's gift shop attendant told us that the story is quite old, dating back to a time when people believed strongly in such things. Indeed, the first known mention of the saga of the White Lady is from 1486 at the old castle of Bayreuth, and the account is revealing. Apparently, whenever the cavaliers wanted to get rid of the visiting ruler and his court, the White Lady tended to show up. Particularly gullible was a Count Friedrich, whom the castle inhabitants enjoyed fooling. In 1488, a ghost arrayed in a white gown began to roam the dark corridors and chambers of the Plassenburg. Actually, however, one of the court ladies had dressed up to play the role, and others began to imitate her (Wachler 1931). One such role player (according to our guide) was a man who dressed in white and appeared at night to chase members of the Hohenzollern dynasty from the castle. There are two versions of what happened next: either he fell down the stairs, probably drunk, or he was pushed by the man he was attempting to scare. Both versions agree that he broke his neck.

Of course, we cannot be certain that these early accounts of ghostly hoaxing are true, but surely they deserve as much credit as later reports of the White Lady's appearances. Besides, as skeptics well know, once the idea is planted that a ghost exists, that expectation can take on a life of its own. The power of suggestion—especially among certain imaginative people—is well attested and can easily be augmented by the ambience of old castles (Nickell 2001).

Moreover, the historical record casts doubt on the basis of the White Lady tale. The only historical person who could be the legendary child killer and penitent was the Countess Kunigunde, who was married to Count Otto von Orlamünde-Plassenburg in 1321. Two years after his death (which occurred

Figures 66 and 67. The Countess Kunigunde before her death *(above)* and after *(below)*, when her malevolent specter began to haunt certain Franconian castles. (The author and his colleagues were given special access to these small frescoes, which are located in the Plassenburg.) (Photos by Joe Nickell)

around 1341), she did enter a monastery; however, it was named Heaven's Throne, not Heaven's Crown, although she had actually founded it earlier. She died there in 1385—not in her thirties, as the legend holds, but in her seventies (Wachler 1931, 31–32).

Most significantly, her two-decade marriage to Count Otto was childless. If there was a proposed second marriage to Albrecht von Hohenzollern, its failure to transpire obviously had nothing to do with her nonexistent children or, probably, with his parents. According to our guide at the Plassenburg, the real story is that Albrecht did not want her because she was impoverished. (By treaty, another count inherited Otto's estate, and she was apparently left virtually penniless [Wachler 1931, 32].) For that reason, reportedly, she was placed in the monastery.

Given the facts in the case, it is not surprising that the Plassenburg's gift shop attendant—who noted that she had not seen the specter herself and that there had been no recent sightings—stated that she believed the White Lady was "only a legend."

References

Knight, Christina, ed. 2002. *Fodor's Germany 2002*. New York: Random House.

Nickell, Joe. 2001. Phantoms, frauds, or fantasies? In *Hauntings and Poltergeists*, ed. James Houran and Rense Lange, 214–23. Jefferson, N.C.: McFarland.

The Plassenburg above Kulmbach. N.d. Information sheets from 2002. Kulmbach, Germany.

Die sage von der Weissen Frau. 2002. www.burghotel-lauenstein.de/sage_wf.html.

Wachler, Martin. 1931. *Die Weisse Frau*. Reprint, Kulmbach, Germany: Freunde der Plassenburg, 1984.

INDEX

Italic page numbers refer to illustrations